Invitation to the Theatre

Brief Edition

Invitation

George and Portia Kernodle

University of Arkansas

to the Theatre

Brief Edition

Harcourt Brace Jovanovich, Inc.

New York / Chicago / San Francisco / Atlanta

ISBN: 0-15-546922-3

Library of Congress Catalog Card Number: 70-145598

Printed in the United States of America

ACKNOWLEDGMENTS

Cover: Gerald Arpino's *The Clowns,* 1969, The New York City Center Joffrey Ballet. Photo Herbert Migdoll.

Chapter-Opening Photo Acknowledgments

Introduction (page 1): *Galaxy, a Dance Theatre Piece.* Choreographed by Alwin Nikolais. Photo Susan Schiff Faludi.

1 (page 5): Paddy Chayefsky's *Printer's Measure.* Wagner International Photos.

2 (page 35): Arthur Kopit's *Indians.* Photo Martha Swope.

3 (page 63): American Ballet Theatre rehearsal. Photo © Max Waldman, 1971.

4 (page 97): New York Shakespeare Festival production of Sophocles' *Electra* at the Delacorte Theatre in Central Park, 1964. Directed by Gerald Freedman. Photo George E. Joseph.

5 (page 113): Sophocles' *Oedipus.* State Theatre production, Darmstadt, Germany, designed by Franz Martz. Photo Pit Ludwig.

6 (page 143): Rossini's *Barber of Seville.* Juilliard Opera Theatre production, designed by Ming Cho Lee. Photo Nathan Rabin.

7 (page 173): *Bluebeard,* written and directed by Charles Ludlam. Presented by the Ridiculous Theatrical Company. Photo © Max Waldman, 1971.

8 (page 201): Model of setting for Harold Pinter's *Landscape* and *Silence* by Douglas W. Schmidt, based on designs by John Gunter. Repertory Theatre Company of Lincoln Center, 1970. Photo Martha Swope.

9 (page 221): Molière's *The Miser,* Repertory Theatre Company of Lincoln Center, 1969. Photo Martha Swope.

10 (page 243): Wagner's *Die Walküre,* New York Metropolitan Opera, 1967–68. Photo E. Fred Sher.

11 (page 271): Ryszard Cieslak as *The Constant Prince,* from the Polish Laboratory Theatre (Ryszard Cieslak, Rena Mirecka, Antoni Jaholkowski, Zbigniew Cynkutis, Zigmunt Molik, Stanislaw Scierski), under the direction of Jerzy Grotowski. Photo © Max Waldman, 1970.

Text Acknowledgments

The authors wish to thank the following companies for permission to reprint material used in this book.

Atheneum Publishers, Inc., for material from *The Persecution and Assassination of Jean-Paul Marat as Performed by the Inmates of the Asylum of Charenton under the Direction of the Marquis de Sade,* by Peter Weiss. Copyright © 1965 by John Calder Ltd. English version by Geoffrey Skelton. Verse adaptation by Adrian Mitchell. Reprinted by permission of Atheneum Publishers.

Calder and Boyars Ltd. for material from *Marat/Sade,* by Peter Weiss.

J. M. Dent & Sons Ltd. for material from *Under Milk Wood,* by Dylan Thomas. Reprinted by permission of J. M. Dent & Sons and the Trustees for the Copyrights of the late Dylan Thomas.

Faber and Faber Ltd. for material from *Waiting for Godot,* by Samuel Beckett, and *Murder in the Cathedral,* by T. S. Eliot.

Samuel French, Inc., for material from *The Adding Machine,* by Elmer Rice. Copyright, 1922, 1929, by Elmer Rice; copyright, 1923, by Doubleday, Page & Co.; renewal copyright, 1949, 1950, 1956, by Elmer Rice.

Elaine Greene Ltd. for material from *Death of a Salesman,* by Arthur Miller.

Grove Press, Inc., for material from *Waiting for Godot,* by Samuel Beckett. Translated from the original French text by the author. Reprinted by permission of Grove Press, Inc. Copyright 1954 by Grove Press.

Harcourt Brace Jovanovich, Inc., for material from *Murder in the Cathedral,* by T. S. Eliot. Copyright, 1935, by Harcourt Brace Jovanovich, Inc.; copyright, 1963, by T. S. Eliot. Reprinted by permission of the publisher.

William Heinemann Ltd., Publishers, for material from *On the Art of the Theatre,* by Gordon Craig.

Houghton Mifflin Co. for material from *J. B.,* by Archibald MacLeish.

New Directions Publishing Corp. for material from *Under Milk Wood,* by Dylan Thomas. Copyright 1954 by New Directions Publishing Corp. Reprinted by permission of New Directions Publishing Corp.

Random House, Inc., for material from *Actors Talk About Acting,* by Lewis Funke and John E. Booth. Copyright © 1961 by Random House, Inc.

The Society of Authors for material from *Man and Superman,* by George Bernard Shaw. Reprinted by permission of The Society of Authors for the Bernard Shaw Estate.

Thames and Hudson Ltd. for material from *Actors Talk About Acting,* by Lewis Funke and John E. Booth.

Theatre Arts Books for material from *On the Art of the Theatre,* by Edward Gordon Craig. All rights reserved. Used with the permission of the publisher, Theatre Arts Books, New York.

The Viking Press, Inc., for material from *Death of a Salesman,* by Arthur Miller. Copyright 1949 by Arthur Miller. Reprinted by permission of The Viking Press, Inc.

Preface

In preparing a brief, up-dated revision of *Invitation to the Theatre,* we have had in mind the students in a one-semester introduction to the theatre course or in a humanities course that covers more than one art. We have kept the same general plan as in the first edition, presenting first, in historical perspective, the kinds of plays—realism and romance, tragedy and comedy, disruption and reconstruction—and then describing how the director, actor, and designer work together to create the play. The last chapter is mostly new, describing in some detail the recent experiments in new forms of theatre. Recognizing that most of the plays a student sees are on the screen, we discuss many examples from movies and television drama. A number of the photographs in this edition are new, and there is a new section in color. A short bibliography appears at the end of the book.

We wish to thank Richard K. Knaub for his perceptive and helpful comments on the manuscript.

George and Portia Kernodle

Contents

Introduction

In the last ten years several explosions have shaken the theatre, making it seem that the old theatre might be replaced by dynamic rituals of primitive intensity for a fully participating audience. Young enthusiasts deserted theatre buildings to be in the streets "where the action is," carrying masks and monsters in confrontations before draft boards and military-industrial headquarters. Or they gathered in old barns and warehouses to stage "happenings" or "love-ins," celebrating aggressive nudity, four-letter words, and drugs in joyous defiance of "hypocritical" restraints, exploring "total environment," surrounded by grotesque animated shapes, projected scenes on shaped screens, and dozens of loud-speakers each with a different sound track. They went to the "now" movies to "dig" the immediate experience of scenes cut in at a fast pace without plot, character, motivation, or any other conventional development. The new theatre was to be socially "relevant," opposing war, imperialism, racism, pollution, and police brutality. Some extremists wanted to use a dynamic theatre to destroy society, the "establishment," and all rules, rationality, and restraint. Yet the theatre has not dissolved into spontaneous folk festival or political action. Its old forms have been modified but not destroyed. As good directors, actors, and designers discover how to adapt traditions to new needs, old plays often seem more relevant than new fads.

It has been a time of angry debate, with many different ideas contending in the arena. Sometimes these ideas seem to cancel each other out as different groups move in opposite directions. For instance, some directors and most technicians want a "total theatre" of "multi-media," mixing live performers with movies and slides, surging backdrops and sections of floor that rise and fall, and electronic sounds to envelop the audience in a dynamic "environment"—all this requiring elaborate equipment to control light, sound, and space. On the other hand, Jerzy Grotowski's Polish Laboratory Theatre has created "poor theatre," with no scenery, few properties, only two lights, and no sounds except those that can be created by the actors themselves. The "socially relevant" theatre turns outward to make an impersonal attack on the evils of society, but Antonin Artaud, the recently discovered wild prophet of the 1930s, called for a metaphysical theatre of "cruelty," incantation, and ritual, and Grotowski's small group turns inward to uncover the deepest and most personal feelings of the soul. The Living Theatre of the Becks shattered the fixed separation of auditorium and stage, urging the audience to take part: to touch the groping, suffering actors, to help move the dead bodies, to step on stage and pull off their own clothes in defiance of social norms. Grotowski's "poor theatre," in contrast, while it brings its small audience close, presents a finished work of art that never spills over into the lap of the audience. Although none of these ideas is likely to dominate the future, they suggest new evaluations not only of old plays but of the experiments and trends in the arts of the theatre for the past hundred years.

In part this new ferment is a continuation of an old quarrel, that of drama versus theatre. The people who read drama expect productions of their favorite plays to be as they imagine them from reading, with a minimum of interpretation or spectacular embellishment. They think that the purpose of a theatre is very simply to "put on the play" and only recognize the art of the actor if he subordinates himself to the playwright. On the other hand, the theatre people insist that there is an art of the theatre, that any playwright worth his salt writes for performance, and that the play as printed is like the ground plan of a building, on which the builder must erect

Two current trends in the theatre, the group celebration and the festival theatre. *Top: Hair,* New York, 1968. Photo Martha Swope. *Bottom:* New York Shakespeare Festival production of Ibsen's *Peer Gynt* at the Delacorte Theatre in Central Park, 1969. Directed by Gerald Freedman. Photo George E. Joseph.

Four recent college productions. *Top left: Black Dragon Residence*, University of Colorado production of a Peking Opera, 1970. Directed and choreographed by Daniel S. P. Yang and designed by Roger Klaiber. Costumes imported from Taiwan. Photo Daniel S. P. Yang. *Bottom left: Celebration,* Wayne State University production, 1969. Directed by Russell Smith, designed by Russel Smith and Norman Hamlin, and costumed by Stephanie Schoelzel. *Top right:*

Shakespeare's *Twelfth Night,* University of Iowa production using a turntable stage, 1962. Directed by George R. Kernodle, designed by Jerry Emery, and costumed by Janice Wroth. *Bottom right:* Anouilh's *Thieves' Carnival,* University of Arkansas theatre-in-the-round production, 1968. Directed by Cleveland Harrison, designed by Preston Magruder, costumed by Paula Orsborne, and lighted by Clay Orsborne.

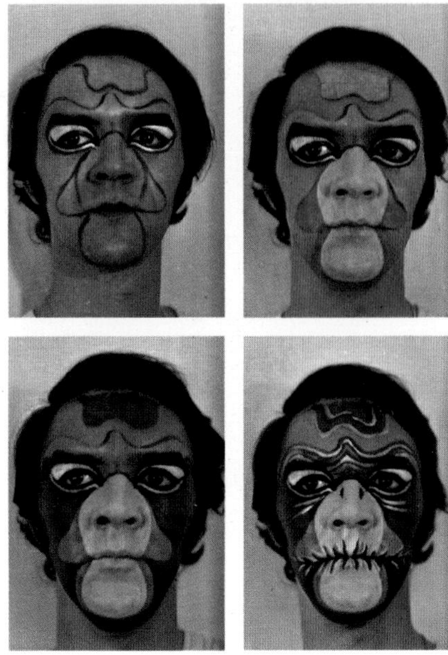

Fantasy in make-up and costuming, from three productions designed by Irene Corey for the Everyman Players of Pineville, Kentucky. *Top:* stages in make-up of the Tortoise in Alan Broadhurst's *The Tortoise and the Hare,* from outlining the face to the character in costume (with the Hare, at left). *Bottom left:* the Lion in Fauquez' *Reynard the Fox. Bottom right: The Book of Job,* adapted and designed by Orlin and Irene Corey. Photos from Irene Corey, *The Mask of Reality* (Anchorage, Ky.: Anchorage Press, 1968).

Imaginative and effective use of masks and make-up in Genêt's *The Blacks,* New York, 1961.
Photo Dennis Stock–Magnum, 1961.

The brittle sophistication of the musical *Company* (New York, 1969) is reflected by the plexiglass and steel used in Boris Aronson's mobile setting. Photo Friedman-Abeles.

Two recent Metropolitan Opera House productions. Rough texture and informal composition are used in Bizet's *Carmen (top)*, 1967, while Strauss's *Der Rosenkavalier (bottom)*, 1969, is characterized by romantic elegance. Photos E. Fred Sher.

The "multimedia" approach to theatre. *Top:* The setting for the Humboldt State College première of John Pauley's *September Tea* (1970), which used dynamic groups of actors, pools of light, fragments of scenery, projected images, voices, and sounds. Directed by Richard Rothrock, designed by David Brune, and costumed by Ethelyn Pauley. *Bottom:* The New York City Center Joffrey Ballet's production of *Astarte* (1969), which used psychedelic lighting and living dancers against multiple images projected on billowing plastic screens. Choreographed by Robert Joffrey. Photo Herbert Migdoll.

a superstructure of shapes, rhythms, textures, and colors. At the beginning of this century, when painters, architects, and dancers were stripping off the surface ornaments of the Victorian age to discover the fundamental principles of their arts, Gordon Craig and Adolphe Appia insisted that the theatre is an art of movement, space, line, color, and rhythm, created by one director who controls all aspects of the production. They both dreamed of omitting the playwright, and Craig wanted to control the actor like a supermarionette. In the 1930s Artaud's cry was "no more masterpieces" as he dreamed of a performance built from disconnected phrases or wordless sounds and ritual movements in order to regain the cruel intensities of a primitive ritual.

A production is never just putting on a play. Although it usually begins with the text of a play, it is often as complex an organization of sights and sounds as a film or an opera. Even the compact, well-made drama in which a few characters confront each other in a single room requires careful planning and control so that the sequences of movements, tones, and rhythms of the actors may proceed in a meaningful and exciting way.

This book is concerned with the produced play and its effect on the audience. The first seven chapters distinguish six kinds of plays according to their purposes—a sense of reality, color and romance, exaltation, a hearty laugh, thoughtful laughter, or an understanding of the disruption of the modern world.

Each kind of play presents a different attitude toward life, a different way of answering some of the age-old questions that are still very pertinent in the 1970s. The realistic play deals with the problems of man's physical and social environment, inviting us to take a serious, scientific attitude as we watch man, this creature with animal drives, trying to rebuild himself and his world. The romantic play, the opera, the ballet, or the musical invites us to forget the drab everyday world and follow the charmed paths of romance into the dream world of the primitive unconscious. A great tragedy exalts our spirit with pride as we see a man dare to pursue his spiritual destiny in the face of a challenging universe. Some plays present the miscalculations and frantic schemes of human beings in such a farcical way that we laugh heartily and see what fools we are to take life too seriously. Another kind of comedy provokes more thoughtful laughter as we see sophisticated characters making a game of their disagreements, trying to impose logic and philosophy on the changing patterns of human relationships. Many recent plays ask us to look at the disruption of the modern world, sometimes to shudder at its cruelty and terror, sometimes to laugh at its meaningless chatter, and sometimes to seek reconstruction.

In developing a particular attitude toward life, each kind of play makes different demands on the theatre, the designer, the actor, and the audience.

The size and shape of the theatre building and the form of the stage setting help to determine the expectations of the audience. For realistic plays we have built small, intimate theatres and developed a low-voiced, realistic style of acting. For operas, ballets, and musicals we expect a large stage filled with painted scenery—a romantic picture world, set at a distance behind a proscenium frame. For elevated moods we study the Greek and Elizabethan plays and reshape theatres, settings, and acting to catch something of their tragic grandeur.

In Chapters 8, 9, and 10 we examine the arts of the modern theatre—directing, acting, and design. We show how the director analyzes the text of the play and decides what structure and texture he hopes to create in the production and how he works with the designer and the actor to achieve his purpose. The play that seems so effortless in performance takes many weeks of planning and rehearsal by many workers with special skills, all brought into focus in one overall art of the theatre. But when the lights go down in the theatre and characters emerge from the darkness, the audience does not stop to think that a light man is moving levers to bring on focused spotlights. As the characters move about the stage, the audience is not conscious that the floor has been carefully laid out, varied in levels by platforms, steps, and ramps, and backed and shaped by vertical planes and structures that look like sky, tree, rock, or wall. Nor does the audience consider that the characters who seem so spontaneous, creating the "illusion of the first time," are actors whose speech and movements must have the concentration and control of a dance or a song.

Some students ask why the illusion should be spoiled, why one should look behind the scenes to discover how the magician creates his effects. They think it may be better to know nothing about the arts of the theatre. It is true that if the student pays too much attention to some minor aspect of production, his attention may be diverted from the main course of the play. But the distraction is only momentary. As he learns more about all the arts of the theatre, he finds a double pleasure in a performance. He can be just as involved in the events of the play as the naive theatregoer, but at the same time he can appreciate the skill of the performance and understand just what view of life this particular play is trying to present.

The final chapter of the book, on new forms of theatre, shows how the art of the theatre has been modified in the past few years as architects and designers have created more open forms of auditorium and stage and as poets, directors, actors, and dancers have made experiments that show us not only new techniques but also new ways of looking at man and his universe. The theatre is still one of our most important ways of defining reality, but both the theatre and our definition of reality have changed radically since realists set out a century ago to present a scientific world view.

The Theatre of Realism

1

Realism in the theatre began a hundred years ago with the efforts of a few dramatists to create an "illusion of reality" in which the unadorned truth was to be shown, without artifice, formulas, styles, or interpretations. Settings, properties, costumes, speech, and movement were to correspond so exactly to the world outside that the audience would forget it was in a theatre, supposing instead that it was looking into a real room with one wall removed—the "fourth wall" convention. Playwrights were to avoid all the cliches of heroes and villains, of comedy and tragedy, and to show people as they are, complex, unpredictable, and baffling. Where Aristotle described art as an imitation of life and Shakespeare spoke of holding the mirror up to nature, the realists wanted an actual reproduction of life and an exact reflection in the mirror. Of course it was soon found that actual life could never be put on the stage, that the most dedicated realist had to select his material and interpret it, if only unconsciously, from some point of view. Moreover, it gradually became clear that the central intent of realism—to show man in relation to his environment—could be accomplished in a number of ways, not all of them new to the theatre. During its century of existence, the realistic tradition has been modified and redefined, and in recent decades it has absorbed many of the techniques that were once considered nonrealistic. In the 1970s realism remains the strongest ideal of the theatre—its vitality seems inexhaustible, and audiences still respond to the plays that "tell it like it is."

This chapter and the next will describe six closely related ways of creating the illusion of reality in the theatre. In this chapter we will describe realism as it was first developed in the late nineteenth-century and early twentieth-century theatre and in movies and television. In the next chapter we will consider two early modifications, selected realism and stylized realism, which appeared in the 1920s, and three later ways of dealing with reality that have had a growing importance in the past forty years: abstract realism, the Oriental realism of make-believe, and epic realism.

Realism and Naturalism

Realists in the nineteenth century turned away from the far away and long ago of the romantics to a concern with the here and now, from fantasies of heroic adventure to a journalistic study of how ordinary people live, from idealistic speculation to pragmatic concern with actual problems. A few plays in the 1850s and 60s made tentative explorations in a cheerful, shallow realism, but the main theatre fare continued to be artificial comedies, romantic spectacles, and melodramas. In 1873 Émile Zola wrote a preface to his play *Thérèse Raquin* in which he heaped scorn on the unreality and pomposity of the conventional nineteenth-century theatre, with its "medieval scrap-iron, secret doors, poisoned wine," its middle-class sentimentality, "kidnapped children, recovered documents, immodest boastings." He believed that the outmoded romantic theatre would be replaced by a new realistic theatre based on the scientific study of the actual world.

The scientific spirit of the century indeed transformed the theatre. It taught writers to be objective observers, carefully studying real people living in real places. Where the romantics conceived of their characters as embodiments of large, clear passions, the realists watched for the influence of environment on the basic drives. From the beginning of the nineteenth

1-1 Realism in setting, directing, and acting. The actors, seen in a box set, are absorbed in the detail of the environment, making a clear, balanced picture, but one without obvious design. Odets' *Awake and Sing.* New York, 1935. Photo Vandamm.

century, increasing interest was shown in biology, the study of how creatures live and grow and especially of how they react to their environment. The climax of biological study came in 1859 with the publication of Charles Darwin's *Origin of Species,* which offered the theory that all animals, including man, evolve from lower forms and that, by "natural selection," or "survival of the fittest," only those animals that best adapt to their environment will survive. Another powerful influence on nineteenth-century thought was the materialism that seemed an inevitable concomitant of the science, technology, and the great industrial development of the era.

The quite visible effect on the theatre of these new attitudes was the absorbing interest in properties and little pantomimed business on the stage. Objects became as important as actors. They not only documented the authentic qualities of the environment but also gave the actor a sense of reality as he interacted with the environment. Anton Chekhov, perhaps the greatest Russian dramatist, created his characters out of their little daily actions. One of the directors who worked with him wrote,

> He represented human beings only as he observed them in life, and he could not dissociate them from their surroundings: from the rosy morning or the blue twilight, from sounds, odours, rain, trembling shutters, the lamp, the stove, the samovar, the piano, the harmonica, tobacco, the sisters, the in-laws, neighbors, song, drink, from everyday existence, from the million trifles that give warmth to life.

That last phrase—"the million trifles that give warmth to life"—might be the motto of the whole realistic movement.

In the 1880s a deeper wave of realism, called naturalism, went much further than the exploration of daily life by probing into the violent forces that lie beneath the surface. Victorian ladies and gentlemen were shocked, but the naturalistic realists were determined to make people face the basic facts of hunger, greed, and sex—drives it would be dangerous to ignore. A Viennese physician named Sigmund Freud insisted that if the basic drives are not given normal outlets they may emerge indirectly in distorted and destructive ways, and that the only healthy approach is to make the conscious mind aware of those hatreds and drives that have been suppressed because they are not pretty or respectable.

Naturalism was based not only on an interest in exposing the more brutal aspects of man's animal nature but on an explicit philosophy of determinism—the belief that man has no freedom of will or choice but is "determined" by heredity and environment. Many plays from the late nineteenth century to the present day could be described as either realistic or naturalistic, but we will use the term *naturalism* only when the deterministic philosophy is apparent and when such basic animal drives as sex, hunger, and greed are important in the play.

Artists who were influenced by the naturalistic philosophy were determined to break through the cheerful surface of early realism, with its conventional pictures of the humble poor, and to show the hatred, frustration, and debauchery of the victims of poverty, who survive through forlorn delusions and dreams of escape. Maxim Gorki wrote one of the most powerful naturalistic plays, *The Lower Depths* (1902), to show the suffering, the hopeless dreams, and the depravity of the human dregs in one cellar room.

One of the greatest objections made by serious realists to nineteenth-century melodramas and farces was that they never faced a real problem. After several acts of suspense the missing papers were recovered, the accused hero was proved innocent, the long-lost child was found, the uncle returned with a fortune, or lightning struck the villain. No one had to face a major loss or adjust to people who had both good and bad qualities. Naturalistic plays shocked late Victorian and early twentieth-century audiences by actually facing such problems. When the Victorian idealist said, "Keep your eyes on the stars," the scientific naturalist added, "And fall into a ditch!"

With *A Doll's House* (1879) and *Ghosts* (1881), Henrik Ibsen became the European champion of truth versus conventional hypocrisy. In *A Doll's House*, when Torvald discovers that his charming little wife, Nora, has innocently forged her father's name and that he might be disgraced by the exposure, he turns on her in anger. But when he finds that someone is willing to cover up the scandal, he forgives her. Repelled by his selfishness and hypocrisy, however, and realizing that he has never treated her as an adult, she walks out of the house to try to find herself, with a slam of the door that was heard all over the Western world. *Ghosts* made an even more shocking attack on convention by bringing the subject of venereal disease to the stage and by indicating that the leading character, Mrs. Alving, should have left her debauched husband. In the end she is faced with the horrible dilemma of giving poison to their son, whose mind has given way, or of caring for him as an idiot. Naturalistic characters must make painful choices, not merely toy with the picturesque problems of romantic heroes.

In writing about the serious problems of real people, Ibsen perfected the "well-made play" with which the French dramatist Eugène Scribe had been very successful a half-century before—a very compact play of few characters, with careful exposition, logical progression, great suspense, and strong conflict, all leading up to surprising climaxes and effective curtains. However, unlike Scribe, Alexandre Dumas *fils*, and several others, who used the well-made play to present such problems as the fallen woman, divorce, and financial and family crises, Ibsen used it to show men and women who rebelled against the basic attitudes of nineteenth-century society.

1-2 Realism. Variety and subtle detail give convincing reality to a group of girls in a boarding school. Hellman's *The Children's Hour.* New York, 1934. Photo Vandamm.

1-3 Realism or naturalism showing the influence of environment on character. The grouping is complex and varied, clear but not obviously designed. Kingsley's *Dead End*. New York, 1935. Directed and designed by Norman Bel Geddes. Hoblitzelle Theatre Arts Library, University of Texas.

Much realistic and naturalistic literature was informed by a zealous determination to tear off the mask of respectability and show man in his real nature, to face facts, to expose corruption and hypocrisy. Chekhov said, "To make a man better, you must first show him what he is." European cities, after a century of industrial revolution, were a mass of slums filled with poverty, depravity, and misery. But the Victorian middle class, seemingly happy with the idealized stereotypes of its sentimental literature, refused to look. Bernard Shaw showed respectable people some of the unpleasant facts of economic life; in *Major Barbara*, for instance, he showed that slum properties, from which churchgoing landlords collected their rents, bred disease and crime and that society would do better to build a decent world for the workers than to depend on such charities as the Salvation Army to keep the workers from rebelling. The radicals of the time looked for a revolution, a war between labor and capital. The liberals put their hope in new laws, labor unions, schools, settlement houses, and slum clearance. Both groups welcomed the new realistic art, whether in the simpler form of realism or the grimmer form of naturalism. They believed that only by seeing actual conditions and particular cases—in paintings, in novels, in plays—would the general public become aware of the problems and even recognize that slum dwellers had human feelings. Since that first enthusiasm, realistic art has helped to bring about so vast a transformation of man's environment in all the industrialized nations of the world that it is no wonder that emerging nations, from Russia to Africa, regard "social realism" as the most important form of art.

In America, where the impact of industrial and urban development on literature came later than in Europe, there was some interest in realism from the 1880s on. But the greatest interest came after the First World War, in 1918, and especially in the decade of the depression, from 1929 to 1939. The shocking plays *Tobacco Road* (dramatized in 1933 from Erskine Caldwell's novel) and Sidney Kingsley's *Dead End* (1935) reinforced the hopes of the New Deal of the Franklin D. Roosevelt era. Both exploded the myth that the poor can help themselves. *Tobacco Road* made even its grossly comic hillbillies seem human and touching. The old Georgia farmer, Jeeter Lester, in his attempts to continue after having exhausted the economic and moral resources of his environment, demonstrates the failure of laissez-faire economics and the need for outside help. As his daughters ran away to the cities to become prostitutes, the ribald old man was left to starve to death on the deserted farm. *Dead End,* though equally shocking, was more hopeful. Bringing together on the stage a slum alley and the courtyard of a luxury apartment house, it studied the effects of these entirely different environments on each other. The play shows in detail how alley boys learn to be gangsters. An alumnus of the slums, now a famous killer returning home for the last time, teaches the boys how to follow in his footsteps, thus goading the young architect to work toward improving the housing of his slum neighbors instead of dreaming of escape with the rich. But the main progression of the play is not the story of the architect or the gangster but a succession of moods, blending together many small conflicts and discords.

Impressionism, the Aesthetics of Realism

A similar emphasis on moods can be found in many other plays. Most realistic and naturalistic plays, in fact, are organized, directed, and acted by techniques that correspond very closely to the techniques of impressionism in painting and music. While we have not been in the habit of applying the term *impressionism* to realism, we can understand realism far better if we notice that painting, music, and drama responded in much the same way to the same historical developments of the late nineteenth century,

1-4 Realism and impressionism. A mood of reminiscence and indecision is suggested in this twilight setting. Chekhov's *The Cherry Orchard.* Carnegie Tech Theatre production, directed by Lawrence Carra. Photo Daniel P. Franks.

and that the aesthetics of impressionism in painting and music are much the same as those of realism and naturalism in the theatre. Hence we may speak of the many plays of realism and naturalism in which strong conflicts are kept muted as impressionist plays. Even those plays in which violence breaks out at some point may employ impressionistic techniques.

Impressionism was developed in the second half of the nineteenth century in reaction to the strident intensities of romanticism. Instead of choosing heroic subjects for large canvases, painters became interested in the passing moods of the local landscape, the atmosphere of various times of day, and the special qualities of jugs, tables, and fabrics. Claude Monet wanted to catch in his paintings the impression of a cathedral half lost in the haze of early morning or a bridge in a foggy London twilight. The French composer Claude Debussy was fascinated by sea, clouds, mist, and rain, by the thought of a cathedral with its chimes deep under the sea or by the local color of a Spanish town at festival time. In the 1890s he was working out a music of new harmonies, weaving many little themes into rich textures of mood and avoiding most of the conventional harmonies and expected progessions.

Now, more than a half-century after impressionism reached its first flowering, the basic attitude toward life that produced it is clearer. The techniques of impressionism—in painting, the tiny dots of color, the bold brush strokes, the blurred lines that blend gardens, bridges, trees, and people into soft-focus images; in music, the overlapping sequences, the massed chords, the exotic harmonies that blend the fragments of melodies into muted discords; in the theatre, the details of setting and properties, the overlapping bits of dialogue and background sounds, the tentative gestures and movements that blend the characters and the locality into rich moods—express the belief, explicit in the plays and implicit in painting and music, that man has no freedom from the environment of which he is a product and a helpless victim—a belief that is, as we have seen, basic to naturalism. Foreground disappears into background, melody into accompaniment, and individual decisions into unconscious natural and social forces. Man may struggle to escape his environment, he may be in conflict with it in many ways, but he is himself one of the threads of its complex web. In impressionist plays, as in impressionist music, there is never a decisive beginning or end, never a clear-cut climax or turn, because man is not expected to make a major decision. Violence may smolder beneath the surface and even erupt offstage, but the main characters are bewildered victims who do not understand their own feelings. In presenting such passive people, the playwright weaves a complex pattern from suggestions of mood, hints of half-formed desires and impulses, and fragments of abortive action, which can be more expressive than the strong plot of a typical nineteenth-century play.

Chekhov's plays show how impressionistic patterns were worked out in the theatre. They are all mood studies of groups of people caught in situations they can do nothing about. In *The Three Sisters* (1901), the sisters fret through four acts at the dullness and oppression of the provincial town they live in and plan constantly to escape to Moscow, but they never do because they find themselves trapped by family ties and by habits they cannot change. A thousand and one conflicts arise and stir people deeply, showing slightly on the surface and sometimes catching the attention of other characters, sometimes going unnoticed in the continuous flow of little actions. At times all the characters on stage are caught by the same mood of joy or sadness, but often several characters carry on their own separate sequences. In spite of the deep melancholy of Chekhov's plays, the author insisted that they are comedies. The greatest appeal of an impressionist play is usually its combination of comedy and tragedy. Once the idea is accepted that life goes on no matter how many hearts are broken, there can be deep sympathy for failure and suffering along with laughter at the absurd context of the suffering.

Chekhov's *The Cherry Orchard* (1904) is a very touching, sad, yet funny study of a group of people trying to hold on to the moods and meanings of an old estate. (See Figure 1-4.) Madame Ranevsky, the owner, returns to the estate after spending all her money on a worthless man in

Paris. If only she will subdivide the estate and lease the lots for summer villas, she can have a good income. Her business adviser, the son of one of her father's serfs, is ready to help, but she and her brother cannot make up their minds. In Act I, arriving at daybreak, she cannot bring herself to do anything. In Act II, on a twilight walk, listening to distant music, she still cannot do anything. In Act III, at a big party, she is waiting for news that the estate has been sold. In Act IV she departs for Paris again. Around her are her brother, daughter, foster daughter, the governess, old friends of the family, the business friend who buys the estate, the former tutor of her drowned boy, and the upstart valet who is glad to be going back to Paris—all laughing, teasing, dreaming of the past and dreading the future, doing anything to avoid adjusting to a changing world. They are hopeless, helpless people, but the author looks at them with great warmth and affection. It is not surprising that Chekhov's great popularity has been in the West, where the complexity of modern life is so confusing and frustrating.

Some of the moods and techniques of impressionism appeared in America as early as 1916 in Susan Glaspell's one-act play, *Trifles.* Moods of frustration were not common dramatic material in the 1920s, but with the depression of the 1930s and the darkening clouds of impending war, large numbers of Americans could understand and respond to such moods. In two movies of the 1930s John Ford used the soft-focus techniques of impressionism to create a compassionate picture of groups of people struggling to escape from an oppressive background. *The Informer* (1935) traces the mute sufferings of a Dublin tough who stumbles to his death in the night fog after betraying his friend in the hope of escaping to America. In *Grapes of Wrath* (1939) the Joad family does escape from an Oklahoma desolated by drought and depression and makes an epic journey to California, only to find itself embroiled in the struggle of the migrant farm laborers. The play that catches beautifully the depression decade's feeling of weary helplessness is Tennessee Williams' *The Glass Menagerie* (1944), a rich mood-study of a group of helpless victims, loving and torturing one another but unable to change or break away. Uprooted from the security of a plantation in the Mississippi Delta and deserted by the father, the Wingfields—mother, son, and crippled daughter—seethe and quarrel in a dreary apartment in St. Louis. The mother dreams of departed glory and of a rich gentleman caller who will marry her daughter. The daughter, too fragile to cope with the modern world, escapes into the world of small glass animals that she collects. And the son, trapped in a dreary job and tortured by his family problems, dreams of following the example of his father and running away. The darkening international situation gives encouragement to his hope of exploding out of his frustrations, and he has already taken out papers in the merchant marine. But this is no final solution for the family's problems. Unlike most naturalists, however, Williams does not show to the last detail the suffering and defeat of his characters, but softens the harsh impact of the play by presenting it as a nostalgic review of the past. The son tells the audience that he has wandered restlessly over the wartime world and has been unable to escape his memories, but the audience sees only as much as he allows himself to remember.

Thus impressionism accepted the idea of man's helplessness in a baffling world but sought for understanding and compassion. If it could not trace any clear purpose or larger meaning in the absurd contradictions of life, it could at least discover a rich, vibrant texture in man's relation to his environment. Impressionism and realism are not identical; there are realistic plays of clear decision and melodramatic action, with characters who are not helpless. But many of the principles of acting and directing realistic plays are based on principles that are found in impressionistic music and painting.

Intimate Theatres for Realism

Impressionist plays—indeed, all the new plays of realism and naturalism—demanded not only a new kind of playwriting and acting but a new kind of theatre. No form of realism had a chance in the large nineteenth-century theatres, which were built to accommodate from two to four thousand people and included from three to six balconies. In such a theatre the large stage, on which were sometimes presented spectacular operatic scenes with horses and hundreds of people, was a vast open space with scenery consisting of painted flats and backdrops. For interiors, pieces of furniture from the property rooms were spread around the bare stage floor in conventional arrangements—a sofa here, a table and two chairs there—supplemented at times by furniture painted on the wings and backdrop. The actors expected to act close to the footlights, where their large gestures could be seen and their oratorical voices heard clearly throughout the house.

The new movement for a more intimate theatre started with a few bold, enterprising groups late in the nineteenth century and was so successful that by the 1920s practically all the new theatres in Western Europe and America were small, with at most 1,000 to 1,500 seats. Today, the newer college theatres of America usually seat three or four hundred. The idea of the intimate theatre has won out, and in spite of a hundred experiments in new directions, the realistic approach still dominates the theatre.

The first great step toward both realism and intimacy in the theatre was taken in London in 1865 when Squire Bancroft and his wife refurbished a small neglected theatre, gathered a group of young actors, and found a new director and playwright, T. W. Robertson. Robertson put his actors in the midst of real furniture and properties, real doors, ceilings, and windows, using the upstage as well as the downstage areas. He achieved a more subtle and more realistic ensemble acting than had been known before, making his sentimental scenes with everyday people very convincing by "new school" acting. His critics made fun of his "teacup and saucer" realism, however, and soon it came to seem mild and superficial.

A stronger impetus was given by the Norwegian rebel Henrik Ibsen. Although he himself founded no theatre, he furnished the inspiration for new theatres throughout the world. The first of the new "free" theatres—that is, free from commercial control—was the Théâtre Libre in Paris, founded in 1887 by André Antoine, who made his living working for the gas company. In a tiny hall, using real furniture, some of which he carted through the streets from his mother's dining room, he and a group of amateur actors made a strong impression and in a short while attracted a sizable audience. In 1889 a similar free theatre (Freie Bühne) opened in Berlin with Ibsen's *Ghosts* and soon was presenting Gerhart Hauptmann, a realistic German playwright of major importance. In 1890 London followed with the Independent Theatre, and it too found a native playwright, Bernard Shaw, to follow Ibsen. Dublin's Abbey Theatre was at first devoted to the poetic, mythical plays of William Butler Yeats, but John Millington Synge soon gave the rich, poetic language of Ireland a realistic turn. Then in the 1920s Sean O'Casey wrote some of the most powerful and beautiful realistic plays of the twentieth century.

Most important of the new theatres was the Moscow Art Theatre, founded in 1897 by Constantin Stanislavsky. Anton Chekhov was the new playwright who ensured its success. The only one of the pioneer theatres that was able to establish itself as a lasting institution, it is still the principal theatre in Moscow.

In New York the intimate theatre came a little later. From 1916 to 1920 the Provincetown Playhouse introduced the naturalistic one-act plays of its gifted playwright, Eugene O'Neill. A converted stable on MacDougal Street, the Provincetown Playhouse was even smaller than the realistic theatres of Europe, but it made an enormous impression. As an acting institution it did not last long, but soon the Theatre Guild, a more successful organization, and even the commercial producers adopted its ideals of honesty and realistic acting.

Like the off-Broadway theatres of recent decades, the "free" theatres started on a small scale, with ideals of acting, directing, and playwriting

1-5 Realism. Diagonal lines and dynamic variations of level weave the individuals into the web of environment. Inge's *Bus Stop.* Mankato State College production, directed by Ted Paul and designed by Burton E. Meisel.

quite different from those of the big boulevard theatres. Though short-lived, they pointed the way for others, and proved that a new audience was ready.

In the intimate theatres the proscenium arch was simplified or, in many cases, eliminated as a decorative element, leaving only a functional opening for viewing the "slice of life." Footlights, with their distasteful associations with glaring romantic spectacle and ham acting, were eliminated or hidden under removable sections of the floor for the few times when some artificial effect might be needed. The Cleveland Playhouse of 1927 set the pattern for intimate community theatres, with no decorative proscenium and no footlights but only two or three plain, dark steps leading the audience, in their minds, right onto the stage.

The box setting is the basic one in realism, using three walls and a ceiling, with the illusion that the fourth wall has been removed. Though actors have occasionally supposed a fireplace and even windows in the missing wall, most groups soon found it better to ignore that wall and to keep the actors facing not toward the audience but toward the properties and action on the stage.

With the changes in theatres and plays came new principles of directing: keep the actors focused on some center of interest on the stage; make full use of many different playing areas, especially the upstage areas; enrich the action with frequent use of properties and bodily reactions. The visit of the Moscow Art Theatre company to New York in 1923 left a lasting impression as the ultimate in art that hid all art. Nothing was obviously arranged, yet everything was meticulously clear. The actors seemed to have their backs to the audience constantly and to be absorbed in something behind the furniture or the other actors; no one ever moved out into a clear open space; no one ever seemed to turn toward the audience. Yet behind the casualness was such careful planning that for every important line the speaker just happened to have his face visible. Despite what appeared to be informal composition and random movement, the attention of the audience was always carried straight to the important person or action. Though each character seemed completely independent of the others, so strong was the basic rhythm that they all became part of one compelling action. There was no star, no predominant character, but rather a perfect ensemble. The foreground and background were one, and properties, costumes, doors, lamps, window curtains, and lights—no less than the actors—performed their parts.

The Stanislavsky Method of Acting

The impressive triumphs achieved by the Moscow Art Theatre company were made possible by a new approach to realistic acting that stimulated the inner life of the actor, so that the drama might be revealed in voice tone and body tensions—beyond, between, and sometimes in contradiction to the lines. As director of the company, Stanislavsky developed the principles of the "method," which has become the basis of most acting schools in the United States as well as in Russia. Assuming that his students were familiar with traditional techniques and were working many hours a week in courses in movement, dance, fencing, voice placement, singing, and diction, he concentrated on the inner preparation of the actor, which he has described fully in *An Actor Prepares*, the most admired book on acting in modern times.

Stanislavsky wanted to free the actor from distractions and false actions, to teach him to relax each part of the body from unnecessary tensions, and most of all to free him from conventional techniques of projection inherited from the nineteenth century. By concentrating on properties and the sequence of realistic business, the actor would forget the audience and his own tensions and would have no excuse for stately tread, loud declamation, or resounding intonation. The actor must analyze the character's "objective" in each scene and hence define the "spine" of the character for the whole play, then search for his own "emotional memories" of experiences that might be similar to those of the character. He must visit the kinds of houses, streets, and neighborhoods associated with the character, absorbing the sights, sounds, smells, and moods of the environment. Using the "magic if," he must, alone and with the other actors, improvise scenes, spending days thinking, feeling, acting, and speaking *as if* he actually were the character. In some cases he might substitute his own improvised words, but when he used the words of the playwright he created an "inner text" that added a complex richness to the actions and voice tones that went along with the words. With long practice and concentration, the actor might transform himself and make a complete new creation of each role.

The "method" school of acting has been most effective in intimate theatres and box settings for creating complex, inarticulate characters who are baffled or overwhelmed by their environment, whether the desperate slum characters of Gorki's *Lower Depths* or the equally helpless upper-class characters of Chekhov. Its first triumph in America was achieved by the Group Theatre of New York. Starting work together in 1931, this group of young actors dedicated themselves to the serious year-round study of acting, to the development of good ensemble playing, and to the production of serious new American plays. They broke up in 1941, but after the war one of their directors, Lee Strasberg, founded the Actors Studio, an institution not for production but for actors both young and old to continue serious study. For the next three decades the Actors Studio and the Stanislavsky approach dominated the training of American actors.

The main reason for the success of Stanislavsky's method is the precision with which it expresses the naturalistic vision of man—trapped by heredity and environment, victim of his baser drives, his will thwarted, unable to express his thoughts in words even when he is profoundly moved. The mute violence stirs through his inner being, coloring his daily movements and breaking into his ordinary voice tones. Without deliberately raising his voice or asserting a gesture, the method actor can move an audience deeply by the dark, inarticulate tragedy he holds in. But the repressed victim is not our only stage character, so Stanislavsky's method is not always appropriate. The assertive heroes of musical comedy, dance, and opera freely express their feelings; the exalted characters of Greek or Shakespearean tragedy, while they must be honest and convincing, live their emotions on a scale quite different from the underplayed, frustrated, indoor characters of Chekhov; the characters of Bertolt Brecht are not victims immersed in their environment but activists provoking political reactions; the absurdist antiheroes are broken off from all explainable character development; and the participants of the theatre of confrontation are exploding fragments hurling themselves on some image of the "establishment." These dramatic forms call for acting techniques either completely different or radically modified from the naturalistic techniques of the Stanislavsky school.

In spite of many kinds of new plays and many ways in which realism has been modified over the last half-century, the basic impulses persist and naturalistic playwriting, setting, and acting are still vital. Most of Tennessee Williams' characters are raw and naturalistic, driven by violent forces of sex and greed that they do not understand, shaped and hemmed in by their environment but in violent conflict with it. Arthur Miller made his first success in 1947 with a typical, Ibsen-like naturalistic play, *All My Sons.* After two decades of exploring several other forms—epic theatre, period tragedy, stylized monodrama, and even a modern Western for the movies—Miller returned to the simplest form of naturalistic drama. *The Price* (1967), with one setting and four characters, is as tight a well-made drama as any of Ibsen's, with two brothers reexamining in great detail their relation to their dead father and to each other, trying to come to some understanding of how their past and their environment have shaped them and what price they have had to pay for the choices they unconsciously made years before.

Thus, with its new intimate theatres and its Stanislavsky method acting, realism won a great victory over popular, escapist entertainment and ham acting. For half a century the serious drama student was committed to realism. He might indulge in a visit to opera, musical comedy, vaudeville or the movies. He might indulge occasionally in a "stylized" revival of a classic or an "experimental" expressionistic play. Until the last decade he expected to devote most of his attention and respect to faithful stage representations of real life.

Realism in the Movies

In providing entertainment for the masses, moviemakers have tried to reconcile conflicting impulses: to indulge the audience in sentimental daydreams and to use the camera to put parts of the real world on the screen. Of all the arts the cinema seems to be the almost perfect "dream mode." In the darkened theatre, immersed in waves of atmospheric music, the moviegoer sits back while images flow over him from the screen as easily as in his dreams. The camera swings freely through time and space, bringing him luxurious surroundings and illusions of success, power, freedom, or adoration. He identifies with the perfectly groomed and made-up hero and heroine. Hollywood, "the dream factory," took over the mass audi-

1-6 Realism in the movies. A small, crowded street is arranged for a candid-camera impression of reality in the filming of *Collision.* Even in daylight some extra lighting is needed. Twentieth-Century Fox. Photo Culver Pictures.

ence from the nineteenth-century melodramas and gave them all the clichés of conventional morality, sentimental pseudo-sorrow, and easy happy endings.

Yet even the melodramas, with their sensational stories and artificial heroes and heroines, were given a dimension of reality by the camera. No matter how romantic or sentimental the story, the movie can put it in real-looking houses and show scenes of actual streets and buildings. Many a movie is like a conducted tour, showing the traveler the fountains of Rome, the rich homes of the Riviera, the slums of Chicago, or the dives of Hong

Kong. The spectacular effects of melodrama could be made very convincing by the camera. The chariot race of *Ben Hur* was astonishingly realistic in the stage production, with horses and chariots on a treadmill in front of a moving canvas of painted buildings and painted spectators. But the scene was far more realistic in the movie, with a real crowd and real dust. And who would ever again want to see a heroine lashed to a piece of track on a stage floor with a miniature cardboard train bumping toward her once he had seen her on the screen on a real track with a real locomotive bearing down, or on the edge of a real cliff, plunging into a canyon to escape the pursuing villain?

The Western, the most stereotyped of all Victorian melodramas, with its sentimental, pure heroines, unmotivated bad men, and impossibly brave heroes, took on an unexpected reality with the camera and has continued decade after decade as the mainstay of popular movies and television. Even if the hero is not real, he rides a real horse over the hills in a wide expanse of

1-7 The underworld of violence and power. In a typical gangster film the criminal leader and his men defy the law and threaten the wealthy. *Little Caesar*, 1930. Museum of Modern Art.

western plains and sky. The big Western epics, from *The Covered Wagon* of 1923 on, if weak in psychology, have succeeded in suggesting the epic reality of American history—the exploring and settling of a wide continent. If some naive audiences today try to relive in imagination a pioneer past of quick-shooting tough men before the arrival of schools, churches, and peaceful neighbors, others have sense enough to see that whatever reality the Western has is the reality of a simple era that is now far in the past. But the mountains and plains give the Western an aura of contemporary authenticity.

The glamorous dream movies took on a new life in the 1930s with the development of color and sound, but they still gave little indication that this was the decade of economic depression, the rise of Hitler, and the Spanish Civil War. Yet a new type of picture, the gangster movie, did present some raw reality. Though it exploited sadistic violence and the old melodrama clichés of gang loyalty and betrayal, its tough city characters were played with sharp directness by new actors with irregular, individual features rather than romantic good looks—Paul Muni, George Raft, James Cagney, Edward G. Robinson, and others. In the midst of the thrilling suspense, there was some insight into the twisted personality of the criminal and a great deal of reporting on the modern city, from its raw streets and slums, rich dives and night clubs, to back-room gatherings of corrupt politicians and ruthless businessmen.

The "documentary," which presents real people, with no fictional story and no professional actors, is quite distinct from the story film, yet its approach to reality has had great influence on movies, on television, and on epic theatre. The documentary in a crude form has existed ever since the first man with a movie camera filmed a street parade, but it was not recognized as a separate genre until the 1920s. While Hollywood was producing Cecil B. De Mille's colossal spectacles, superromantic films with Rudolph Valentino, and equally unreal pictures about the social game of wealthy people, Robert Flaherty filmed *Nanook of the North* (1922), showing the daily life and trials of a real Eskimo family. He created an even more compelling documentary in *Man of Aran* (1934), showing life on an isolated island off the coast of Ireland. Flaherty's photography and editing made these studies of real life as absorbing as any fictional film.

Three memorable documentaries of the 1930s were short films that did not center on individuals but studied wide problems that challenged public policy in the days of Franklin D. Roosevelt and the New Deal: the misuse of water and land and the decay of cities. *The Plow That Broke the Plains* (1936), *The River* (1937), and *The City* (made for the New York World's Fair of 1939–40) were impressive and beautiful films. Beginning in 1934, *The March of Time* was a popular documentary, a regular news report in some depth that continued for more than two decades in radio, movies, and television. Its function has been taken over by special reports on the regular television networks. Among numerous documentaries and semidocumentaries in the 1960s, three effective feature-length films summarized, largely through news reels and scenes of actual events, the careers of Winston Churchill, Eleanor Roosevelt, and John F. Kennedy. Just as such writers as Truman Capote and Norman Mailer have treated factual material with the same artistic devices that they had used in fiction, the makers of documentaries use human interest as well as symbolic montage and illustrative background material to give shape and power to their subjects. Conversely, the makers of fictional films and TV shows have added authenticity by cutting in photographed shots of places and events. For example, between the fictional scenes of *Medium Cool* (1969) Haskell Wexler used actual scenes of street violence in Chicago during the Democratic Convention of 1968.

At the end of the Second World War the movies rediscovered the harsh reality of direct realism, but not in Hollywood. Hollywood made *The Best Years of Our Lives* (1946), about the men coming back from the war, telling a real story and including an actor who had had both hands shot off in action. But it turned out to be the same old slick formula film. The new Italian films, on the other hand, offered something vital. Roberto Rossellini finished *Open City* in 1945 as the Germans were leaving, presenting actual street scenes and using harsh black and white film because he could not afford better. But the sun-drenched Roman streets, the sharp shadows, the tenement rooms, and the fresh, nonprofessional performers made a very exciting, unsentimental picture of violence and terror at the end of the war. Italian audiences were not much interested in the frank presentation of their poverty, but American audiences were fascinated by the real people, real streets, real economic problems, and real political passions. Since 1945 the Italian film has been one of the strongest influences in Western cinema. Vittorio De Sica filmed *Shoeshine* in 1946, with street urchins as actors, and when a bricklayer's face caught his fancy, a man who had never acted before became the star of *Bicycle Thief* (1949). The masterpiece of Italian realism was Federico Fellini's *La Strada* (1954), a most touching study of tramp carnival performers. A coarse wandering entertainer, Zampano, played by Anthony Quinn, picks up a young, not very bright girl, Gelsomina, played by Giulietta Masina, Fellini's wife. He buys her, in fact, from her impoverished mother. She learns to play a trumpet, to dance, and to do her part in making their living, accepting Zampano's rough treatment and infidelities. They join a troupe of carnival people, and an acrobat befriends her. When Zampano kills the acrobat and he and Gelsomina are outcasts on the road, he decides to abandon her. Obsessed with memory of the girl,

1-8 Oriental study of fine feelings in a real world. Apu falls in love. *The World of Apu,* 1959, the third film in a trilogy directed by Satyajit Ray. Harrison Pictures.

he eventually finds the village where she had wandered, only to learn that she is dead. In the last sequence he stands on the shore of the gray sea, overcome by grief and despair. Here, with excellent naturalistic acting and directing, are the basic elements of nineteenth-century naturalism—inarticulate characters driven and destroyed by crude natural forces, in harsh but rich-textured surroundings, invoking not our moral judgment but our compassion and objective understanding.

In Sweden, Ingmar Bergman has created his own kind of symbolism, but many of his movies reflect the grim, relentless seriousness of the naturalistic plays of August Strindberg. His trilogy of the early 1960s—*Through a Glass Darkly, Winter Light,* and *The Silence*—follows his characters through the winter twilight of tortured guilt and destructive emotions. India's very large film industry produces conventional romantic spectacles, but the one Indian filmmaker who has found a Western audience, Satyajit Ray, presents with great originality the simple, everyday life in the Bengal villages and the slums of Calcutta. Neither Bergman nor Ray is interested in the social reform aspects of naturalism but rather in the complex feelings of a few real people in their everyday surroundings.

In England, too, there was a resurgence of realism in the 1950s and 60s, led by the playwrights but of enormous importance in the film industry as well. As in the earlier surges of naturalism, it brought in new material, especially about the life in the industrial cities and of such groups as North Country and Jewish families—material that seemed fresh and robust to a London audience used to genteel plays about the upper classes. The resurgence started suddenly in 1956 with the electric response to John Osborne's first play, *Look Back in Anger.* We will discuss Osborne in Chapter 7, on the theatre of disruption, but this play is in most aspects a naturalistic piece. Jimmy Porter, the main character, is caught in an environment he hates, but he is not inarticulate. He spits back with a fiery anger that gave a name to a generation in Britain—the Angry Young Men. The welfare state is a boring fact that leaves him still frustrated. The old establishment is still intact and he is still outside the regular social order. Jimmy is not fighting for any social cause; his problem is spiritual, as shown in his changing relationship with his wife, Alison. He torments her and drives her out, and he can accept her only when she too is humiliated and crushed by intense suffering. Though Osborne's play does not have the wide scope of Sean O'Casey's or Eugene O'Neill's plays, its depth of suffering, its cry for compassion, its vividness of speech almost put it in the class of their best naturalistic plays.

Even more startling in its frank depiction of raw human nature was Shelagh Delaney's *A Taste of Honey,* which appeared on the stage in 1958 and in film in 1961. Set in the slums of a northern industrial city, it presents a lonely young girl, pregnant from a passing affair with an American Negro sailor, who finds she would rather turn to the homosexual boy with whom she has formed a platonic friendship than to her irresponsible mother.

Postwar American films reflected no such resurgence of realism as in other countries, yet in America, too, the field of subject matter was widened to include real-life topics that had been forbidden. American filmmakers had been handicapped by censorship and by the widespread feeling that since the movies were entertainment for the masses nothing should be shown that might startle a conventional American family. Under the threat of censorship that followed a notorious Hollywood scandal in 1922, the producers had set up a "code of decency" that prohibited, among other things, scenes of passion, sexual perversion, white slavery, miscegenation, venereal disease, and childbirth. The camera could not even show a double bed in a married couple's house. Of course profane or naughty language was taboo. Not until *Gone With the Wind* in 1939 was the word "damn" heard from the American screen. There could be any amount of overt violence or oblique indications of sex, but no serious treatment of the darker aspects of human psychology. But after the Second World War, major changes took place. The stage drama and the novel had made great advances, and many people were not happy when the Hollywood film adaptations prettified or emasculated the main scenes. In a series of decisions government censorship was thrown out by the courts, and in 1953 the Supreme Court ruled that the screen shares with the press the protection of free speech guaranteed by the first and fourteenth amendments to the Constitution.

In the first decade after the war the overwhelming power of the Hollywood studios was broken, partly by legal action separating production from distribution, partly by independent producers working in foreign countries and exploiting new material. But the biggest blow to Hollywood was television. By the 1950s television had become the mass entertainment of America, and thousands of movie houses closed down as the movies became a minority art. When the movies and radio in the 1920s had taken the mass audience, the legitimate theatre had lost its wide support, but as a minority art it greatly improved. It did not have to conform to the lowest common denominator of taste or the most conventional ideas of what is proper. In the same way the moviemaker had far greater freedom as a worker in a minority art. But the battle of realism constantly recurs as writer and director try to break through taboos and conventional ideas to show man and his world as they are. In its earlier days Hollywood had neglected or greatly modified the naturalistic plays of Eugene O'Neill, but in the 1950s and 60s the even more shocking plays of Tennessee Williams were put on the screen without flinching from the themes of cannibalism, castration, and homosexuality.

In the 1960s American moviemakers continued to move in two directions. On the one hand, as they followed the path of naturalism in showing with the utmost honesty people as they are, there was a great extension in subject matter. The taboo on four-letter words was relaxed; nudity, the rage of the off-Broadway shows, appeared in brief glimpses on the screen, and themes of sexual and drug experimentation competed in frankness. In the films about rebellious youth that were so popular at the end of the sixties, the wild psychedelic party became a cliché. Moralists continued to cry out in alarm, but a large audience, especially the young people, was ready for freer expression. Movie attendance increased in the late sixties, approaching the figures of pre-television days, with a large preponderance of moviegoers in the age bracket from eighteen to twenty-five. But on the other hand there was still a wide conservative audience that wanted undisturbing films with simple plots and cheerful, conventional characters. Such sentimental costume musicals as *The Sound of Music* and *Mary Poppins*—excellent demonstrations of camera techniques but with subject matter that would not upset the most prudish viewer—were the big moneymakers.

In trying to please both audiences, Hollywood was likely, even when

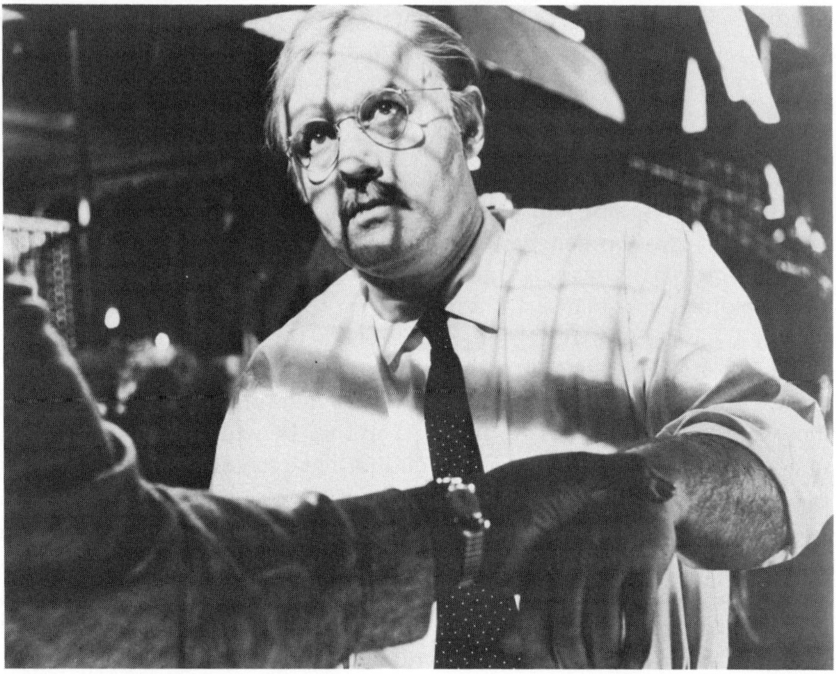

1-9 A high point in acting for the screen. In Sidney Lumet's *The Pawnbroker*, 1965, Rod Steiger plays a victim of Nazi persecution who finally allows himself to feel. Photo Commonwealth United–Entertainment, Inc.

it tried to present a new point of view—as, for instance, on race relations—to use old stereotypes of character and attitude. There is not much fresh realism in *Guess Who's Coming to Dinner* (1968), with the glamorous dignity of Katharine Hepburn and Spencer Tracy as the slightly surprised white parents and the glamorized, impersonal dignity of Sidney Poitier as a black scientist about to marry their daughter. There is much stronger realism in *Who's Afraid of Virginia Woolf?* (1967). No Hollywood studio would have attempted this shocking revelation of frustration, impotence, and vituperative cruelty if the famous actors Elizabeth Taylor and Richard Burton had not insisted, and though in the film there was some softening in the night lighting, there was no softening in the relentless exposure of the characters.

Independent producers of the same decade had previously created some arresting examples of film realism. *David and Lisa* (1962), an unpretentious film written and directed by Frank Perry, is a poignant study of how two psychotic adolescents in a small institution learn to trust each other and to trust reality. Much more painful is the naturalism of Sidney Lumet's *The Pawnbroker* (1965). Rod Steiger gave one of the best performances of the decade as a pawnbroker in Harlem, a survivor of a Nazi extermination camp who is determined never to feel again. The camera catches the rich textures of the slums and a cross section of Harlem people, scared, sullen, cruel. Only when a Negro boy he was beginning to know is killed by gangsters does the pawnbroker allow himself to feel and suffer. The emotion is powerful, but it has been achieved by the indirect suggestion and objective surface of realism.

Other realistic pictures of the late 1960s have been less violent than *The Pawnbroker*, yet they have gained power by their honesty in dealing with unsophisticated people in ordinary surroundings. Both *Rachel, Rachel* and *The Heart Is a Lonely Hunter* will be long remembered because, without the magic of glamorous stars, they arouse a deep compassion for humble people, frustrated in their dreams, forced to accept the compromises of a real world. As in the best impressionist plays, the lonely moods are haunting as sensitive individuals struggle to free themselves from the web of their surroundings.

Movie realism can be as powerful as stage realism, and with photography of actual places, it can seem even more real. By cutting in scenes of skies and trees, light and dark, the film can create powerful impressionistic moods. By going outdoors as easily as indoors, by including work, eating, play, the film can present much more of the environment than can be brought to life on the stage; the screen, though two-dimensional and often without color, seems to be the most perfect medium for presenting the real. Many people have argued that since the camera can so far surpass the stage in showing reality, theatre people should give up realism and try to put on the stage only the fantastic, the artificial, the truly theatrical—only those things that are peculiar to the stage. Yet the film, by so easily using its textures of reality to validate fantasies, sentimental stories, conventional characters, and shopworn ideas, constantly caters to the idle daydreams of the masses. Only the more determined authors, directors, and moviegoers—ardent fighters with the spirit of Zola and Ibsen—can forget easy entertainment and deal with real life.

Realism on the TV Screen

Realism has had to battle for a place on the home screen, the mass medium that brings dramas—nearly a hundred a week—to almost the entire population of America. Through radio, broadcast drama grew up as a distinct form, and its relation to the audience is quite different from that of the movie or play. The millions of viewers have not gone out for a special occasion. They are sitting at home, drinking or eating or talking with family or friends, expecting every week or every day, in the midst of countless commercials, the same familiar news broadcasts and variety shows in neat half-hour or one-hour programs. The drama that catered to such a relaxed audience was more like vaudeville than like either realistic drama or the movies, borrowing from the neighboring programs the narrator-announcer, some of the stereotyped characters, and the casual, informal relationship with the audience. To this day the popular TV personalities, especially the comedians, often include a dramatic skit with their songs and jokes—excellent light entertainment for the mass audience but not a serious treatment of reality. Nevertheless there have been some notable achievements in realistic broadcast drama.

In the minds of the audience a broadcast conveys a far stronger sense of reality than either the stage or the movies—a sense that what they are hearing is not fiction but news of an actual event. When an English radio station in 1926 presented a parody of an announcer describing a supposed riot, the broadcast was taken seriously. In this country in 1938, when Orson Welles produced a dramatic program about an imaginary invasion from Mars, using some of the techniques of announcers and interviewers, listeners were disturbed and many ran out of their houses in terror. Conversely, even the most factual documentary has some elements of fiction and dramatization. During the first space flight the three major television networks spent an estimated ten million dollars, which included not only the cost of televising the launching and the recovery of the capsule from the ocean but also the cost of many shots of models, some of them created in the studio, showing not the actual capsule but how the equipment probably looked in use. Some critics thought that drawings might have been more honest in clarifying whether a shot was of the real space ship or of a model. On the stage there is no question of the relationship between specific fact and generalized truth, since all is clearly not actual fact, but representation on a particular level of honesty or fantasy. But the TV camera blurs this distinction, and for that reason judges and congressmen have been reluctant to allow a television camera in court or Congress. Sometimes a fictional representation, as in a drawing or a drama, is "truer" and more just than simple facts. Still, a TV broadcast, even of a drama, seems not a generalized truth, but an immediate event.

The late 1940s and 50s saw a remarkable development of live TV drama in America. "Playhouse 90," "The Philco-Goodyear Playhouse," "Studio One," "The Kraft TV Theatre," and several other programs brought to the home screen new plays on an average of once a week. Some were adaptations from stage plays, novels, or short stories, but many were the work of a new school of playwrights who explored the documentary realism and quiet intimacy of radio drama to develop a new form that was especially effective for television. In these plays, as in the impressionist plays of Chekhov, the quiet characters are in conflict with their environment at many little points, trying to find a small area of freedom while accepting the web of fate that holds them. At most there is a muted sadness, never such sharp defeat as in the realism of O'Neill or Williams. One of the finest plays was Tad Mosel's dramatization of the James Agee novel *A Death in the Family*, called on the television screen, as on Broadway and in the movie, *All the Way Home*. The family, faced with the sudden accidental death of the husband and father, finds new strength through deep and uncomplicated affection for the dead man and for one another. In Mosel's *The Haven*, a middle-aged woman, discovering an infidelity her husband committed years before, realizes that she is caught in the web of daily life herself and must work out a new pattern. In Horton Foote's *Trip to Bountiful* a little old Texas lady escapes from the shoddy city home of her son and daughter-in-law to hunt for the farm home she left some years before. When she discovers that her closest friend has died and the farm is overgrown with woods, she gives up. Having made her protest, she is willing to accept her fate.

The high point of this intimate realism, the miniature television masterpiece of the 1950s, was Paddy Chayefsky's *Marty*, put on the air in 1954 with Rod Steiger in the title role and later made into a successful movie with Ernest Borgnine. Marty is a short, fat worker in a butcher shop who lives with a possessive mother but spends much of his time with rootless young friends drifting from bars to public dance halls. One night Marty meets a lonely, unattractive girl who is ignored by the other men. The two, in their loneliness, find that they are congenial. When his companions make fun of the girl and his mother disapproves, Marty hesitates. But after looking again at the life led by his friends, with their ideals of flashy feminine beauty and cheap popularity, he asks the ugly duckling for a date. He has a chance for a family of his own on the back streets of the big city.

Thus, in what has been called the "golden age of television drama," a school of playwrights learned to make effective use of the techniques particularly characteristic of television. There were a number of realistic insights—conflict between mothers and sons, frustration and anger in crowded apartments and boarding houses, conflicts between the values of the big city and the small town or old city neighborhoods. But such insights were not enough to save this form of drama from the simultaneous expansion of the national economy and the television audience in the late 1950s and the 60s. The wider, more affluent audience was not interested in little plays about little people or in the themes of frustration and the acceptance of limitations—the themes of intimate realism since Chekhov. The advertisers, for their part, did not want the public to dwell on acceptance of life in small towns and on grubby back streets but to dream of the glamorous elegance of new automobiles and hair sprays. In the intimate dramas the central characters are repelled by slick city ways, but luxury buying was what the advertisers wanted, and American television depended entirely upon the advertisers.

As a substitute for the individual television play, producers and advertisers of the 1960s relied on the packaged drama series with the same familiar characters and the same pattern of action, continued week after week. This format held the audience better than individual plays, and it was more likely to put the audience in a mood for buying. Like the commercials themselves, these series portrayed rich, successful people. In "Peyton Place" there were old crimes, prison records, and misunderstandings that might have come from nineteenth-century novels or daytime soap operas, but the women had beautiful hairdos and, for a small town, rather up-to-date homes and wardrobes. Doctors, nurses, and psychiatrists in other series generally had rich patients. "The Beverly Hillbillies" retained their rural twang but had money to throw away. The Cartwrights of "Bonanza" were not pioneers struggling to build a home in the wilderness but affluent owners of an enormous ranch and defenders of an established security against evil intruders and eccentric wanderers. In the serious TV series, poor people with foreign accents were merely passing problems for the lawyers, social workers, and legislators to do something about. So the anthologies of live drama—the hope of the 1950s—dropped out, leaving local characters to the broad comedians and spontaneity to the Jack Paars, Johnny Carsons, and other "talk show" personalities.

The most interesting achievement of realism on the television screen came in the early sixties with a marriage of myth and reality, the domestication of the most far-fetched of popular romantic fantasies—the savior-figure who brings rescue or aid to suffering humanity. In the 1930s, radio listeners from eight to eighty, hearing the *William Tell Overture* and the sound of pounding hooves, settled down comfortably for another episode of "The Lone Ranger." They knew the formula. Some questionable character was threatening the rights of the good settlers, and it was time for the masked stranger to appear on his horse, Silver. He arrived with the Indian Tonto, spoke in a deep, rich baritone, and shot the gun out of the hand of the villain. Although he had supposedly been a Texas Ranger, nobody really knew who he was. Accepting no thanks for his services, he cried, "Hi-ho, Silver, away!" and rode off into the mysterious void, to be seen again only when his help was needed. On other nights, the Lone Ranger of the Machine

Age, the Green Hornet, arrived in a purring roadster with his house boy Kato to the theme music of *The Flight of the Bumblebee.* He could put a villain to sleep with a green whiff from a nontoxic gun. Besides these rescue melodramas, the 1930s discovered the appeal of hearing real people in trouble advised by an expert. A Bronx cab driver (who was, incidentally, very unsuccessful in his own marriage) set up a Marital Relations Institute and went on the air as John J. Anthony. Every Sunday night husbands and wives wept as they reviewed their quarrels for the gaping ears of America. It was the newspaper advice-to-the-lovelorn column come alive. Psychologists and social workers might be contemptuous of the program's simple, clichéd advice—"Mother knows best," "Follow the Golden Rule"—but Mr. Anthony knew how to draw out the confessions and guide the squabbles, so that the audience had a sense of seeing into human misery and was given reassurance that some solution—some magic advice or unexpected financial aid—could be found.

In the early sixties a hybrid character appeared that combined the Lone Ranger and Mr. Anthony and added the complexity of naturalism. The modern rescue hero—doctor, lawyer, reporter—gave mature, professional advice and undertook to face complex problems that could not easily be solved. A fair amount of realism had already appeared in the courtroom dramas about Perry Mason, but the people he unfailingly rescued from the district attorney were involved in conventional situations of deception or misunderstanding, and the program's interest centered on clever devices of courtroom strategy. But the high school teacher in the "Mr. Novak" series found that many students had problems he could not solve. The social worker in "East Side, West Side" dealt with difficult problems of slum children and old people, with poverty, greed, even abortion and insanity—problems too serious and too genuine to win top rating for the program. It was dropped after one season. Other rescue series that were less disturbing to the average viewer but still honest and serious managed to survive a little longer. "Slattery's People," showing an idealistic young statesman working on public programs in a state legislature, had a rich, smooth social setting, but it portrayed a rescue figure in a real world. In "The Defenders," the two lawyers, father and son, had to explore all aspects of the modern city in order to help their clients. "The Reporter" gave a strong sense of reality, though often the rescue was not much more subtle than Superman's leaping tall buildings at a single bound. Even some of the lighter, more sentimental series of the early sixties had a touch of reality. "The Andy Griffith Show" was set in a conventional small town where family and community problems were solved not by a legal or medical expert but by an old-fashioned, good-natured sheriff.

The "problem" type of television series was a major attempt to create serious social drama for a wide public, offering the continuity of a few appealing characters for audience identification, a repeated pattern that made understanding easy, and considerable variety and complexity in the problems that needed solving. The attempt was partially successful. These programs found an audience of many millions, and "East Side, West Side," "Slattery's People," and "The Defenders" won high praise from thoughtful people. But even a small degree of realism was too much to attract the largest audience. By 1965 the advertisers had become slaves to the rating system. If the rating services found by their samples that a program had fallen a few points below the rival shows, that program was dropped as soon as a replacement could be found. Public favor and advertisers' support had veered away from the realistic "problem" series to the more conventionalized suspense drama, to the agent-spy-defender, who was more stereotyped than the realistic lawyer, social worker, or doctor, to the simpler kind of battle against mythical international conspirators or old-fashioned bandits and cattle thieves.

The realistic approach is still a very vital tradition, but, as we shall see in the next chapter, it has been greatly modified and influenced by other developments of the twentieth century. There are now many different kinds of realism. Realism has had a strong impact even on ballet and opera, and as we have found, it has a place in the mass arts of cinema and television. Even as the popular arts show people the old stereotypes of how they would like to live, realists insist on showing them the patterns and forces that actually shape their lives.

New Ways of Presenting Reality

2

In almost all the realistic or naturalistic plays we have mentioned so far, man is seen as the victim of an environment that thwarts his wishes. His angers and hopes may smolder in frustration, but all he can do is face destruction or fret as his life is eroded by time. But there are other ways of showing man's relation to the environment, other kinds of realism in which the victim does not so docilely accept defeat. He may decide to stand up to his environment and either control it or destroy it. Two variants of realistic theatre, similar in some ways, express this confidence. One, which may be called *selected realism*, depicts man's partial victory over his environment; things no longer overwhelm, and the local color, though it may be rich in mood, is not so stifling as in naturalistic plays. The other variant, which may be called *stylized realism*, shows a more direct, more explosive attack on the environment. Although they followed rather different lines of development—selected realism leading to a comedy of social problems and stylized realism to expressionism—they can be considered together as modifications of realism that no longer treated man as a passive victim.

Selected Realism and Stylized Realism

Escape has not always seemed a futile dream, as it does in Chekhov's plays. Many people have escaped from slums and small towns. Many people have become rich and moved away from their cramping environment or have asserted themselves and improved it. Many popular novels and plays have presented a serious struggle with environment leading to at least partial triumph. If the main character has been defeated, there is often hope that the next generation will succeed. That was the pattern of the most talked-about novel of the 1920s, *Main Street*, by Sinclair Lewis, in which small-town conformity won a temporary victory but stirred the victim to the secret determination that her young son would someday succeed where she had failed. In Sidney Howard's *The Silver Cord* (1926), the conflict between a possessive mother and her sons builds to violent scenes, which end in the defeat of one son but the successful escape of the other. Escape is gloriously successful in *The Barretts of Wimpole Street* (1930) by Rudolf Besier, in which Robert Browning, like a medieval knight, rescues his love, Elizabeth Barrett, from her father, who has tried to keep her an invalid under his own morbid control.

On the other hand, some plays suggest that the environment may not be so bad as it has seemed, that escape may not be necessary. Perhaps nature is not always the enemy of man. Perhaps it does not really matter that the hero, wishing to escape, is held back by the unconscious forces of nature and that his conscious wish is defeated. In Shaw's *Man and Superman* (1903), though the tone is that of a vigorous high-comedy quarrel between a man and a woman, the theme is the same naturalistic one of an attempt to escape. Jack Tanner, feeling that marriage would be the end of his intellectual independence, struggles to escape the wiles and powerful appeal of Ann Whitefield, who seems the essence of blind nature, determined to use him and destroy him just to propagate the race, without regard for his human, intelligent purposes. Yet when he does capitulate there is no defeat. He has had a dream of a great debate that his predecessor, Don Juan, holds in hell, a dream that ends with Don Juan and Donna Anna leaving the comfortable world of hell to tackle the difficult job of creating a higher,

2-1 Selected realism. The details of a middle-class Norwegian home are simplified and organized into a design of dignity. Alla Nazimova and Harry Ellerbe in Ibsen's *Ghosts.* New York, 1935. Photo Vandamm.

more intellectual man—a superman. When Jack realizes that woman, the blind force of nature, may also will the intelligent, as Donna Anna did, he no longer objects to giving in to nature by marrying.

In several American comedies of the 1920s, a comic hero suffers an exasperating defeat, which pleases the audience. One of these is Ben Hecht and Charles MacArthur's *The Front Page* (1928), a fast-moving play about newspapers, crime, and politics, which had a very successful revival in New York in 1969–70. A young reporter is trying to wrap up his scoop on a murder case so that he can be free to marry and can escape from his hectic career. When he finally gets on the train with his fiancée, however, his boss calls the police to bring him back, and the audience knows he will never get away. But why should he escape such an exciting environment?

In plays like this the human personality is not absorbed by the background. A few bold characters assert their will with sharp comic acting that is more positive than "method" acting. The stage setting does not present the full, overwhelming detail of naturalism but only enough detail for the action or for local color. If the play indicates that the characters have some control of their destiny, it is fitting that the setting reflect the artistic control of the designer. It can have elements of good composition: good line, form, proportion, rhythm, color, and even a fair amount of symmetry—elements that would be neglected or hidden in a naturalistic slice-of-life play.

Both naturalism, in which the individual is overwhelmed by the details of the environment, and selected realism, in which the individual has some control, still kept an objective view of one real place at a time. But that objective view did not suffice when the naturalistic character felt menaced by the machine age and when his irrational fears burst into his conscious mind. It was not so much the immediate surroundings that terrified him as the isolated images: rhythmic mechanized sounds, dehumanized groups of people, fragments of many past experiences. This explosive conflict called not for selected realism but for stylized realism, which kept the central character intact but, in order to present the violence of the conflict, used abstraction and distortion to break up the environment into fantastic fragments.

Eugene O'Neill's *The Hairy Ape* (1922) is an excellent example of stylized realism. Yank, a ship's stoker, is a typical naturalistic character who makes a blind attack on his environment, ignorant of how that environment might be improved but acutely aware of the spiritual anguish of not belonging to it. He has tried to identify himself with the steel, the coal, the power and speed of his time, but he finds that the machine age needs only his muscle: he has become a dehumanized brute. When the daughter of the shipowner calls him a hairy ape, he leaves the ship in a rage, throwing himself against the rich people coming out of a church on Fifth Avenue. But they are not human. Without looking to right or left they walk along in rows, repeating in stylized, mechanical rhythms the phrases of their inane chatter. In some productions they wear masks. The street and the people are shown not objectively but subjectively, stylized and distorted as they would appear to Yank's bewildered mind. It is only the environment that is unreal, however; Yank remains a naturalistic victim, but one who refuses to accept his fate and explodes in violence. Deep in his puzzled mind he realizes that his alienation cannot be cured by any slight improvement in the environment. He has been thrown out of the office of a labor union, where he offered to help blow up the city; violence does not "belong."

The expressionistic distortion in *The Hairy Ape* is only incidental, intended to show the mental state of the main character. The more extended and systematic stylization of the environment makes O'Neill's *The Emperor Jones* (1920) an expressionistic play. Yet in this play too the main character is a naturalistic victim in explosive conflict with his environment. A clever black Pullman porter, Brutus Jones, exploiting the ignorant natives of an island in the Caribbean, has made himself Emperor. When his subjects become restless he tries to escape, but in the terrors of the jungle night he loses his veneer of civilization and is destroyed, not so much by the natives as by his own fears. As in Vachel Lindsay's poem "The Congo," the primi-

2-2 Stylized realism and expressionism. Jones in his fantasy sees the crocodile god. O'Neill's *The Emperor Jones.* Design by Donald Oenslager for Yale University production. Photo Peter A. Juley and Son.

tive jungle repossesses modern man. The environment is stylized in the regular drumbeat—one of the most famous theatrical devices of early twentieth-century theatre—which starts early in the play and continues without interruption through the brief intermissions to the end. The environment, as much subjective as local, is stylized also in the phantoms that appear to Jones each time he pauses in his flight. Each hallucination goes further into his past, peeling off another level of his consciousness. First there are just vague shapes, then the crap games, fights, trials, and chain gangs of his own past, and finally the crocodile gods of his primitive ancestors—all stylized in mechanical, terrifying, rhythmic movement. By using an abstract and symbolic form, O'Neill makes his play suggest the primitive violence that lurks beneath the surface of modern man and the violence of colonial peoples, ready to turn on their exploiters and destroy them even when, as here, both exploiter and exploited are black.

Such monodramas, with one real character contending against the stylized fragments of a hostile environment, have been important in the 1950s and 60s. Some of the monodramas of Eugène Ionesco and John Osborne will be discussed in Chapter 7, on the theatre of disruption. A brilliant example was the movie *Midnight Cowboy* of 1969. As the Texas cowboy, played by Jon Voight, is baffled by the confusing appearances of New York, we see either stylized fragments of the New York scene, the bleary colors of a psychedelic party, or the fast, distorted flashbacks of his memories of Texas. As he dreams of sexual conquests, there are flashbacks to his childhood, with his grandmother building him up as a charmer. When he is in the hands of a religious fanatic, we see gruesome flashbacks to a Texas baptism. When he is cornered or threatened, his terror is expressed in horrifying flashbacks to the night he had taken a girl to an abandoned house, and had been captured first by a gang of hoodlums and then by police. Gradually the dying city rat, played by Dustin Hoffman, comes into focus, and for awhile there are two real people against the hostile, disconnected outside world. On the bus trip to Miami, it is the crippled city boy who sees Florida's beaches stylized in his forlorn hopes.

Stylization is a kind of abstraction, but the theatre before the middle of this century had developed other kinds of abstraction that were more thoroughgoing than selected realism and more flexible and subtle than stylized realism. We will now look at three other ways of presenting reality, ways that have usually been classified as nonrealistic but that are now being absorbed into the main tradition of realism: abstract realism, Oriental realism of make-believe, and epic realism.

Abstract Realism

In 1938 Thornton Wilder called on the New York audience to take a new view of reality, to see the daily details of American life abstracted from the usual box setting of the realistic environment. His *Our Town* used no front curtain, no scenery, and no properties except a few chairs, a couple of ladders, and some trellises pushed out at one point "for those who think they have to have scenery." The Stage Manager came out to chat with the audience and point out what they were to imagine on the stage—two kitchens, a back yard, or a drugstore counter, with the rest of the town imagined in the background. He moved chairs as they were needed and occasionally became a minor character—the soda fountain clerk or the minister for the wedding. The play was equally free in time as the Stage Manager introduced scenes or stopped them, mentioning what was going to

2-3 Abstract realism. Death and eternity are suggested by simple theatrical means. The living characters stand with umbrellas around Emily's grave, while she joins the rows of the sitting dead. Wilder's *Our Town.* New York, 1938. Photo Vandamm.

happen to different characters or what had happened in the past. Since there is no strong plot, Wilder freely arranged his series of scenes to demonstrate in three separate acts three aspects of one theme.

The first act shows the daily life of the town, from the first preparations for breakfast and the arrival of the newsboy and milkman to the return from choir practice in the moonlight and the settling down for the night. In the second act, the daily kitchen and breakfast activity is concentrated on getting ready for the wedding of Emily and George, but before the wedding scene itself there is a flashback to a drugstore scene showing the first time the couple knew that they were made for each other. With the method of make-believe well established in two acts, it is easy to move on to the cemetery in the third act, the chairs now set in rows to represent graves where the dead sit and speak. Emily, a new arrival, realizes that she can revisit the living and decides to look at her own twelfth birthday. A few feet in front of the sitting dead, she watches her mother start the day, until the pain of seeing her youthful self in the light of later time becomes too strong, and she gladly returns to take her place on the hilltop.

Free from the limitations of a realistic setting and actual properties, Wilder can show each individual moment against a wide panorama of time and place. The imagination conjures up the streets, stores, churches, trains, and milk wagons of the town, the twins born over in Polish town, the grandparents in the cemetery on the hill, the early settlers, the Indians, the rocks of the mountains, millions of years old. The Stage Manager sends the mind back to the daily life of Babylon and Rome, and forward to the future of these small-town American people and to people who may look back at them thousands of years from now. Each action of Emily and George and their parents and neighbors in Grover's Corners, New Hampshire, is the center of concentric circles of waves extending into time and space as far as the mind can conceive. The first act ends with the younger sister's awe-struck recital of the address on a letter her friend has received: "It said: Jane Crofut; the Crofut Farm; Grover's Corners; Sutton County; New Hampshire; United States of America; Continent of North America; Western Hemisphere; the Earth; the Solar System; the Universe, the Mind of God—that's what it said on the envelope—and the postman brought it just the same." The last act ends with the dead quietly talking about the stars and the millions of years it takes their light to reach the earth. Everyday life, seen by so many naturalistic writers as restrictive, petty, and degrading, takes on a glow of importance when thus abstracted from realistic scenery and set in a wide perspective of time and place.

Wilder derived the device of looking at a single moment from two distinct points in time from the novels of Marcel Proust. For Proust, time was destructive and experience meaningless except as isolated moments of the past might be recaptured and enjoyed in memory through the recollection of how senses, feelings, and moods had been aroused in the original experience. In Wilder's wide perspective of time, however, the little events of daily life are not meaningless or disconnected. In *Our Town*, the sentimental recognition that time passes is painful to Emily, but it makes her see human life more clearly in a wider philosophical framework. Wilder does not accept a grubby, materialistic view. "It ain't houses and it ain't names, and it ain't earth, and it ain't even the stars—everybody knows in their bones that something is eternal, and that something has to do with human beings." Even the people in the cemetery are waiting "for the eternal part in them to come out clear." By his abstract staging, Wilder makes the timeless human quality of his characters come out clear.

Our Town has played all over the world, and its influence has been enormous. Its success has encouraged other playwrights and producers to use more flexible, imaginative staging, with open platforms and no scenery or only suggestive pieces, using narrators or masters of ceremonies who interrupt the actors or bring them on stage as the theme requires, in any plan of time or space that the audience can be persuaded to imagine.

Oriental Realism of Make-Believe

It was the Chinese theatre that suggested to Wilder his new approach in *Our Town*. He had grown up in China, where his father was an American consul, and he was fascinated by the free, highly imaginative methods of the Oriental theatre. From the Chinese theatre he learned that even the

2-4 Oriental make-believe. Masks of the Japanese Noh theatre. Drawn by Bobbie Okerbloom.

important events of everyday life can be presented by actors on an open platform, reacting not to a realistic setting but to the private thoughts and personal relations of the characters.

A few Chinese plays had been known in the West before *Our Town*, but they were considered the opposite of realism and had been presented in such a way that audiences might laugh at the unfamiliar stage conventions or might be entranced by the bright-colored costumes, the painted faces, and the ancient exotic stories. After *Our Town* was produced in 1938, the West began to see Oriental theatre not just as a ceremonial and playful treatment of human relations, but as a fundamental way of treating reality. The Chinese theatre in particular has had such an impact on the tradition of realism that it is logical to discuss it in this chapter rather than with the Western theatre of color and romance.

Still a living art, the Chinese theatre uses plays that are three hundred to seven hundred years old and traditions that were well established by the Tang dynasty, more than a thousand years ago. The Chinese stage has no front curtain, scenery, or realistic properties. A temple canopy, sometimes held up by two lacquered columns, decorates the acting area, and the back of the stage is a decorated screen or beautiful embroidered cloth that carries the imagination into romantic realms of fancy but tells nothing about the individual scenes. Both the orchestra and the property man are on stage and visible at all times.

The Oriental method of presentation is essentially children's make-believe raised to a high art. It recognizes that reality in the theatre is entirely a matter of the mind and imagination of the audience, of what it wants and expects to believe. Adults are not basically different from children, who in their imaginations freely turn chairs, rocks, sticks, tools, boards,

2-5 An Oriental platform for actor, chorus, and musicians. A traditional Japanese Noh theatre on the estate of a feudal lord. Drawn by Bobbie Okerbloom.

or any old clothes and pieces of cloth, into the palaces, weapons, jewels, and costumes needed for their stories. On the Chinese stage, the actor, entering by one of the conventional doorways in the back cloth, comes down to address the audience and tells exactly who he is and what his motives and plans are. If he is to enter a house, he indicates by an elaborate pantomime that he is sliding the two doors apart, stepping over the threshold, and then closing the doors after him. If he is to sit, the property man brings a chair to put under him, and neither the actor nor the audience pays any attention. The same standard chairs and tables serve for many different levels—hills, walls, river banks, platforms. The property man sets the chairs on the table, and the actor climbs a high mountain pass. To indicate a journey by chariot, the actor crouches and trots between two flags on which wheels are painted. It matters little if he has only a whip to suggest that he is riding a horse. It matters much more what skill he shows, with the aid of the whip, in suggesting the essence of a man getting on or off a horse.

The few scenic effects are highly conventionalized. To indicate mountain country, small panels painted with the traditional mountain and stream pattern are brought out and leaned against a chair or table. To show an attack on a gate, attendants hold up a long pole from which hangs a painted cloth representing a section of wall with a gate, and behind it the defending general climbs on a chair and table to speak from above the wall. But such scenic devices are subterfuge; it is the actor who creates the reality—marching, riding, shouting, brandishing his weapons, whirling, fighting furious duels with all the rage of battle but rarely coming close enough even to touch weapons with his opponent, shivering to create the illusion of a storm while a demon of winter dances and the property man shakes paper snow from a box.

The characters also sing many songs, so that the drama almost seems to be an opera, and there are formal dances and stylized movements. The orchestra accompanies everything, reinforcing the melody and rhythm of the songs, giving shape and rhythm to the action by marking each step, gesture, and movement, using numerous instruments: flutes, violins, gongs, drums, bells, cymbals, and blocks of wood. The famous Peking actor Mei Lan Fang, on his tour of America in 1930, demonstrated that the conventional method of the Oriental theatre can create an illusion of reality just as convincing as our theatre of realistic detail, and perhaps more compelling. In spite of—indeed, by means of—these indirect conventions—men acting girls' parts, song instead of colloquial speech, sustained dance movements instead of fumbling starts and stops, traditional gestures with hands, sleeves, and head—he created his own world of heightened reality.

In American college theatres, Oriental plays, with elaborate costumes, painted faces, and many of the Oriental conventions of relating the actors to the audience, have been given very successful performances. These productions have usually shown, on the proscenium stage, a colorful structure

2-6 Scenic spectacle combined with make-believe for the popular Japanese theatre. Eighteenth-century Japanese Kabuki theatre. Drawn by Bobbie Okerbloom.

suggesting Chinese architecture and the formal extrance and exit doors of the Chinese stage. They have used English prose, spoken in a slightly exalted style with a light suggestion of Oriental music as a background, especially for the more poetic passages, and much percussion for entrances and movements. Two Chinese plays have been widely popular. *The Circle of Chalk* is the Oriental version of the story of the wisdom of Solomon (see Figure 2-8). To determine which of the claimants is the mother of the child, the Emperor uses the test of the circle of chalk. The child is placed within it, and the women are told that only the mother can remove him. Actually the Emperor knows that the true mother will not hurt her child's arm by jerking him away from the other woman; therefore he correctly declares that the woman who removes him is not the child's mother. There is more conventional romance in *Lady Precious Stream,* which made a great impression in both London and New York in the 1930s in an adaptation by S. I. Hsiung. The young heroine chooses to marry the gardener and, when he goes away,

2-7 The traditional Chinese platform theatre, showing property men and orchestra on stage. The play shows a general arriving in a chariot before the gate of a city. Drawn by Claude Marks.

2-8 A colorful imitation of the Chinese stage, with the property man at one side and the orchestra at the other. *The Circle of Chalk.* University of Iowa production, directed by Harold Crain, designed by A. S. Gillette, and costumed by Berneice Prisk.

waits faithfully in poverty, despite the machinations of her wicked brother-in-law. But when her husband returns, pursued by the loving Princess of the Western Regions, she makes him play some high-comedy games before she will take him back, and the Princess has to agree to be only a second wife. In the English adaptation, the Princess wears Russian costume and has helped make the gardener her king but has not yet married him, and she agrees to remain his friend and to respect the position of the little wife.

By the 1960s the American interest in Oriental plays had increased to the point where many directors and actors wanted to go beyond Western acting with a slight Oriental flavor. The mere addition of incidental songs was no longer enough. The splendid Broadway production of *Lute Song* in 1946, with Mary Martin singing vaguely Chinese songs, was still American musical comedy. Why not learn some real Oriental dancing and singing? Not only the University of Hawaii, with its large East-West program, but several American universities on the mainland, have in the last decade brought in specialists to teach American actors some aspects of the music and dance of Oriental theatre (see color section). Undoubtedly American production of the great plays of the East will continue, with varying amounts of authentic color and techniques adapted to the American stage.

More and more, the Western theatre in the twentieth century has

2-9 Theatre of make-believe in the West. Actors are costumed as lion and oxen, and stylized units of scenery serve to indicate the city of Rome. Shaw's *Androcles and the Lion.* New York, 1946. Photo Vandamm.

moved toward the freedom and imagination of the Oriental theatre. As recently as the 1920s an actor scrupulously avoided any contact with the audience, and the audience was never allowed to see how the scenery was moved; to show a stagehand in action would have been shocking indeed. But now audiences are delighted to watch stagehands or actors change the settings. Authors write monologues and direct addresses to the audience, and some even include audience participation. The use of masks, symbolic props, and fragments of settings is now familiar. Time and space can be made completely flexible. In Friedrich Duerrenmatt's *The Visit* (1958), the events of many days are telescoped into a few scenes, and the train, town councils, and crowd scenes are suggested by the actors as freely as in an Oriental play. Imaginary darkness, suggested by the actors in full lighting, was startling in the storm scenes of Peter Brook's production of *King Lear,* but in Peter Shaffer's *Black Comedy* the audience could easily suppose the visible actors to be in a room totally dark from a blown-out fuse. Even animals can now be represented on the stage in an Oriental fashion. In Bernard Shaw's *Androcles and the Lion* (1913) the lion was played by an actor (see Figure 2-9), and recently, in the musical *Camelot,* the serious drama *Becket,* and the epic drama *Indians,* some of the leading characters came prancing on wearing the frames of hobbyhorses around their waists. Clearly, modern Western audiences are becoming accustomed to make-believe and consider it an acceptable way of dealing with reality.

Epic Realism

In epic realism we find the Western synthesis of all the forms of realism and all the techniques that have modified the early conventions of realism. Epic theatre differs so greatly from the realistic theatre of 1880 to 1920 that many people consider it one of the revolts against realism. Yet in attempting to piece all its fragments together into one meaningful picture of the real world, it also differs from such revolts as expressionism and the theatre of the absurd.

The notion that an "epic" has a wide scope in time and space, with many characters and many episodes, while the "dramatic" concentrates on the final climactic struggle of one hero, goes back to Aristotle, who knew Homer's epics of the Trojan War and the ten-year journey of Ulysses and supposed that the theatre should never attempt stories of so large a scale. In the novel, of course, the writer can present his characters as part of the social and historical events of the day, sometimes trying to blend the description of background into the narrative events, sometimes interrupting the story of the main figures to cut in formal short sketches such as the famous "news reel," "camera eye," and poetic biographies of important people of the day that John Dos Passos put between his narrative episodes in *U.S.A*. In a similar way the movies began very early to cut in brief scenes of public events as background for a story, soon adding *montage*, a technique of piling up images, one after another, or of simultaneously presenting several images on a divided screen. Montage can show not only the passage of time but also the changes wrought by time. One of the first things a scriptwriter does when he sets out to make a movie version of a play is to "open up" the action. Where the playwright has had to concentrate long scenes of talk in a single set, the screen writer moves the characters into a more varied environment of streets, offices, public buildings, and distant places.

Since the movies can make such an effective combination of a dramatic foreground and a documentary background, why should the theatre even try to follow such a pattern? Any attempt to use regular naturalistic scenery is bound to fall short. Gerhart Hauptmann's *The Weavers* (1892) was a very impressive play that explored, in five acts and five very real settings, different aspects of the violent revolt of a group of workers. But five acts were not enough to show all the motivation for the rising anger of the workers. Many scenes had to be left offstage and were presented only indirectly in the dialogue. One possibility for such a complex play was to put at least one full realistic set on the central part of the stage and then to present at the side short background scenes, songs, or monologues staged in a suggestive or symbolic way that would not require heavy scenery. But that was only a compromise—a naturalistic play with skimpy documentary decorations at the edge. The only real solution was to omit the naturalistic central setting or to reduce it to a simple, half-symbolic structure, like the skeleton of Willy Loman's house in *Death of a Salesman* or the simplified four-story tenement house in *One-Third of a Nation.* Then the symbolic, flexible technique of the side scenes could be applied to the whole production.

Epic theatre is the stage's answer to the cinema. It is a different kind of realism, not trying to give the illusion of actual places, but more than making up with actors, speeches, and symbolic groups what it loses in photographic reality. The movie of *Oh! What a Lovely War* seemed vastly inferior to the stage show. The camera gave a real background for the soldiers of 1917–18, and made a light, witty entertainment into a heavy movie about a war. On the screen were real people singing in 1918, while on the stage were modern performers wildly singing and dancing about the ironic contrast between heroic show and bloody actuality.

Epic theatre can deal with a wide subject as well as movies can by making a virtue of its economy, which concentrates the attention on the stage rather than allowing it to wander over a wide range of reality. Properties, cut-down or miniature sets, and simple screens and curtains can be brought on as the action requires and moved by whatever means is easiest, whether let down from above, rolled in on wagons or turntables, or brought in by the performers. The details are often realistic, and rich textures, such as rough wood, old cloth, or leather, may be used. Or the setting may consist of one vivid symbol. There is no need to hide lighting equipment, and spotlights are often placed and moved in sight of the audience. If a moon is needed, why paint it on the backdrop in nineteenth-century style or use the early twentieth-century illusion of an actor standing in light from an unseen moon? With the frankness of the Oriental theatre, epic style accepts a disk hung by a conspicuous chain or supported by a visible framework. Where naturalism seemed an impoverishment of the theatre, using muted Stanislavsky acting and the subdued lighting of local moods, epic theatre brings back the more exciting and colorful devices of masks, music, songs, dances, monologues, asides, and announcements, to which may be added projected slides, charts, posters, slogans, tableaux, and movies, which appear, disappear, or move with whatever speed or rhythm is required. Most interesting of all these mobilities is the demonstration group or choric mass, which may come on stage or stay on the stage and at any moment step into the roles required by the action. In *The Caucasian Chalk Circle* (1948), Brecht used only three completely individualized characters. The play begins with a choric mass of people sitting at one side of the stage listening to a storyteller. As he gets into the story, the main characters leave the choric group and begin to act out the story. As the action expands, some or all of the choric group rise, put on half-masks and a shawl or other suggestion of costume, and step into the action, becoming townspeople, soldiers, or whatever else is needed. Between episodes they sit down again and watch or listen to another beginning by the storyteller. It is no wonder that epic theatre is sometimes called narrative realism. It has the speed and mobility of a vivid story.

In the 1920s the left-wing German director Erwin Piscator made a tremendous impression in Berlin with a dramatization of a satiric novel about a stupid Czech soldier, *The Good Soldier Schweik.* In a long series of episodes he showed the journey to the war, with people, furniture, and miniature settings moving by on a treadmill, backed by a screen on which were projected movies of the towns and war camps the soldiers passed, satiric cartoon sketches by George Grosz, and slogans, ironic facts, and other bits of information. To the bitter, defeated, inflation-ridden Germans of the 1920s, this objective panorama seemed to epitomize the idiocy of war.

A French poet, Paul Claudel, was also at this time experimenting with techniques that, as we now see, were moving in the direction of epic theatre. While he was French ambassador to Japan, he became interested in Japanese theatre. His experiments, partly inspired by this influence, took him outside the regular theatre into opera and dramatic oratorio. Not until they were revived in mid-century, however, did they have an impact on theatre audiences. His *Joan of Arc at the Stake,* with music by Arthur Honegger, presents a trial or hearing to which Joan and other witnesses return. The actors sometimes sing their lines and sometimes speak them against the musical background provided by the chorus and orchestra. By reenacting the main events and yet commenting on them from outside, they give a sense of the wide sweep and significance of the events that no series of separate realistic scenes would give (see Figure 2-10).

Another of Claudel's epic plays, *The Book of Christopher Columbus,* had a few performances when it was first set by Darius Milhaud as a full opera. But after the Second World War, when Jean-Louis Barrault produced it with new incidental music by Milhaud, it proved to be a very effective piece of epic theatre for both French and American audiences. It too is a hearing, a judgment, with an expositor who calls the forlorn, old Columbus out of a lowly inn in Valladolid to come onto the forestage and watch as another actor, playing Columbus, presents the story. The techniques employed include moving pictures, symbolic images, vague shadows projected on a screen, ballads, and narratives, and dialogue that both occurs within the event and describes its significance from a later time. The play reviews Columbus' long career, showing his departure from his home in

2-10 Lyric theatre in epic form. The chorus of cows serves as witness at the trial of Joan of Arc. Claudel and Honegger's *Joan of Arc at the Stake,* with Vera Zorina as Joan. University of Kansas production, directed by Jack Brooking. Masks by Don Ferguson.

Genoa, his appeal to the King of Spain, the mutiny of his sailors, the curses of the gods of the New World, and finally an apotheosis as Queen Isabella leads him toward the gates of glory. It is like a trial, with accusation and defense spoken directly to the audience, then illustrated by the dramatic scenes and made theatrical through music, movement, mobile scenery, and projections.

In the depression decade of the 1930s, such large problems as public health, housing, wages, and farm income seemed more important than stories about individuals, and America developed its own documentary form of epic theatre. Sidney Howard's *Yellow Jack,* produced in 1934, was a landmark. It set on the stage a series of episodes in the long fight to control yellow fever, from laboratories in London and West Africa to tents in Cuba, where soldiers died from fever or served as guinea pigs for the long experiments. Clifford Odets' *Waiting for Lefty* (1935) interrupts the strike meeting of a taxi drivers' union to cut in on the forestage five short scenes of the desperate home lives of five drivers, while the whole circle of union members is dimly visible in the background—a reminder that individual frustration could be relieved only by union action. For the Living Newspaper, one of the most exciting of the many government-sponsored projects of the New Deal, journalists joined with theatre workers to present in documentary form reports on national problems. The first Living Newspaper, *Triple-A Plowed Under*, dramatized the farm problem, with angry farmers, city customers, and government officials contending and asking questions. There was more human appeal in a later issue called *One-Third of a Nation*, a Living Newspaper about housing. In a large setting of a four-story tenement, a fire and a family tragedy led a little man, Mr. Buttonkooper, to ask police, politicians, and inspectors how conditions had gotten so bad, why property owners did so little to improve them, and what might be done by government-supported rehousing. Many demonstration scenes were brought onto the forestage. One of the most vivid showed the history of the city in miniature, as land dealers set up a little plot of grass, with street signs a few feet apart, and sold off one lot after another to the crowds of immigrants who arrived and sat close together on the stage, each filling his plot of land. Far more than the first Living Newspaper plays, this one gave glimpses of individuals with whom the audience could sympathize and identify. While some Europeans, following Bertolt Brecht, seem to feel that too much emotional identification and illusion keep the audience from seeing the wider meaning of the play, Americans like to have a few individuals they can know and care about, even when the issue is a general one.

Wilder's *Our Town* uses many epic techniques, but his *The Skin of Our Teeth* (1942) is an even better example of epic theatre. It is not always categorized as such, because instead of social, economic, and political problems it deals with historic and mythical events and philosophical, religious, and metaphysical ideas. But its purpose is the same as that of other epic dramas—to break through the shell of the particular in order to reveal wider implications. We shall examine the play in more detail in Chapter 7, in relation to the theatre of the absurd, but the epic techniques found in this play are worth noting here. The play dramatizes man's perennial need to pick up some threads of civilization and start over again after a catastrophe—here, the ice age, the flood, and war. The epic method includes the use of an expositor speaking over a loud-speaker, slides, allegorical figures, myths and parables, and a parade of actors quoting passages from Plato, Spinoza, and the Book of Genesis.

Most discussion of epic theatre is concerned with the plays and theories of Bertolt Brecht. But, as we have seen, many other playwrights have made sizable contributions to the movement. Brecht's techniques are no longer novel, but he is still appreciated for his characters and—ironically, since he was forever preaching against illusion or too much sympathy—for his poetry, and for the anguished plight of his main figures.

Brecht started writing in the chaotic, disillusioned Germany of the 1920s, when in both politics and theatre old ideas were being questioned and new forms tried. During the war he had been a medical orderly helping to patch wounded men up quickly, so that they could go back into the trenches and be shot at again. After the war he saw the lines of unemployed, the abortive attempts of labor groups to gain control, the terrible inflation that wiped out all savings, the corruption, venality, and exploitation in the cities. He enjoyed the satiric songs of the cabaret and the rowdy give-and-take of the sports arena. He saw Max Reinhardt's productions of *The Circle of Chalk* in the Chinese style and of the eighteenth-century comedy *A Servant of Two Masters* in the improvised-platform style of a *commedia dell' arte* troupe. The dadaists in France were showing their contempt for established order. The popular image of America was a vivid one of a land of great enthusiasm for sports and great attainment in science and technology but with shocking contrasts between corrupt millionaires and exploited laborers, and Brecht looked on it with both fascination and horror. Long before he moved to America, he tried to capture in his plays both the lively freedom of an American sports arena and the shock of social conflict in America.

Brecht's most sensational success came in 1928 with *The Three-Penny Opera,* a bitter musical satire based on John Gay's *The Beggar's Opera,* which had been the sensation of London in the 1720s and had had a spectacular revival there in the 1920s. Brecht created his own grotesque picture of the world of beggars, thieves, and corrupt officials, of love, exploitation, and betrayal, with many bitter comments on human depravity and with forebodings of destruction. The young composer Kurt Weill, creating his own German version of American popular music, wrote songs for it that are still sung.

Whereas this early play showed a cynical, demonic individual, Macheath, or "Mack the Knife," triumphing in a ruthless world, *Mother Courage and Her Children* (1941), like most of Brecht's later plays, shows a more sympathetic character trying to survive in a world that outrages all sense of what is human. Dragging her peddler's wagon across central Europe through the Thirty Years' War, Mother Courage loses her sons to the corruption of war and sees her daughter scarred, maimed, and finally shot for trying to save victims of the war. After each blow, she hides her feelings and bravely takes to the road. The many songs, instead of giving charm to the piece, increase the ironic sense of the futility of war.

Two of Brecht's later plays that have been widely produced in America take the form of parables, and both borrow in method from the Chinese theatre. In *The Good Woman of Setzuan* (1943), a kind-hearted girl, set up in a shop by three roaming gods, finds that her kind heart has no place in the world of business. To save herself from complete ruin, she disguises herself as a male cousin so that she can deal ruthlessly with her kinsmen

2-11 The ironies of war. The individual woman in her peddler's wagon tries to survive in the chaos of the Thirty Years' War. Brecht's *Mother Courage,* with Anne Bancroft in the title role. New York, 1963. Photos Martha Holmes.

and her trading associates. But she finds no way to reconcile the two ways of life. The gods only smile and tell her to go on being good, leaving the audience to conclude that perhaps they themselves should change the world of starving dependents and ruthless trade and not ask one young woman to try to lift the universe. The other parable, *The Caucasian Chalk Circle* (1948), gives an entirely new ending to the old Chinese play. Another tender-hearted girl, running away from the palace during a revolution, rescues the young prince abandoned by the heartless mother. Although the child repeatedly causes her trouble, she loves him and takes care of him. Later the mother, needing her child to claim large estates, demands him from the girl. But a picturesque judge, the village rogue Azdak, sets up the old test of the circle of chalk. The real mother easily pulls the child out,

2-12
Complex multiple setting for epic theatre, using rough textures, like junk sculpture, for a "confrontation" style. The gods descend in a rickety elevator in Brecht's *The Good Woman of Setzuan.* University of Texas production, directed by Francis Hodge and designed by John Rothgeb.

because the one who really loves him refuses to risk injuring him in the inevitable struggle. The judge gives the child to the loving foster mother, repudiating old ideas of legitimacy and showing that people and things belong where they can be best cared for, "the children to the motherly, the carts to the good drivers."

Much of Brecht's theory was developed in negative form as an attack on the established conventions of the realistic stage. He despised the conventional audience looking for emotional thrills and identifying with helpless heroes on the stage. Such an audience, he felt, did not think or judge, but only drifted in pity and empathy. The play showed them man as a known entity, his fate settled and finished. Their emotions were stirred, then exhausted, and at the end they were reconciled to their imperfect world. But Brecht wanted to wake up his audience, to make them think, compare, question, and see the implication of the play for their own world and not just lose themselves in the psychological problems of the leisure class. Hence he theorized a great deal about breaking the illusion, about devices of interruption, about keeping the emotions in check. He wanted on the stage the objectivity of a lecture by a scientist, with important demonstrations, to be watched thoughtfully. He disliked the naturalistic or Stanislavsky approach to acting, in which the actor lost himself in complete identification with the character. Brecht felt that the actor could indicate a character and his social implication far better by standing at a distance.

Brecht's term for this objectivity, *alienation*, has caused much confusion; many people suppose that he wanted to give only a cold, dull lecture. He invented the term when actors thought that talking directly toward the audience or changing scenery before the audience would break the illusion. But Brecht, confident that the theatre would be better without that kind of illusion, was perfectly willing to break it. Today, when we so easily accept the methods of epic theatre, we realize that an actor can create a new kind of illusion, even with the interruptions and the fast epic pace. Certainly the central characters of Brecht, when they are well played, create a high degree of sympathy and identification. It is not cold acting but the interruption by the narrator or by the contrasting scenes that sets the characters at a greater aesthetic distance, in *Our Town* as well as in Brecht's plays.

What emerges in a Brecht play is a heightened sense of the individual struggling heroically in a chaotic world. In the back of his mind, Brecht looked to a Marxist revolution and the coming of communism, but his plays do not celebrate any communist order; they show the failure of a corrupt bourgeois world to maintain humane values. Many of Brecht's principal characters have no motivation at all; they are merely symptoms of a fragmented society. Hence the portrait of the central character is drawn by presenting a number of confrontations with the fragments of the society—symbolic characters, who are often more functional than individual, and facts, statistics, and localities. No one fragment is all-determining; there is no need for a full, enclosing, naturalistic setting. Yet each fragment must be convincing, with the right feel, smell, texture, and dialect. The audience itself has to put all the fragments together and, while concerned over the plight of the individual, ask how a better social order can be built. Thus, epic drama, with its insistence on fact, belongs to the main tradition of realism. The goal in epic theatre is the better understanding of the actual world, with the hope of improving it.

In 1965 two very striking British epic plays were brought to New York, and both have had many productions in American colleges. Peter Shaffer's *The Royal Hunt of the Sun* and Peter Weiss's *Marat/Sade* went much further than Brecht's plays in mixing fantasy with history and in using all the intensities of music, dance, and poetry. Like Brecht's plays, they are concerned with violence and revolution, but they also deal much more with the spiritual dilemma of the individual. In *The Royal Hunt of the Sun* (see Figure 5-13), the cynical, greedy Spanish conqueror Pizarro finds new understanding of faith and trust as he sees his men kill the Peruvian sun-emperor, Atahuallpa. We will discuss this play again in Chapter 5 as an example of modern tragedy, but it is also an excellent example of epic theatre. The play's many scenes are presented continuously on a bare sloping platform, with the emperor standing majestically on an upper stage framed by a twelve-foot medallion of gold, the symbol of the sun. The choric group of soldiers and Indians mime the climb up the Andes, the battles, and the processions, and chant songs of worship or lament. Visual elements are used not as background but as symbols. The curtain that ends the first act, for instance, is not a standard theatre curtain but a vast blood-stained cloth, dragged from the middle of the sun medallion by howling Indians to billow out over the stage and mark the completion of the mime of the great massacre.

Even more striking use is made of a choric group in *Marat/Sade*, or, to use the full title, *The Persecution and Assassination of Marat as Performed by the Inmates of the Asylum of Charenton under the Direction of the Marquis de Sade*. Since the characters are supposedly played by the inmates of an insane asylum, a great range of bizarre intensities, macabre tones, and group rhythms is possible. Here Weiss outdoes Brecht in making the audience take an objective and distant view as the contradictory and ironic political debates are spoken in the midst of the distorted sounds and movements of the insane. This is more bitter and disillusioned than that early epic play on the French Revolution, Georg Büchner's *Danton's Death*

2-13 Political leadership in a mad world. History, politics, and psychology are treated in epic form with theatrical intensity. Peter Weiss's *Marat/Sade.* Royal Shakespeare Company production, directed by Peter Brook and designed by Sally Jacobs. Photo Morris Newcombe.

(1835), and yet it challenges the audience to try to achieve the objectives of social revolution without the madness of the revolutions of the past.

The epic form is especially useful for the wide subject of race relations. For *In White America* (1965) Martin B. Duberman arranged passages from letters, diaries, and public documents of American history to dramatize what it has felt like to be black. A more fiery image was created by LeRoi Jones in *Slave Ship* (1969), which concentrated in one ship the surging hatred that cannot be appeased by religion but leads to active militancy. A more complex epic was attempted by Arthur Kopit in *Indians* (1969). Kopit had written the funny absurdist drama *Oh Dad, Poor Dad, Mama's Hung You in the Closet and I'm Feelin' So Sad,* and he includes many absurdist ironies in his epic play. But *Indians* is a very serious picture of the misun-

2-14 History, fantasy, realism, symbolism, and dance combined with Oriental freedom for an epic drama about race relations. Kopit's *Indians.* Stacy Keach as Buffalo Bill, making a show of the Wild West (above) and then trying to intercede for the Indians (at right). New York, 1969. Photos Martha Swope.

derstandings between the white man and the red man. The hero is Buffalo Bill, prancing on his hobbyhorse, friend of the Indians, friend of the President, creator of the popular image of the sharpshooting scout of the West. In his Wild West show he presents Indians, real and fake, to white audiences all over the world, but he gradually breaks through the mask he has created to realize what he, and all white men, had done to the confused red man, and he tries hard to help correct the injustices. Serious scenes of a congressional delegation trying to understand the Indians are interwoven with buffalo-hunting scenes, buffalo dances, Indian dances of self-torture, and scenes from Buffalo Bill's Wild West show, some completely fake and one of an actual chief who is required to reenact his final, tragic appeal for help for his dying people before their surrender to the white soldiers. The play opens and closes with a scene of glass museum cases showing wax figures of Buffalo Bill and the Indians, and at intervals vanishing masked gods of the plains are brought on. If the stage cannot, like a film, show a

cineramic battle and the massacre of thousands, it can show a powerful dance-mime of a dozen Indians spreading a great sheet of snow, on which they lie down to be frozen in their final anguish. The stage can use realistic scenery when it needs to, but by using only symbols and fragmentary scenes it can give more of the meaning of a large subject than a film can.

Epic theatre seems in some ways the most characteristic and effective theatrical form of the twentieth century. It borrows some of the best features from theatres of the past—primitive, Oriental, Greek, and Elizabethan—and absorbs many of the modern attitudes of the other arts—expressionism, abstraction, surrealism, and symbolism. As we have seen, it can accommodate both history and fantasy; it can deal with religious and metaphysical ideas and wide social, economic, and political forces while keeping a vivid concern with the immediate; and it can relate the inner life to the outer experience. Where naturalism and early realism found no place for most of the intensities of art, epic realism has restored to the theatre exciting words, colors, movements, and rhythms—elements that early in the century could be found only in revivals of old plays or in the escapist theatre of romance. At its best, epic theatre is far more than a flexible device for propaganda or for demonstration of diverse facts and ideas on the stage. It can be a very rich and exciting theatrical experience, tracing the development of human character in relation to many events, both subjective and objective. It is one of our mid-century approaches to what we sometimes speak of as "total theatre," a theatre that appeals to the eye, the ear, the mind, and the soul.

The Theatre of Romance

3

Some people go to the theatre not for a realistic picture of the world they live in but for color and romance. They want exotic scenery, music and dance, and a bittersweet story of long ago or far away. They want to escape from the petty, the dull, the usual, to find release from daily frustration. They want to identify with the romantic hero, who does big things, makes exciting journeys, takes great risks. Where the ordinary man fritters his life away in thwarted impulses, tentative efforts, irrelevancies, and delays, the romantic hero lives life to the fullest. He makes no compromises, appeases no one. Every issue is clear and of the utmost importance. Chance brings him great opportunities, and he takes full advantage of them. In defeat he goes down fighting, sure that his cause is just and that some day the evil will be overcome.

It is an axiom of the romantic theatre that no one is tongue-tied or clumsy. Romeo pours forth his soul to Juliet in the inspired verse of Shakespeare or in gorgeous operatic song. Gravity and other laws of the universe are ignored as skaters swing around curves and leap over obstacles with complete power over space. Ballet dancers rise into the air and land again without a suggestion of weight or muscle. In the movie of *South Pacific*, Lieutenant Cable, a perfect swimmer, pursues his lovely native girl into the water and under the water with a freedom known only in dreams. To see a romantic play is to forget the limitations of the material world and move into a world with laws and ideals of its own.

Development of the Romantic Ideals

The two greatest ideals of romance, developed in the Middle Ages and still of primary importance in our concepts of what man should be, are the ideals of the knight-champion and the knight-lover. Feudalism created an ideal of a knight loyal to his lord and ready at all times to fight to protect the castle. The Crusades developed that champion into the knight-errant, ready to recover the Holy Land from the infidel or to go about rescuing innocent maidens and the poor or persecuted. In a sacred ceremony, he dedicated his sword and himself to the protection of the weak and the endless fight against evil.

Under the influence of Eleanor of Aquitaine, who was for a time Queen of France, then for many years Queen of England, the troubadour poets created another version of the knight that has had even more influence on the modern world, that of the knight in love. It is no exaggeration to say that the modern concept of passionate, dedicated, transforming love was the invention of the poets of the twelfth and thirteenth centuries. Before that time, love had been a youthful adventure or a family partnership. Now the worship of woman became a new religion, with the woman on a pedestal and the man an abject slave at her feet. This "Court of Love" game, which gives us the words *courting* and *courtship* as well as *courtesy*, puts love at the center of man's life. It is one of the major attempts made to shift the emphasis in the relations between the sexes from the physical to the spiritual. It calls for the woman to be very difficult and distant. The young man gets one glimpse of her beauty and is transformed forever. He shows a long list of medical symptoms—he can't eat or sleep, he grows pale, he wanders in melancholy groves by moonlight. He may write poems for his lady or serenade her, but he actually sees little of her. She sets him difficult tasks that may take years to perform. Sometimes he pictures her as so far removed from the real world that it would be a sacrilege to win her and touch her. It may be better to yearn unhappily for the ideal than to desecrate it by turning it into reality. That dilemma has greatly complicated the psychology of love to the present day, but it has been a great inspiration to romantic art; melancholy, absence, and longing make for excellent songs.

Romantic love was invented outside of marriage. It was assumed that the lady was already married to someone else; hence the attachment must be secret. There seemed to be no chance for real love in marriage. By the strict doctrine of the medieval church, all passion, even in marriage, was a sin; marriage in feudal times was an alliance of convenience, not of choice, and true love must be free and spontaneous—a gift, not a bond or duty. It was not until three hundred years later, in Shakespeare's time, when the rising middle class was developing new ideals, that it became possible to think of romantic love in marriage. *Romeo and Juliet,* written about 1594, was the first great poetic drama to celebrate the union of love with marriage.

Dedication to love and adventure made Shakespeare's plays the first great romantic dramas. The historical plays have many romantic elements. They are full of wars and rebellions, sieges of castles, challenges and duels, threats and denunciations. There are songs and clowns, and intimate scenes alternate with splendid processions and coronations. The whole range of human experience is shown with magnificent costumes and pageantry. Shakespeare's Richard III is a scheming villain, wicked enough for a child's tale of adventure, and a young champion kills him in the end. The poetic young King Richard II is defeated and killed, but the idealistic Prince Hal, leaving his tavern revelry, comes to the rescue of his father and becomes the successful warrior-king, Henry V, who conquers France and returns with the French princess as his bride. Shakespeare added characterization and ironies that transcend the basic plots, but one finds in his plays the eternal themes of romance.

Shakespeare's comedies are set in the faraway never-never land of romance: the enchanted moonlit woods of *A Midsummer Night's Dream,* where the Fairy King and Queen hold their revels and the mischievous Puck helps delude foolish mortals; the Forest of Arden; the seacoast of Illyria or Bohemia; the fabulous orchards, gardens, and courts of an Italy Shakespeare had never seen. There are handsome princes and charming ladies, wicked usurpers and envious villains spreading terrible lies, powerful magicians and magic herbs, long-lost brothers found again, and statues that come to life. It is a bittersweet world where "parting is such sweet sorrow," where "the course of true love never did run smooth," and where "present mirth hath present laughter" because "youth's a thing will not

3-1 Romantic setting in a large nineteenth-century theatre. Sheridan's *Pizarro* at Covent Garden Theatre, London, 1804. Radio Times Hulton.

endure." It is a world of accident, chance, evil, and delusion, where everything is transitory and beauty and virtue pass too quickly. But it is also a world of faith, love, and hope, of noble purpose and high adventure.

After the French Revolution, a new romantic movement gave fresh impetus to the old formulas and introduced new themes and characters. Following Rousseau's exaltation of the free man, the hero became a rebel against a corrupt society, either stirring up wars of liberation or seeking out high mountains or deep caves where he could question the meaning of the universe. Goethe's *Faust* most fully expressed the rebellious spirit of the time—the release of irrepressible yearning, the rejection of old rules, and the angry attack on all the institutions of society. Faust is torn between God and the Devil, between day and night, between creation and destruction. Magic is only one of the mysterious, irrational forces he appeals to. He wants all experience, but when he gains the love of Marguerite he destroys her and feels more lonely than ever in his guilt. In poetry, fiction, and drama, the rebel dominated the imagination. Lord Byron, most daring and turbulent of the English poets, created heroes in his own image, proud and rebellious, maimed and tortured by secret guilt.

Throughout the nineteenth century the romantic play dominated the popular theatre. *Cyrano de Bergerac* (1897), by the French dramatist Edmond Rostand, summed up many of the best features of the romantic play, using poetry, historical costume, duels, serenades, battles, and crowds. Cyrano is a brave and dashing French soldier of the time of Richelieu and the Three Musketeers. He is endowed with unlimited strength, ability, and wit, but he has one great defect, an enormous nose. His soul is full of love for his cousin, Roxane, but he dares not speak to her of love because he is mortally afraid of being laughed at for his grotesque nose. When he finds that Roxane is enamored of Christian, a handsome new cadet in his company, he hides his own feeling and composes for Christian the letters that win her, even whispering of romance under her balcony until Christian can climb up and take her kiss. After Christian is killed in battle, Cyrano still sustains Roxane's delusion, and only years later, as he is dying, does she learn that it was Cyrano's mind and soul she loved. He bravely defies his enemies to the last: "What's that you say? Hopeless?—Why, very well! / But a man does not fight merely to win. / No—no—better to know one fights in vain!"

Melodrama

The *melodrama* was the poor man's romantic play. It simplified the complex hero, the romantic rebel with both good and bad impulses, by dividing him into two characters—a spotless hero and a deep-dyed villain. It kept the guilty hero but made the guilt false, a lie invented by the villain. Sometimes the hero himself thought he was guilty, but always at the end he was cleared by the proper papers or the villain's confession. As its name implies, the melodrama used music, not only songs and dances but background music, to accompany the emotional scenes and sometimes to set off each movement, gesture, or speech. Often long sequences were performed in pantomime, and when a group action led to a climax, the tableau would be held still for several seconds. The most exciting sequence was the chase, as the heroine fled from the villain—out windows, over roofs, off bridges into the water, through fires, floods, earthquakes, explosions, and train wrecks. To thrill the spectators the old wing-and-backdrop scenery inherited from the Renaissance and the seventeenth century had to keep moving and make room for all kinds of platforms, steps, towers, trap doors, and trick effects. Burlesque revivals of old-fashioned melodramas amuse sophisticated audiences today by exaggerating the trite sentiments and expressing all emotions in a few patterned gestures. Nineteenth-century actors had a far greater range of gestures and were completely convincing to their devoted fans. The melodrama built one of the widest popular

3-2 Melodramatic action in the nineteenth-century theatre. The heroine escapes from the villain by leaping into the water of a cave. Poster for Boucicault's *Colleen Bawn.*

3-3 Romantic melodrama in Russia. The nobleman abducts a girl from the poor man's house. The State Dramatic Theatre production, Leningrad, 1832. From Derjavine's *A Century of the State Theatre.*

audiences in history and led directly into the movie and television drama of the twentieth century.

Today, on the movie or television screen, the melodrama has the same appeal it had on the nineteenth-century stage. By setting a good hero against a wicked villain, it captures the most elemental sympathies. Whether the villain is a feudal lord mistreating his peasants, a banker threatening to foreclose the mortgage in order to get the heroine in his power, a heartless father driving his daughter and her innocent babe out into the storm, a cattle rustler, a city gangster, or a Nazi or Communist spy plotting to blow up the capital, we know that the hero must come quickly to the rescue.

On the positive side, the hero is often a pioneer in a new land, an inventor of a great boon to mankind, or a savior bringing rescue from fire, starvation, or massacre. In characterization these heroes are very much alike, but put a good-looking actor in the role, one who can speak, sing, or dance well, and he becomes the incarnation of our romantic dreams.

Occasionally a movie has the complex characterization and the anguished, yearning hero of the true romantic play. The French *Children of Paradise* (1945) and the English *The Red Shoes* (1948) have these qualities. The first tells the story of a famous nineteenth-century mime artist who endures the brutal street life of Paris and suffers a hopeless love for a beautiful actress. *The Red Shoes* tells the story of the love of a young composer and a ballet dancer. For a while they work together wonderfully in the glamorous Riviera world of Monte Carlo, the girl dancing to his music and both of them slipping away from champagne parties for long moonlight rides in an old-fashioned carriage on a lonely road by the sea. But their two careers eventually separate them, and, torn between her great love for the composer and her dedication to her career, the girl kills herself.

But most of the big movies have followed the old formula of the melodrama, not the true romance. Choose a brave hero and a delicate heroine with little individuality to identify with in our dreams; surround them with a few devoted friends and relatives who may be somewhat comic; show them in grave danger from the villain or besieged by hordes of enemies, whether Western redskins, British Redcoats, or barbaric armies of Huns; or, for variety, let the villain make it appear that our hero is guilty so that, like a medieval crusader, he must go on a journey to fight the villain, rescue an innocent victim, and redeem himself in the eyes of his love. Story is all-important and is devised to create great suspense and to carry the characters through sensational, spectacular scenes of fires, earthquakes, erupting volcanoes, and battles at sea, on land, or in the air.

The outdoor sweep of the camera can of course far outdo anything possible in the limited area of the stage. *The Sound of Music,* the great moneymaker of the 1960s, had good songs and some dances, but basically it depended on the simple plot of an old-fashioned melodrama—armies of wicked Nazis, with spies and traitors in the fort, an exciting escape, and a wild flight over the mountains to freedom.

Some critics argue that American audiences will never mature as long as they continue to watch the simple melodramas of the TV screen. Whether the piece is a Western, a spy story, or an action serial about crime on the streets, the conflict is extremely simplified. The people are either "good guys" or "bad guys"; there are rarely good people who are sometimes bad or bad people who have their good moments. The villains, naturally, are monsters, and everyone else is too wholesome to be true. Realists have long pointed out the dangers of the melodrama formula, which has no place in the complexity of human nature. But nineteenth-century producers discovered that the masses wanted a simple moral story of good against evil, and TV advertisers find that popular taste has not changed.

Opera

Romance must have some intensities, and even though we have lost contact with nineteenth-century art and poetry we still have the intensity of grand opera and ballet.

Both opera and ballet began in the aristocratic European courts of the sixteenth and seventeenth centuries. Opera began as an experiment in reviving Greek tragedy, with a stylized, intoned speech called *recitative.* In the seventeenth century the recitative came to be used for dialogue, and passionate *arias,* accompanied by an orchestra, were added for solos, duets, and even large ensembles. When dances were added and scene designers learned how to make spectacular scene changes, grand opera became the most impressive of all Baroque entertainments. The plots were as magnificent as the music and settings. Great heroes struggled with Saracens or demonic magicians until Jupiter himself descended with a heavenly host to reestablish order in the world.

In the eighteenth century, the middle class began to come to the opera and to demand less grandiose music and heroes with whom they could identify. Both farce and sentimental scenes were added. At the end of the eighteenth century Mozart was able to combine all the forms, new and old, comic and sentimental, raising opera to an expressive power it had never known. For many music lovers today, the three best Mozart operas are the high points of all music. *Don Giovanni* is an amazing achievement. The old Don Juan story is about seduction, murder, and damnation and builds to a tremendous scene when the statue of the murdered father comes to take the Don into the open jaws of hell. Mozart lets a comic servant dominate much of the opera, and his Don keeps a brash cynicism almost to the end, yet the whole range of comic and serious feelings is expressed in the most charming, graceful music. In *The Marriage of Figaro* Mozart took a fairly serious French comedy, deepened the feelings of the characters, even the rake-seducer and his lonely, sad countess, and built up to a wonderful finale of lyric self-revelation and forgiveness in what may be the most perfect blend of light and sentimental comedy ever created. In his last opera, *The Magic Flute,* Mozart included an even wider range of characters and emotions in a charming allegory. One of the gayest of all clowns, the bird-catcher Papageno, accompanies a young knight in search of ideal love and virtue. They overcome the wicked Queen of the Night, liberate the girl, and are initiated into Masonic rites of purification.

Mozart perfected the Italian form of opera, enabling highly skilled singers to show off their voices in a wide range of songs—solos, duets, ensembles—tied together by narrative dialogue that was sung in stylized recitative. The songs and recitative dialogue combined to tell a dramatic story. Nineteenth-century composers had only to set to music the fashionable historical romances and melodramas of the day. For most opera fans, romantic theatre means the Italian opera of the nineteenth and early twentieth centuries, especially the works of Giuseppe Verdi. He wrote for singers to show off their voices, and he wrote songs that sound good on the concert platform. He used all the conventional forms the audience was familiar with, yet his arias are extremely dramatic; they create character, express the inner emotions, change dynamically from one part of a song to another, and drive the drama forward from beginning to end.

Most impressive of Verdi's operas is *Aida,* written for the opening of the Suez Canal and first performed in 1871. Great spectacle is possible in this story of an Egyptian princess and an Ethiopian slave girl, both in love with the triumphant young general. There are large processions of military display and solemn conclaves of chanting priests, then midnight love trysts and betrayals in the lush moonlight on the banks of the Nile. Yet there are many passionate, melodic arias for solos, duets, and ensembles. In contrast, Verdi's *La Traviata,* also a favorite, is far less spectacular, indeed almost intimate. It is based on Dumas's novel *La Dame aux camélias,* or *Camille,* about an actual courtesan who fell in love, left the gay social world to join her lover, and died of tuberculosis. At first audiences did not like the opera. A realistic story in contemporary dress, it had no romantic distance. Only when it was revived years later and set in the historic past was it acceptable. Today Italian opera is a great romantic spectacle of the past, sung by virtuoso singers with elaborate, romantic scenic effects. Opera houses have become museums, presenting the great nineteenth-century operas, showing us a world far removed from our everyday lives.

3-4 Opera as spectacle. The magnificent scene of the return of the triumphant hero in Act III of Verdi's *Aïda* at the Metropolitan Opera House. Photo Louis Mélançon.

It is the other operatic tradition, the German opera created by Richard Wagner, that has had a direct influence on twentieth-century theatre. Wagner, in the middle of the nineteenth century, raised the ideal of a serious, romantic, superhuman story to its highest peak. He disliked the use of a "set song" with a definite beginning and end, which was too much like a concert piece that could be sung out of its context. His ideal was a real music drama that combined all the arts, a *Gesamtkunstwerk*, or composite work of art, which moved from the opening of an act through to the end with no place for a pause. The result was a continuous, uninterrupted symphonic poem. He enlarged and enriched the orchestra and wrote the vocal parts as single strands woven with the instruments of the orchestra into a complex web. Instead of separate arias, he developed his symphonic poem with short, bold melodies called *leitmotifs*, or leading motifs. Each motif is associated with a particular character or idea—an ingenious way of making the music carry the story and even the inner drama. A character's motif is heard not only when he is speaking but also when someone else is speaking or thinking of him.

Of Wagner's operas, the most impressive accomplishment is *The Ring of the Nibelungs*, a series of four long operas tracing a legendary story of men and dwarfs contending for a magic hoard of gold deep in the waters of the Rhine. It includes the story of Siegfried, who kills the dragon and wakes the princess who has been sleeping within a wall of magic fire. It involves the northern gods, who are also contending for the gold. With the rippling waters of the Rhine, the murmuring of the forest, the magic fire, the birds and rainbows, the mists around Valhalla, and the mountain castle of the gods, there is enough descriptive music to hold an audience for hours watching the display of changing scenery and lighting and grouping. Yet there are also joys and sorrows, and the strong-willed conflict of superhuman beings. For even the gods are swept along by passions greater than themselves. At the end Valhalla sinks, carrying the old gods down in flame and water to make way for a new world.

Some people find the highest achievement of Wagner's operas not in the complex mythology of the *Ring* but in the simple love story of *Tristan and Isolde*, perhaps the most powerful drama of passionate yearning ever written. Isolde is the King's bride, but she is bound to Tristan by a love potion. Their moonlight love scene is interrupted by the King and Tristan

3-5 Opera spectacle in the nineteenth century. Full romantic detail of trees, rocks, clouds, and sky painted on wings and backdrop, with some three-dimensional structures in the foreground. Wagner's *Götterdämmerung* at the Bayreuth Festival, 1876. Painting by J. Hoffman. Photo Richard Wagner Gedenkstätte der Stadt Bayreuth.

3-6 Modern emotions in opera. The helpless little man sings his lonely anguish in a world that is absurd and cruel. Berg's *Wozzeck* at the Metropolitan Opera House. Photo Louis Mélançon.

is wounded. On a lonely island the dying Tristan looks back on his life and comes to a new realization of the spiritual meaning of love. Isolde arrives and they sing their *Liebestod*, "love in death."

Wagner has had a great influence on the modern theatre both by his theoretical writing and his example; not only for particular reforms, such as darkening the auditorium so that the audience could more completely lose themselves in the drama, but for the concept of total theatre, with all aspects of the production coordinated, and for the concept of an inner life of the drama. This inner life is not the words nor even the plot as conceived by the playwright, but a dynamic sequence, constantly surging in rhythmic waves from the beginning to the end. The actor must follow that inner sequence, and his words, tones, and movements, as well as the accompanying music and sound effects, must follow and express that surging rhythm. Adolphe Appia, in working out his approach to settings and lighting, followed the lead of Wagner and showed how, by means of changing plastic lighting, all the visual elements could follow the same inner life.

Ballet

An even purer form of romance than opera is preserved in the ballet. No other form of art so directly expresses our simplest, most frequent daydreams. Nowhere else is reality so refined and idealized. Nowhere is the human body more charmingly displayed. But the silk tights and the tutu skirts, the precise movement so perfectly keyed to the music, and the soft lighting transform the erotic into romantic yearning. All is seen behind the veil of the imagination.

Ballet movements are abstracted from movements of real life—stepping, leaping, landing, kicking, turning—but they are carefully selected and simplified. In this ideal of beauty, charm, and dignity, the back is held rigid, the head high, the toes and legs are turned out, and the feet and hands are limited to a few precise positions. Every movement begins and ends in a set pose. Only occasionally in the solo character parts does personality or emotion or even facial expression find a place. One of the pleasures of a good ballet is the exact duplication as a line of ballerinas, dressed alike, make exactly the same movements in unison, sequence, or opposition.

Ballet has a tradition of more than four centuries and has gone through three major stages of development; the Renaissance courts gave it pattern and stateliness, the classic academies of the seventeenth and eighteenth centuries formulated its technique, and the romantic theatre of the nineteenth century gave it soul and drama. During the Renaissance it was practiced by the aristocrats themselves, who liked to dress up and act the parts of shepherds and nymphs or Greek gods and heroes. They liked a "classic" costume, derived from a soft, diaphanous "nymph" costume such as we see in Botticelli's famous painting *Primavera* ("Allegory of Spring"). During the seventeenth and eighteenth centuries ballet became more strictly disciplined, calling for systematic training in the five basic positions

3-7 Ballet as a dream of enchantment. Act II of *Giselle.* Indiana University production, designed by C. M. Cristini and choreographed by G. Reed.

3-8
The ballet dancer as an ethereal being from the world of dreams. Marie Taglioni, who created the first of the diaphanous charmers in *La Sylphide* in 1832, is about to lure the Scotsman James away from the world of everyday reality. Dance Collection of the New York Public Library.

of the feet and the neat and elegant positions of the head and arms. The skirt was shortened to show the elaborate foot movements, and both men and women wore a stiff bodice or tunic.

But it was the nineteenth century that made ballet the perfect expression of romance. The main theme of romantic ballet is the irresistible lure of the ideal, which draws man away from the real, often to his destruction. In the first great romantic ballet, *La Sylphide* (1832), James, a young Scotsman, sits by the fire on his wedding day dreaming of an ethereal creature, a *sylphide* who dances with him but always eludes him. At his wedding she snatches the ring and lures him out to dance on the moors. When he tries to catch her with a witch's scarf she dies, leaving him to discover that his earthly bride has married another man. In *Giselle* (1841), the luring spirit is the ghost of a country girl who had killed herself when she discovered that her love was a prince and that he was engaged to a noblewoman. She tries to save the prince from the other ghosts, who lure men into the lake, but the Queen of the Wilis orders her to lead him into wilder and wilder dances. He tries to follow her to the grave, but dawn interrupts, the Wilis fade away, and he is found and consoled by his earthly love. In *Swan Lake*

(1877), for which Tchaikovsky wrote such seductive music, the hero falls in love with the Queen of the Swans, maidens who are under the spell of a wicked magician. The two lovers finally plunge into the lake, thereby breaking the spell, and are seen in an enchanted bark, united forever in the world of the ideal. These romantic stories gave opportunities for much classical dance, with formal lines of dancers, solos, duets *(pas de deux),* and both small groups and large, creating an ideal world of charming ladies with perfect discipline and control.

In the twentieth century a new chapter of romantic ballet began in Paris when the impresario Sergei Diaghilev, with a group of Russian dancers, began to produce a variety of short ballets. Diaghilev attracted some of the best dancers in the world, and from 1909 until his death in 1929 he brought dancing, painting, and music into a new creative union. This *Ballet Russe* was able to adopt new modes of modern art as Picasso, Bakst, Rouault, and Derain designed settings and as Poulenc, Milhaud, Strauss, and Ravel composed music for Diaghilev. Stravinsky wrote his three most famous compositions for this ballet company. *The Firebird* (1910) was an exotic version of the romantic story of a youth in an enchanted wood who destroys a wicked magician with the help of a supernatural girl in the form of a bird. *Petruchka* (1911) was made from a story

3-9 The charm of soft skirts and classic group form. The New York City Ballet in *Symphony in C,* choreographed by George Balanchine. Photo Fred Fehl.

of a sensitive puppet, defeated and killed by the more successful Moor, who runs off with the ballerina—an image of the helpless "little man" struggling in vain against the dull, practical, powerful man. The third Stravinsky score, *The Rite of Spring* (1913), was so shocking in its primitive movements and violent rhythms that it caused a riot, but what once seemed only noise and dissonance is now accepted as a rich symphonic poem echoing our interest in primitive rhythms. The great contribution of the Diaghilev ballet was to create a new art of the theatre, comparable to the concepts of Craig and Appia, in which all the elements—setting, costume, lighting, movement, and music—would produce an artistic unity and harmony. More than any other man of his time, Diaghilev brought into the theatre the creative forces of twentieth-century literature, art, and music.

Ballet came slowly to America. Anna Pavlova danced her dying swan from coast to coast and the Ballet Russe and its several successors played the major cities to a small but devoted following. Even as late as 1940 ballet was still an exciting importation from Europe; no one would have predicted that by the 1960s America would be a world center for ballet. Yet now there are schools all over the country, and ballet has taken several new directions that seem particularly American. The American Ballet Theatre, founded in 1939 and subsidized for years by the millionairess Lucia Chase, continued the eclectic, international trends of Diaghilev's Ballet Russe, using national folk idioms and theatrical characters. Antony Tudor devised some striking psychological ballets for the Ballet Theatre, and Agnes de Mille widened the style of the company to include the masculine vigor of the American West in *Rodeo*.

Most surprising has been the development of an American classicism in the ballet, the achievement of George Balanchine and the New York City Ballet. Starting with a school in 1933 and a ballet company in 1946, Balanchine has created one of the top ballet companies in the world, with its own home in the New York State Theatre in the Lincoln Center for the Performing Arts. Where other choreographers had turned against the classic tradition to widen and loosen the old techniques, Balanchine returned to the strict classic form. He has made far less use of story, pantomime, and gesture than is found in the more romantic ballets, depending more on the abstract form of music than on the characterization and narrative form of literature. Where the simpler romantic ballets presented a fairy story of a man trying to capture a dream, the newer ballets even in their charm show the surrealist nightmares, anxieties, and fears of twentiety-century man (compare Figures 3-9 and 3-10).

Antony Tudor and Jerome Robbins have gone much further than Balanchine in creating psychological and surrealist ballets, with images of alienation, dread, fear, and flight, of neurotic Greek legends, of strange

3-10 Psychological tensions developed in a modern ballet, with haunting motifs from Greek mythology. The New York City Ballet in *Agon*, choreographed by George Balanchine, to music by Stravinsky. Photo Fred Fehl.

gardens haunted by memories, missed opportunities, and frustrations, of Freudian shapes, masks, and monsters, of dark journeys and phantom corridors. Yet for all these modern touches, ballet, even more than opera, has been a museum of eighteenth- and nineteenth-century art. Most people expect the ballet to serve them the same charming daydreams and floating fairylands that pleased their great-grandfathers. A living museum is marvelous, but it is no wonder that ballet often seems effete to those who hope for a closer relation between art and the modern world. It seemed so to the pioneers of modern dance, one of the important new forms of theatre that we will discuss in Chapter 11.

The Musical

For the last four decades the musical has been the principal form of romantic theatre in America. Most people have called it musical comedy, but it often carries such deep emotion, such rich characterization, and even so much serious thought, that it is more than just comedy. For London and Paris audiences, American musicals surpass those of all other countries and seem the most distinctive theatrical contribution of America. Borrowing from the sentimental Viennese operetta, from the satirical Parisian comic opera and revue, even from the English Christmas pantomime, and using ideas from vaudeville, music halls, and burlesque, Americans have created a form that catches the energy and dash, the combination of skepticism and faith, the naive heart on the sophisticated sleeve that is the active image of America. Until recently serious critics looked down on the musical, but finally they have come to recognize that when story, characters, music, dance, and spectacle are all integrated in a musical, it is one of the highest dramatic achievements of the modern age.

Even more than the actor in the legitimate play, the skilled performer in the musical is the center of the piece; libretto, lyrics, songs, and dances must all be planned to set him off at his best. Audiences are used to songs and dances in night-club acts and television shows and expect a wide variety of vivid numbers even if the heroine has to take a trip to China or Spain as an excuse to bring in a new scene. What is amazing is that the best musicals do have unity and most of the songs and dances do grow out of the plot and express what the characters are feeling but could not express in any other way. When Eliza in *My Fair Lady* at last begins to pronounce

3-11 Comic musical fantasy of changing race relations in the South. Melba Moore, Cleavon Little, Novella Nelson, and Sherman Hemsley in *Purlie*. New York, 1970. Photo Zodiac.

her vowels correctly, she turns her practice sentence about "the rain in Spain" into a tango, and she and her two teachers celebrate their triumph in a wild release that is one of the high points of the play.

A type of song that fits the musical well and that was used very wittily by Gilbert and Sullivan is the self-introduction. The same audience that wants a drama to be indirect and implicit—to be "natural"—is delighted when a character in a musical comes right out and tells in song who he is and what he thinks, as Sir Joseph Porter in *H.M.S. Pinafore* does on his first entrance:

> I am the monarch of the sea,
> The ruler of the Queen's Navee
> Whose praise Great Britain loudly chants,

followed by the chorus "and so do his sisters, and his cousins, and his aunts," and a frank recital of his indoor training for a naval career:

> When I was a lad I served a term
> As office boy to an attorney's firm.
> I cleaned the windows and I swept the floor
> And I polished up the handle of the big front door.
>   I polished up the handle so carefulee
>   That now I am the ruler of the Queen's Navee.

No musical is complete without its romantic love song. It may be as direct as "O, Rose Marie, I Love You" from *Rose Marie* or it may be sung alone, as the nurse from Little Rock sings "I'm in Love with a Wonderful Guy" in *South Pacific* and Eliza sings "I Could Have Danced All Night" in *My Fair Lady*. Not until the end does Higgins sing his reluctant "I've Grown Accustomed to Her Face." During most of the musical he and Eliza express their hostility—their form of love—and in the meantime Eliza turns to Freddie for her simple love songs.

Between the individual songs the musical is shaped by the big production numbers at the beginning, the middle, and the end, with choruses of singers and crowds of dancers in picturesque formations, bright costumes, and colorful settings and lighting. Spectacle is a great pleasure in itself, but it can also create a sense of community and build a social and geographical background for the main story. Put together "There Is Nothing Like a Dame" for the lusty American Seabees, "Bloody Mary" for the madam, "Bali Hai" for the exotic native girls, and "Dites-moi" for the French planter's children, and you have the whole background for Lieutenant Cable's sad love and Nellie Forbush's more hopeful love in *South Pacific*. Since Eliza and Higgins come together at the end of *My Fair Lady* in a quiet mood, there can be no big production number, but just before the end

Eliza's father is the center of the noisy celebration as he sings, "Get me to the church on time." In Jule Styne's *Gypsy* (1959), the very orchestration develops with the progress of the story, from the tinkly piano and percussion as the girls are making their start in vaudeville to the much fuller orchestration as they gain success and come into conflict with their mother, whose last songs have a full brass setting of Wagnerian magnitude.

Since the first big American musical, *The Black Crook* (1866), which combined a noisy romantic melodrama with a bevy of ballet dancers, dance has been as important as music; but for a long time dances in musicals consisted mainly of well-drilled lines of brightly painted chorus girls stepping, kicking, and whirling, or prancing the can-can. But there has been a revolution in the twentieth century as choreographers have absorbed both ballet and modern dance and have learned to integrate the dance into the plot and style of the whole show. A number of shows have been directed by the choreographers. Ballet made the first impact. In 1936 a quite sizable ballet, "Slaughter on Tenth Avenue," was the high point of *On Your*

3-12 The musical sensation of the nineteenth century. *The Black Crook* of 1866 started a tradition of daring display of the female form combined with many songs and dances in lavish settings, all vaguely united by a story. Museum of the City of New York.

Toes, a Rodgers and Hart musical with Ray Bolger and Tamara Geva as show people in the raw underworld of the city. George Balanchine was called in to direct the dances. Then in 1938 a ballet dancer played the heroine in *I Married an Angel,* with the same combination of Rodgers and Hart and Balanchine. But for the general public, the first real ballet that seemed completely right and overwhelmingly effective was Agnes de Mille's in *Oklahoma!* in 1943. There was dance throughout the play, reinforcing the cheerful, open-air songs. But the high point of the show was the dream ballet. Laurey's fears that she had been too independent with Curly and had become too involved with the dangerous Jud were acted out in the ballet. Here were beautiful dancing, lovely music, costumes, and lighting based clearly on the main characters and emotions of the play. After *Oklahoma!* Agnes de Mille was in great demand, and a more serious type of dancing—ballet or modern—was recognized as a major part of show business. For *Bloomer Girl* (1944), Miss de Mille created a ballet expressing the feelings of American women as they waited for their men to return from the Civil War. Some think her richest achievement came in the dancing for *Brigadoon* (1947), which allowed a wide range of emotional expression, from the dancing for a funeral ceremony to a ceremonial sword dance at a wedding. Another choreographer, Michael Kidd, in planning the dances for *Finian's Rainbow* (1947), a satiric fantasy about Irish leprechauns, gold at the end of the rainbow in the Kentucky hills, and race prejudice in America, made such a skillful blend of acting and dancing that it was never certain where one gave over to the other.

Still greater achievements in dance were *West Side Story* (1957) and *Sweet Charity* (1966). Jerome Robbins opened *West Side Story* with dance, not a conventional show number with singing and kicking but a tense scene of the gang arriving suddenly in a street and looking around quickly. It was rhythmic, patterned, exact; it was unmistakably dance yet also the simplest, most direct expression of reality. *Sweet Charity* was choreographed in precise movements from beginning to end by Bob Fosse and brilliantly sung and danced by Gwen Verdon.

The musical had come a long way from the Viennese operetta of the late nineteenth century, where all was glamour and charm, with a handsome prince and a beautiful woman in disguise, with sorrow and joy, anxiety and relief, even heartbreaking disappointment—but all very remote and picturesque. It had developed into a remarkably supple form that could express a wide range of feelings, including the harsh realities of city life.

Above all, the musical is a celebration of America, perhaps the best celebration we have. *Show Boat* (1927) is a picture of mid-America of the nineteenth century, with its color, its gambling spirit and quick success, its restless changes and disrupted family life—a picture made sharper by its

3-13 Modern street violence danced to music. Bernstein's *West Side Story.* New York, 1957. Choreographed by Jerome Robbins. Photo Fred Fehl.

background of Negro workers and mulatto girls. One of the brightest shows of the 1930s was *Of Thee I Sing,* which opened at the end of 1931 and continued through the Roosevelt-Hoover campaign of 1932. A sharp but good-natured thrust at American elections, George S. Kaufman's satire is distinctively American. It points up imperfections with the utmost clarity, yet with that amused indulgence which makes fanatical reformers despair of America's ever reaching perfection. To show a presidential election being run as a beauty contest, campaign oratory being spiced up with wrestling, and nine Supreme Court justices hopping into a football huddle to pronounce on the sex of the President's child, is to remind Americans, as Aristophanes reminded the ancient Athenians, that we often do not take public affairs seriously enough. George Gershwin's music, alternately charming and raucous, emphasizes the irreverence and the satire.

In 1935 the great Negro folk "opera," *Porgy and Bess,* brought together a number of traditions. Dorothy and DuBose Heyward created the story of a gentle cripple, Porgy, who wins the trollop Bess from the strong man only to have her lured away by Sportin' Life, the high-stepping dope peddler from Harlem. At the end Porgy leaves home with only his goat cart to search the world for his woman. George Gershwin studied the group rhythms and melodies of the Gullah Negroes and produced the first operatic music that seemed authentically American. His songs express the tenderness of love, a cheerful defiance in "I Got Plenty o' Nuttin'," a humorous reflection on Biblical stories in "It Ain't Necessarily So," and, most powerfully of all, the fears, amusements, laments, and prayers of the crowd. The opera is a celebration of American regionalism and a farewell to it.

The top musicals of the forties—the decade of giants like *Oklahoma!*, *Carousel*, *Annie Get Your Gun*, *Finian's Rainbow*, and *South Pacific*—included the sorrows of separation and death, but even when they were set in picturesque, faraway places they celebrated American strength and faith, that great "willingness of the heart" that has always seemed so peculiarly American. And the old-fashioned, brassy *The Music Man* and the almost completely operatic *The Most Happy Fella* of the 1950s continued the tradition of big, energetic productions set in the romantic America of the past. As for the West, *Annie Get Your Gun* and *Paint Your Wagon* make most television and movie Westerns seem pale and adolescent by comparison.

America as the dream of the European immigrants was dramatized in *Fiorello!* (1959) and *Fiddler on the Roof* (1964). *Fiorello!* is set in a New York City ridden by graft and corruption, where minority groups are struggling to find their place. They are led by that great little hero, Fiorello LaGuardia, the half-Jewish, half-Italian champion of the people, who went to Congress and then served for years as mayor of New York. *Fiddler on the Roof*, taken from the Yiddish stories of Sholem Aleichem, projects the immigrant back to the narrow but colorful ghetto communities of central Europe. The old father Tevye, struggling to keep a balance between the traditions of his people and the new ideas of his children, is finally driven out of his old-world home and moves to America. Early in this century such old-world backgrounds were the subject of broad comedy and ridicule, with clownish comedians presenting Jewish, Irish, and German caricatures. In the years of Hitler and the Second World War, such national dialects and customs were either avoided or treated with awed seriousness. By the mid-sixties, it was possible to look with both amusement and affection at the minorities who brought their local traditions and their high hopes to America.

As remarkable an achievement as showing admirable characters in the sweep of history is the use of less glamorous material—hardened city types, sardonic moods, destructive and antisocial aspects of human character. *Pal Joey* (1940) was so unsentimental and sardonic that it repelled a large part of the regular audience, though it had one of the best Rodgers and Hart scores and the young Gene Kelly as the conniving hoofer who dreams of owning a fabulous night club. It was a wry version of the American success story, showing its stupid and unsavory aspects. But it seemed a new and exciting kind of musical to many people, and when Columbia brought out a recording in 1952, the show was revived in New York and has found a real audience since then. *Guys and Dolls* (1950), with its

3-14 Local color in a folk opera. The main action is reinforced by the acting and singing of the chorus. In this picturesque setting every window is an acting area. Heyward and Gershwin's *Porgy and Bess.* New York, 1935. Photo Vandamm.

tough-skinned but soft-hearted gamblers and racketeers, was a bit more sentimental; its sinners were softened and reformed in the end. But it, too, caught the racy vitality of America and carried the musical a long way from its aristocratic Viennese ancestors. *Company* seemed the complete opposite of romance, with its abstract setting of pipe frames and elevators and its lonely bachelor hero watching his friends' marriages at their worst, but its wit and lively music caught the wry mood of the New York audience in 1970.

Workers and labor unions would seem to be far from the romantic world of the musical theatre, but not in America. In the 1930s, the decade of the depression and the New Deal, labor and industry fought battles that did not stop short of shooting. It was a great day in 1937 when a musical revue called *Pins and Needles*, produced and acted by the International Ladies Garment Workers Union, showed a sense of humor. Its love songs took such forms as "One Big Union for Two" and "Sing me a song with social significance—nothing else will do. It must be packed with social fact, or I won't love you." An excellent recording in 1962 and television revivals brought to life again the songs of a turbulent but idealistic period of American labor. In 1954 it seemed natural for a musical to be based on love and group spirit in a labor union; *The Pajama Game* was a great success in both America and England.

Though *West Side Story* seems to be the most strikingly original and one of the most harmonious of all American musicals, it is yet a summary and perfection of the whole line, giving the audience almost everything it has learned to expect. There are dances and songs of group unity for the juvenile gang, songs of love and of dreams of the future, a half-comic celebration, "America," sung by girls recently arrived from Puerto Rico, and a sardonic-comic song, "Gee, Officer Krupke," mocking the police and social workers. There are satire, violence, gang warfare, and murder, yet such an obvious love of New York, such a strong assertion of the hope of love over hatred, that this musical must be described as a celebration of America. The musical *1776* (1969), shrewd but sympathetic in its appraisal of the mixture of selfish interests, doubts, and idealism in the Revolutionary Fathers, is still a celebration of American traditions. With playful humor, satire, and irony it follows the uneven course of the Continental Congress to its achievement of the Declaration of Independence.

The most striking development of the late 1960s was the rock musical. The Beatles, with their long hair, their new sound in music, their vision of fresh, youthful enjoyment, had set a fashion for revolt around the world. The angry reaction of conventional older people to so harmless a symbol as a fashion in hair helped to convince the young that there was a generation gap, with people over thirty hopelessly devoted to materialism, military police power, and war. If short hair was a symbol of conformity, materialism, and repression, then long hair became a symbol of youthful rebellion, peace, brotherhood, and sexual freedom.

The new musicals brought on the stage not only the rock tunes, psychedelic lighting, flower costumes, long hair, nudity, and protest against war and the military-industrial establishment, but also a much greater freedom in form. The rock musical has less story and far more group celebration than the traditional musical. In fact, it sometimes consists almost entirely of music, with only the vaguest suggestion of a plot.

Hair (1967) exploits this free form to the fullest (see color section). It is performed as an "American tribal love-rock musical" by a cast of about twenty-five. Only a few characters emerge with names. One young man is expelled from school and another is drafted. Both are in love with the same girl. Though she loves the one who is expelled, she goes along with the other. The tribe celebrates the burning of a draft card (which turns out to be a library card), the glory of long hair, the defiance of rules and restraint, and the use of marijuana. The songs and dances weave together images of Hindu love gods, black and white companionship, love-ins, hopes of peace and freedom, draft boards, the war in Vietnam, the Civil War, the Indian wars, Shakespearean actors, Buddhist monks, and Catholic nuns. With an orchestra on one side of the bare stage, actors bringing on suggestive props and symbols as needed, and actors in the group stepping in and out of roles, *Hair* uses the happy, imaginative flexibility of the Oriental theatre and the group mobility of epic realism to celebrate group joy and the hopes of rebellious youth.

Such group joy grows out of a revival meeting in the musical *Salvation* (1969), which has elements of both folk and gospel music in its rock style. But not all rock musicals are mere releases of group energy. *The Last Sweet Days of Isaac* (1970) shows how rock songs along with lively poetic dialogue can express the inner feelings of distinct, appealing characters. Clearly, the rock idiom, which permits a stanzaic form almost as free as a prose declamation, has dramatic possibilities that musicals so far have barely suggested.

It does not seem likely that rock will replace the older musical tradition completely. In the 1920s jazz was also a radically new kind of music, and some musicals were developed from the dance halls and the jazz bands. But gradually writers and composers learned to combine the jazz idiom with the complex patterns of the Viennese operetta. In the 1970s, when costs of production both on Broadway and in Hollywood have made spectacular musicals almost impossible and when only such sure moneymakers as Katharine Hepburn in *Coco* and Barbra Streisand in *Hello, Dolly!* have a chance of paying off the enormous investment, low-cost production methods and the current emphasis on youth make the rock musical very attractive to producers.

Movie adaptations have given stage musicals the usual Hollywood formula, increasing the spectacle, adding many crowd scenes and dancers, using tourist geography—a whole island for *South Pacific*, Austrian mountains for *The Sound of Music*—and increasing the romantic identification of the audience by using many close-ups of the main characters. Yet the total effect of these additions has often been to dull the impact of the music by increasing the difficulty of projecting the songs to the audience. In a movie it is more natural to sing facing the scenery and to blend the songs into the action. But then there is no way to build the song to a big climax that brings the audience to a wild burst of applause. So most songs from stage musicals, like those from grand opera, seem too large and unbelievable for real surroundings; yet when translated to the screen, they are too short and too quiet to achieve the impact they had on the stage.

The most satisfactory movie musicals have been those that were developed especially for the screen. In the 1930s, Busby Berkeley made some remarkable discoveries of what could be done with a camera for spectacular dance effects. In most of the films he directed, he used stories of backstage or night-club life, thus giving a theatrical motivation for the music. Then he expanded the dance effects far beyond anything that would be seen in any actual night club or theatre. Sometimes he used large choruses, photographing them from far above, from below, from the sides, or reflected in complex multiple mirrors. Sometimes with trick lenses he built up elaborate geometrical patterns of dancers on the screen. And sometimes he created startling sequences by combining close-up shots of single dancers or parts of their bodies. He was at his best in expanding the sparkling mirror and rhinestone effects of a night-club act, with songs and dances that were ends in themselves and had little relation to the action of the play.

A far better relationship between drama and dance was created when Fred Astaire and his partner, having reached a point of emotional intensity in the story, would blend the action smoothly into a song and dance, closely integrating the musical number into the drama. For Astaire, the camera caught just the right amount of movement, closely framing his solo beginnings and moving easily backward ahead of him, then expanding to include the larger ensembles. The simple popular songs and Astaire's own brand of popular dance—part ballroom, part theatrical tap and soft shoe—fitted well his light, sophisticated style of comedy.

Dancing in outdoor settings, real or simulated, has been a special pleasure in a number of screen musicals, giving the choreographer a freedom and scope that the stage cannot match. Gene Kelly's dancing in Paris streets was a large part of the urban charm of *An American in Paris* (1950); the gangs in *West Side Story* made effective use of New York alleys; dancers on London rooftops in *Mary Poppins* (1964) bobbed in and out of chimneys; and *Oliver!* (1969) offered two exciting outdoor numbers—a scene in Covent Garden market and one in a Bloomsbury plaza, with groups of street criers, policemen, nursemaids, school children, window-washers, and housemaids expressing in song and dance the joy of a beautiful morning in London.

A Picture Stage for Romance

Whether on the screen or on the stage, romance calls for spectacle and color. For a romantic play, opera, ballet, or musical, the stage presents a series of beautiful pictures that are changed rapidly, often in sight of the audience, and are framed by the permanent proscenium and sometimes also by a brightly painted inner frame hung especially for the show. Modern design and lighting have, of course, brought changes, but in most of its elements the romantic picture stage is a traditional theatre form that has been in use for four centuries—a theatre of illusion.

The picture stage was invented as a solid, three-dimensional architectural setting for the courts of Renaissance Italy. Since there was at first no thought of changing the setting, it was so substantial that in one Renaissance theatre, the Teatro Olimpico in Vicenza, Italy, the scenery is still standing. At the beginning of the sixteenth century, when Italian princes started to revive classic plays and produce new ones in imitation of the classics, they had their architects build this kind of stage at the end of their ballrooms. It was a simple thing to put two rows of small houses on the stage, building for each house only the two sides that would be seen. But the ballroom stage was not large enough to extend the houses to an ideal depth, and the architects realized that a forced perspective would look better anyway. So at the back they added a two-dimensional canvas frame on which was painted a continuation of the street. The stage floor was sloped and the houses at the sides diminished in size to give the right perspective effect. The first completely illusionistic theatre had come into existence. Contemporary reports were ecstatic about the splendor and reality of the picture. In 1545, Sebastiano Serlio, an Italian architect working in Paris, published a book on architectural design with three engravings of scenes and directions for building them, and the stately perspective settings, sparkling with brightly colored lights, were soon used in court productions all over Europe (see Figure 3-15).

In the seventeenth century, however, the masque and the opera replaced the classic play as the entertainment of the aristocrats, and opera won a wide popular following. The Serlian perspective setting, so solid and dignified, was replaced by lightweight, flat, painted wings and backdrops, and scenery that could be changed became the rage. Some operas showed a dozen or more changes of setting. Instead of Serlio's solid wings, the baroque designer used a nest of flat wings. His scene might show first a woodland grove of six flat, painted "wood wings" at each side leading to a cloth at the back painted with more woods. Then, at a signal from the prompter, a hidden stagehand at each nest of wings slid back the front wing, which moved in one groove in the floor and another above, to reveal the next

3-15 Early perspective setting of solid two-faced or angle wings. Two rows of wings on a sloping floor lead up to a painted cloth drop to give the illusion of a long street. The Tragic Scene from Sebastiano Serlio's *Architecture*, Book II. Paris, 1545.

wing, perhaps depicting a rocky cave. At the same time, the back cloth was slid out to reveal the cloth behind it. For the large court productions architects devised an elaborate system for pulling out all the wings and back shutters of each setting with ropes controlled by a capstan under the stage. As higher lofts were built above the stage in the eighteenth century, it became possible to "fly" the back cloth instead of pulling it in grooves; since then the system has been called a *wing-and-backdrop stage*. Baroque audiences delighted in watching the quick changes of setting. The system was excellent for repertory companies, furnishing colorful painted settings at low cost (see Figure 3-16).

It was only when nineteenth-century producers wanted to add realistic three-dimensional effects to the painted wings and backdrop that difficulties arose. For the changing of steps, platforms, and solid structures, the curtain had to be lowered and the continuity of the play was broken. Nineteenth-

and twentieth-century engineers devised elaborate and extremely expensive machinery—pulleys and ropes for flying heavy scenery, wagon stages, jack-knife stages, turntables, and even elevator stages—to speed up the changes. But it still took so long to get a beautiful painted picture ready to disclose to the audience that opera composers sometimes wrote an intermezzo to fill the time.

During the nineteenth century the picture stage reached a peak of painted illusion. Tableau effects became the rage, especially in the popular melodramas, and as many as thirty might be used in a single play. *Ben Hur* started its great career in 1899 with as much emphasis on pictorial effect as there was in later movie productions. The first act alone had fourteen changes, each setting designed by a different painter. The chariot race was run on a treadmill by real horses and chariots as a panorama painted on cloth and attached to huge rollers moved across the back of the stage. The galley scenes that filled the stage with rows of oarsmen faded into a scene of the tempestuous sea, with a boat that sank out of sight through the stage floor, leaving Ben Hur and his captain tossing on a raft.

Similar painted settings were expected for Shakespeare, giving Shylock a very real-looking Venice (see Figure 3-17) and Juliet a beautiful balcony,

3-16 Climax of a seventeenth-century opera. Jupiter and his celestial court are let down in a cloud machine. Flat wings on perspective lines lead to the backdrop. Drawn from Italian sources by Martha Sutherland.

3-17 An elaborate nineteenth-century setting for Shakespeare. Solid steps and downstage structures are combined with painted wings and backdrop. Charles Kean's production of *The Merchant of Venice,* London, 1858. Radio Times Hulton.

even if the audience had to wait for long changes and Shakespeare's cinematic rhythm of many short scenes had to be broken up. It is no wonder that more and more twentieth-century producers have returned to medieval or Elizabethan stage forms, which used few or no scene changes, and let the splendor of Shakespeare appear in the costumes, the processions, and the words themselves.

Romance as Psychological Structure

Romance was under strong attack in the early twentieth century. Overliteral minds were impatient with fantasy and dismissed romance as a child's daydream of old fairy tales and legends. The avant-garde continues to despise it because its old fairy tales are charming and popular. Overserious reformers, especially the revolutionary Marxists, have attacked it as bourgeois, as another opiate of the people that, like conventional religion, distracts workers from their duty to the state and wastes their time and emotions. Realists are skeptical of romance because they think that its impossible ideals make people unwilling to face the world as it is. Does not the romantic lover, like the neurotic Tristan of Wagner's opera, dwell on his unsatisfied longings until he associates his love with death?

The objection that romance is escape is no longer convincing. A fantastic parable, whether as Christian teaching or as a drama of epic realism, may be the best way to understand a real situation. Since Freud, psychologists have recognized that the age-old romantic stories fascinate both children and adults because they express the patterns of the search for identity and destiny in the half-hidden depths of the mind. In art, as in science and philosophy, it is necessary to achieve a distance, a degree of abstraction, in order to see the immediate object in its wider relationships. The person seeing a romantic play may momentarily forget the immediate problems of his life, but he wakes from the dream with a new perspective on the patterns of human aspiration and desire.

For centuries Shakespeare's romantic comedies have given audiences and readers not only the dramatic pleasure of a happy ending after anxious trials and sad distress but also a sense of spiritual renewal. Many critics have commented on the fact that the characters seem to take part in the deep seasonal rhythms of nature and in the religious processes of salvation. Shakespeare surrounds his characters with visual and verbal images drawn from popular folklore and Christian doctrine. As his hero wanders through enchanted forests, endures cosmic tempests, or encounters the baffling magic of moonlight, he finds his long-lost father, brother, or sister. He reestablishes his identity and finds his true love. As he takes part in the rites of winter sacrifice and the festivals of the rebirth of spring, he sees the chaos of the storm replaced by the harmony of music and poetry and the cruelty of nature redeemed by divine forgiveness, grace, and love. It is the old romantic journey into the soul, but the playwright has illuminated and spiritualized it.

The complex, open form of the romantic play has had more meaning for the newer playwrights and directors of the modern theatre than either the classic or the realistic form. Like the romantic playwright, the dramatist of today wants to deal with a complex, baffling universe that is mystical and surreal rather than real, illogical and disconnected rather than clear. To a considerable degree he follows the structure of the romantic drama.

The essence of romance is freedom. Where realism is bound by fact and classicism by logic, the romantic play is bound by neither. The romantic hero, as we have seen, gains freedom by triumphing over the everyday world of fact. The romantic play gains freedom in structure by disregarding the strictly logical organization of the classical form. The compact classic play, whether ancient Greek tragedy, neoclassic tragedy, or the "well-made" problem drama of the past hundred years, is tightly organized by logic, each development linked to the preceding ones with the strongest chains of causality. The three unities of one time, one place, and one action are observed by omitting subplots and restricting the scope of the play to the final, climactic episode of the story. Colorful public events and violent acts are left offstage, and only private decisions and reactions are shown. In the classic view, the individual is summed up in the one great decision he makes. But most romantic plays have a very loose structure, with many different characters involved in many different episodes and treated in a variety of comic and serious moods. The three unities are disregarded. On first impression a romantic play seems to be only a chaotic exercise in irresponsible freedom. The story is told from the beginning with the kind of wandering narrative loved by children. Spectacle is lavishly exploited, seemingly for the sheer love of color and movement. The romantic hero goes from one crowd scene to another with no apparent connection between them. Classic-minded critics object to this seemingly random structure, but writers of romances believe that it is meaningful, and they go to a great deal of trouble to integrate its many elements into one large plan.

The free structure of the romantic play expresses the romantic idea of a complex, infinitely varied, paradoxical, and mysterious universe. And since it is an open universe, unfinished and unmeasured, no one act or crisis is all-important. Each character must try many things, his individuality developing gradually as a result of his wide experience. He must be seen not merely in his private life but also on colorful public occasions. Not one conscious decision—analyzed and debated, then final and overwhelming—but many decisions, made in the heat of action over a long period of time, are what shape the romantic character, who in turn gives unity to the play.

The structure is explicable in aesthetic as well as philosophical terms. Where classic art emphasizes unity, romantic art revels in variety, risking the loss of a strong sense of unity in order to represent the broad scope of human experience, especially the picturesque and the intense. But this variety is not without order and meaning. Comedy is set next to tragedy so that each element may enhance the other by contrast. In combining prose and poetry, clowns and kings, crowd revelry and individual distress, the grotesque and the charming, the playwright increases the intensity of each experience. In the preface to his play *Cromwell* (1827), Victor Hugo wrote an ardent defense of the grotesque in art, emphasizing its value for contrast. Nothing, it seemed to him, could be more insipid than the monotony of the classic play with its one even, noble tone.

Most objections to romance are no more valid than the objections to realism. Many critics have complained that the scope of realistic drama is narrowed by its dependence on fact. But as we saw in the preceding chapter, realism has learned to borrow from many other traditions and even to find a place for the intensities of masks, music, poetry, and dance. In the same way, the romantic theatre—drama, opera, ballet, and musical—which was formerly devoted to the distant and exotic, can deal with many vital aspects of present reality. At the beginning of this century, realism and romance seemed in sharp conflict, but the distinction between them has gradually faded as playwrights no longer try to separate fact from fancy but define new relationships between the inner life and the outer world.

The Theatre of Exaltation: Greek Tragedy

4

The theatre can charm the spirit with romance, but it can also raise the soul to the highest exaltation. Even in a commercial theatre the play may be as powerful as a prayer or a religious ritual in bringing man into contact with the divine. The theatre may become, in Shaw's phrase, "a temple of the spirit."

Religious drama, depicting the most important acts of the gods and the prophets, came into existence thousands of years ago, apparently as soon as there was religion or any concept of man's share in divine purpose. In ancient Egypt each new king performed the central role in a coronation drama celebrating the victory of the young god Horus over the evil spirit Set and his own rebirth as the son of the Divine Spirit. When a king died, either the new king or his priests performed a drama before his tomb every day at sunrise to celebrate the resurrection of the spirit and its journey to the stars. Egyptian drama, though it influenced Greek drama, was completely forgotten and only recently have scholars begun to piece together the fragmentary accounts.

Greek drama grew out of the Dionysian festival celebrating the resurrection of the spring out of the sacrificial death of the old season. The festival opened with a wild, ecstatic procession; its high point was a series of choral dance dramas performed in a large outdoor theatre. To the traditional rowdy satyr plays the Athenians added a very serious new form, *tragedy*, which combined the pain and humiliation of sacrificial death with the joy and exaltation of resurrection. Tragedy was profoundly religious, yet it put the emphasis on man and the values of this world. In accepting the defeat and death of a great hero, the audience felt pride and joy that a man had challenged the universe and measured his finite reach against the infinite.

The Tragic Vision

Tragedy is the most fascinating and amazing of all forms of exalted drama—fascinating because it is the most universal, carrying its appeal on stages of many different kinds to ages and countries far distant from its origin; amazing because this most serious of forms is very successful entertainment and because, while portraying the defeat and death of the hero, it gives pleasure to its audience. This paradox never ceases to puzzle and intrigue students of drama, and each tries to find his own explanation. Tragedy asks several profound questions: What is man's relation to the world, to himself, and to God? What is the meaning of evil and suffering, of choice and responsibility? How can man be both an individual with free will and a part of society and the universe? Those who are shaken deeply by seeing tragedy find that while the first part of the play expresses their impulse to rebel, the ending and the import of the play reconcile them to the mystery at the heart of the universe.

A tragedy progresses through several phases. It is not merely the turn of fortune's wheel that lifts a man to a peak, then plunges him to disaster and ruin; not merely the irony of fate that turns hopes and promises to despair and disillusionment; not merely the miscalculation, the guilt, the tragic flaw that exposes man to overwhelming punishment, though tragedy may contain any or all of these. One of the strongest patterns involves making a choice and then facing the results of that choice, but often, as in Sophocles' *Oedipus the King* and many of Ibsen's plays, the choice and the deed took place long ago and the play itself traces the long trail of consequences that must be faced. Tragedy, like romance, may show a quest for the secret of eternal life—a journey to a dark grove, an underground cave, or a secret place at the bottom of the sea, and a struggle with an evil monster. The hero regains his own soul by bringing back the token of his identity, even as he pays a terrible price for what he has won.

Especially helpful for an understanding of the many possible phases of the tragic pattern is Francis Fergusson's suggestion in *The Idea of a Theatre* that they may be seen as a sequence of three P's: *purpose, passion,* and *perception.*

Purpose

In most tragedies the hero faces a great crisis that challenges him to the utmost. Often that challenge comes near the beginning as he takes on the terrible burden of action. Oedipus finds a fearful blight on the kingdom and his people turning to him to cleanse the land, no matter what the cost. In *Macbeth* the promises of the witches stir ambitions that terrify the hero. Lured on in the "swelling act of the imperial theme," he knows that "to catch the nearest way" must be by murder, and though murder is against his nature he begins the journey from which he cannot return. Willy Loman, the hero of Arthur Miller's *Death of a Salesman,* faces a terrifying failure he cannot understand. He is indignant. He has been displaced from his rightful place in the world. He demands justice—of his sons, of the past, of his long-lost brother, of the night.

Isolation is the immediate price the hero pays for taking up his burden, but it is an isolation, a rebellion, that gives him identity. Beginning with Aeschylus' Prometheus, who stole fire from heaven and succored mankind in defiance of Zeus, the heroes of tragedy have taken a stand against the accepted order, either of man or of the gods. They are men of pride and stature, men who will risk destruction in order to assert themselves. Tragedy, from Clytemnestra and Orestes to Iago, Macbeth, and the heroes of Dostoevski, Sartre, and Camus, has included many of "the great offenders," those who turn to ruthless violence and murder rather than accept the world as it is. The world may ultimately destroy them, but not before they have had their say. Theirs may be a limited freedom, but out of the solid rock of necessity they hew a space for freedom. It is a perilous freedom, gained at a terrible price, but for a moment the hero holds it. He does choose, and his free will is the very basis of his identity. He is ultimately defeated, but that particular battle for that one little plot of freedom will never have to be fought again.

In his isolation the hero cries out against injustice. At the end of Aeschylus' Prometheus trilogy, Zeus, the lord of heaven, learns wisdom and is reconciled with Prometheus, but the one play that has come down to us, *Prometheus Bound*, ends with defiance. As Prometheus is overwhelmed by Zeus's thunderbolts and as the chasm of the mountain is split open to take him far down into the earth, he cries out with his last breath, "Behold me, I am wronged." Nor does King Lear take his treatment calmly. He lays a dire curse on his ungrateful daughters. Then, when he is thrust out into the storm and discovers that the very elements side with his daughters, he turns his rage on the heavens. Macbeth is furious at the mockery of promises and appearances, where foul is fair and whatever is, is not. At the end of O'Neill's *Anna Christie*, Old Chris sits pondering the strange ironies of life. He had tried to save his daughter from a coarse life among sailors, but she was nevertheless drawn into the life of the sea. He is no Prometheus who can foretell that Zeus will change in thousands of years; he controls only a very tiny realm of free will and knowledge. But he can shake his fist at "dat old debil Sea."

To the extent that a man asserts his difference, his ability to stand apart from the universe and declare that it is wrong, he becomes a tragic hero. He is no longer a victim, a thing; he becomes a man by stealing a bit of fire from heaven. He is no longer merely a creature; in his small way, he too becomes a creator, transcending the finite even as he sinks, lost, in the infinite. We are not always sure whether it is pride, duty, arrogance, love of the good, or love of rebellion that drives the hero in his self-assertion, but we glory in his will and his choice.

Sometimes a tragedy is simply a study of the heroic pioneer who blazes the trail for the benefit of the next generation. He succeeds partially and gives his life in the battle in order that those who come after him may succeed fully. In 1945, as the plans for the United Nations were being laid, an impressive movie about Woodrow Wilson showed his struggle to establish a League of Nations in 1919. Wilson was destroyed not merely because he miscalculated the response of American senators but because as a pioneer he was inevitably ahead of his time.

Passion

Before they reach a reconciliation, most tragic heroes undergo tremendous suffering or struggle in which they question the basis of their own being and see the foundations of the world shaken. Terrifying enough when there is the utmost faith in the benevolence of a deity, the glimpse over the edge often comes to the hero when he is in the strongest conflict and acutely aware of the hideous cruelty in the world. The romantic imagination often sees evil in the very positive terms of a demonic universe. George Steiner in *The Death of Tragedy* describes this "otherness" of the universe as an enemy. He writes:

> Call it what you will: a hidden or malevolent God, blind fate, the solicitations of hell, or the brute fury of our animal blood. It waits for us in ambush at the crossroads. It mocks us and destroys us. In certain rare instances, it leads us after destruction to some incomprehensible repose.

Ultimately, most tragic heroes find religious meaning in the universe, but not until they have fully faced the indifference, the malignity, and the devastating play of chance and accident.

Perception

Tragedy is most significant in its final phase, when meaning becomes clear, when the sacrifice is followed by resurrection, when the trial reaches judgment and sentence, when the isolated hero is reconciled to the world he has opposed. Through his suffering he learns to be both an individual and a part of the mysterious larger entity. At last the world that seemed capricious, malignant, and unjust is revealed as moral, meaningful, and ordered, though finite man may never completely understand that order.

On the simplest level, the hero faces the result of his own actions. In O'Neill's *Mourning Becomes Electra,* his modern Electra, after being involved in avenging her father's death and in the suicide of her brother, rejects all active contact with the world and closes herself in the family mansion to live with her ghosts. Mourning is indeed becoming to Electra. Even medieval writers, who did not guess the larger meaning of tragedy, could understand this elementary concept of retribution. When in their passion plays Herod ordered the slaughter of the innocents, he soon found that his own son had been killed. Even the melodramas of the nineteenth century show the fitness of retribution. In the opera *Rigoletto,* the hunchback jester, plotting to kill his enemy, kills his own daughter. Most tragedies, though more subtle and complex, suggest that the hero had it coming. There is assurance that life is not meaningless chance, that results have causes, and that fate in its indirect way has a dependable moral order. There is relief when the trial is over and the verdict is clear.

Aristotle suggested not a ritual purging but a metaphor of medical purging as an explanation of the effect of tragedy. He defined the proper reactions to tragedy as pity and terror and added that by pity and terror tragedy effects "a catharsis of such emotions." The literal meaning of *catharsis* is "purging" or "purification," but since no one knows exactly what Aristotle meant, the word has become the most discussed term in dramatic theory; it has been variously interpreted to mean every kind of emotional release, from the repose of "all passion spent" to a cleansing from all selfish and petty emotions.

The reconciliation of the tragic hero may take either a metaphysical or a psychological form, or both. Tokens of a wider justice break into the tragic world in many ways. The Furies in Aeschylus' *Oresteia,* Mephistopheles in Goethe's *Faust,* the Ghost in *Hamlet,* and the witches in *Macbeth* are vivid examples of supernatural forces that find an immediate echo in the psychological. In *Oedipus* the oracles and the uncanny old soothsayer are very important, and the gods in many Greek plays are brought directly on stage as symbols of forces beyond human control. Romantic writers are skillful in building up an atmosphere of terror and superstitious dread that suggests impending disaster and unaccountable fate. For naturalistic writers, the environment is all-important, and its inescapable influence is suggested by fog, storms, floods, and decay and disease.

In psychological terms, the reconciliation in tragedy is with the self. All masks have been removed as proud assertion is exhausted. At the end of Sophocles' tragedy, Oedipus has passed beyond his Freudian conflict with his father and his ambiguous ties with his mother. He has even worked out his self-loathing by blinding himself. He finds his identity and accepts responsibility for his deeds. Broken as he is, he takes up his burden with great dignity and serenity. In the deep humility of suffering, the tragic hero often discovers a new bond of sympathy with all suffering humanity.

Reconciliation is not confined to the heart of the hero. Just as the world echoes the hero's shock and passion, it also shares his peace. In Shakespearean tragedy, a clear dawn follows the night, the political order is reestablished after the cataclysm, and the survivors find new strength. Even when the universe is indifferent and the individual chooses only for himself, he still finds that another person may be affected by his choice. Even in the existentialist world, as we shall note in Chapter 7, no man is an island.

The peace of tragedy involves both a spiritual and an aesthetic balance. The audience experiences vicariously the spiritual reconciliation between the hero and his gods and the resolution of his inner conflicts. The audience also achieves an aesthetic balance in which all their own impulses are brought into harmony in the richness of the theatrical experience and in the perfection of the artistic form. Whether or not the hero himself gains full perception, the audience can see the magnificence of his assertion and the inevitability of his defeat.

Greek Tragedy

Tragedy was the invention of the Greeks. In their Golden Age, the fifth century before Christ, they produced four of the world's greatest dramatists, new forms of tragedy and comedy that have been models ever since, and a theatre to which every age returns for rediscovery of some basic principle. At that time the Athenians had just rid themselves of a series of dictators and established the world's first important democracy. When the Persian armies invaded Europe, the Athenians led the confederation of little city-states and drove them back. They rebuilt their burned city in marble and made Athens the artistic as well as the political center of Greece.

On top of the fortified rock, the Acropolis, the Athenians built the Parthenon, a beautiful temple to Athena, the goddess of wisdom, but down by the roadside on the southern slope, available to everybody, they built the theatre, a shrine to Dionysus. The center of the theatre was a round space called an *orchestra*, or "dancing place," because the drama was derived from the dithyramb, danced and chanted by a chorus. The theatre could seat seventeen to twenty thousand people. The rows of seats, built

4-1 Night performance of a Greek tragedy in the ancient theatre at Epidaurus. The chorus takes a formal position in the large circular orchestra. Photo by Harissiadis, Athens.

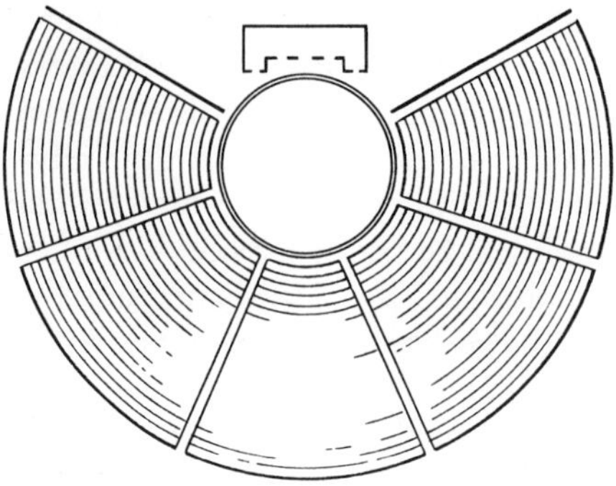

4-2
The general plan of the ancient Greek theatre. The actors entered from the *skene,* to meet the chorus in the circular *orchestra,* or dancing place, almost surrounded by the audience. Drawn by Don Creason.

up the slope of the hill, almost completely surrounded the orchestra; spectators in the first rows could almost touch the performers in the orchestra. The earliest plays centered in an altar in the orchestra and had only one actor, who carried on a dialogue with a chorus of fifty. But soon two more actors were added, and the actors' dressing hut, or *skene,* was moved up to the edge of the orchestra so that its three formal doors could serve for entrances in the action—hence the term *scene.* Eventually a raised stage was built, but in classic times the actors were not separated from the chorus.

4-3 Tragic masks of the Greek theatre. The large, dignified masks made a strong facial expression visible in a vast theatre. Between episodes they could be changed to indicate a change of emotion. Drawn by Martha Sutherland.

Since it grew up amid primitive religious rites, with masks and ceremonial costumes, and made use of music, dance, and poetry, the Greek drama was at the opposite pole from the modern realistic stage. In fact, probably no other theatre in history has made fuller use of the intensities of art. The masks, made of painted linen, wood, and plaster, brought into the theatre the primitive atmosphere of gods, heroes, and demons. Though our nineteenth- and twentieth-century grandfathers thought of masks as very artificial, today we appreciate their exciting intensity and can see that in a large theatre they would have been indispensable. If they allowed no fleeting change of expression during a single episode, they could give for each episode in turn more intense expression than any human face could. When Oedipus came back with bleeding eyes, the new mask could be more terrible than any facial makeup the audience could endure, yet in its sculptured intensity more beautiful than a real face.

The Chorus

Most essential of all intensities, and hardest for us to understand, was the chorus. It is easy to see that during the episodes played by the actors the chorus could provide a background of group response, enlarging and reverberating the emotions of the characters, sometimes protesting and opposing but in general serving as ideal spectators to stir and lead the reactions of the audience. We are familiar with such group response in the crowds of our romantic plays and the choruses of our operas. More difficult to imagine is the treatment of the choral odes. Since the action of most tragedies is complete without the odes, the modern reader either skips them or supposes that they served as some kind of lyric punctuation, like intermissions between the acts of a play. They include philosophical reflections on the meaning of human destiny and poetic references to ancient gods and heroes. They have usually been translated in such dignified, old-fashioned language that in presenting a Greek tragedy some directors have the chorus speak formally in a half-chant, standing in static groups, or moving slowly to express lamentation, sympathy, shock, or despair.

But we now know that the choral odes were complex performances, with sung or chanted words, musical accompaniment, and vigorous, sometimes even wild, dances and symbolic actions that filled orchestras sixty to ninety feet in diameter. At first the playwrights used choruses of fifty but later set the number at fifteen. We know that the playwrights had a sophisticated audience and highly trained performers, for each of the ten tribes of Athens entered a dithyramb of fifty men or boys in the annual contest, rehearsing them in song and dance for weeks. In the plays the chorus sometimes expressed simple horror or lament. Sometimes it chanted and acted out, in unison and in precise formations of rows and lines, the

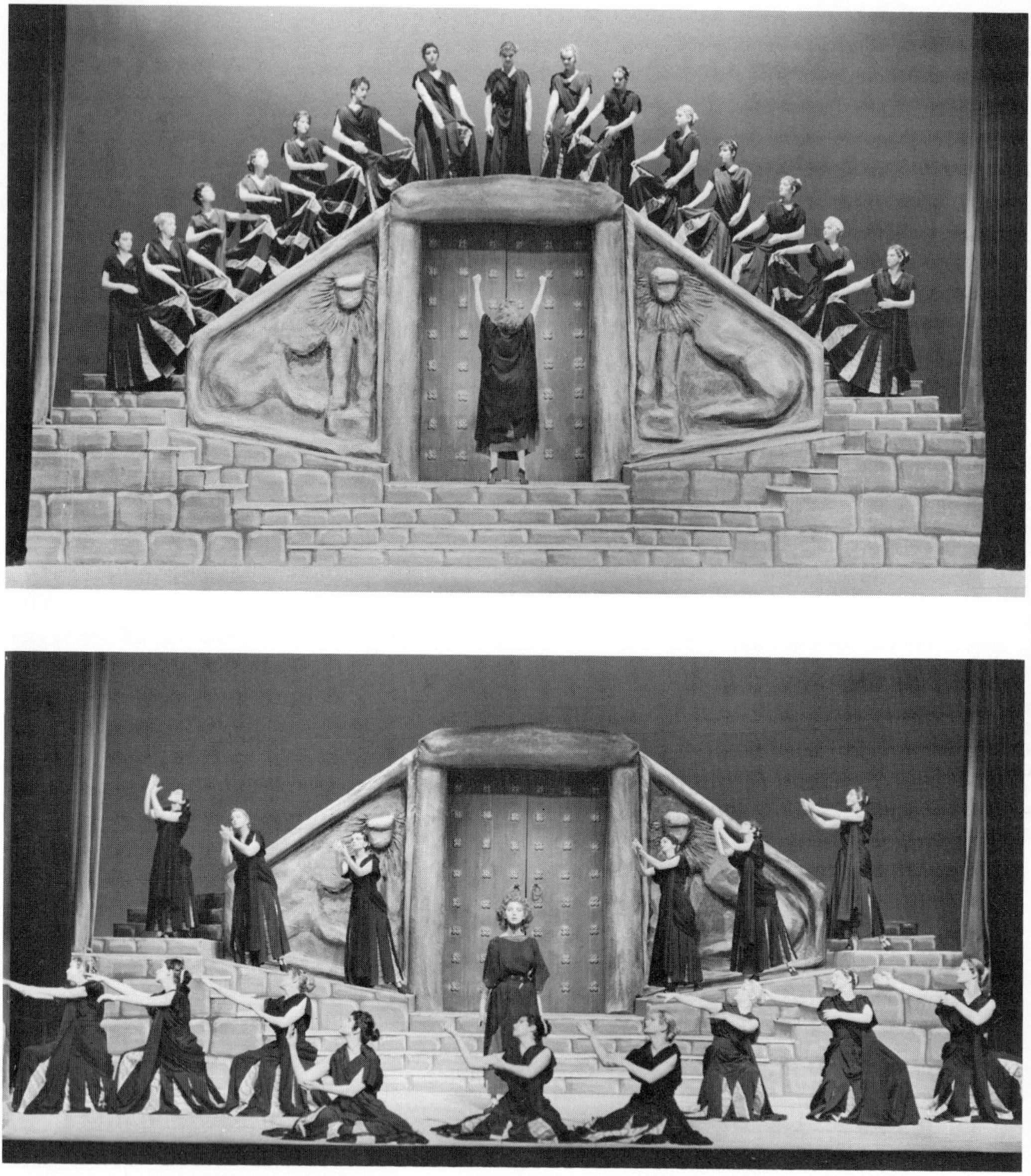

4-4 Chorus used to enlarge the emotions of the main characters. The formal grouping adds stately beauty and a sense of control to the large emotions. Sophocles' *Electra.* University of Michigan production, directed by William P. Halstead, designed by Ralph W. Duckwall, Jr., costumed by Elizabeth Birbari, and choreographed by Nancy Enggass. Photo Ouradnik.

acts of violence the characters were enacting offstage. When Phaedra rushed offstage in *Hippolytus* to hang herself from the rafters, all fifteen members of the chorus performed in mime and chant the act of tying the rope and swinging from the rafters. Sometimes the chorus related or reenacted an incident of history or legend that clarified the situation of the play. Sometimes the chorus put into specific action what was a general intention in the mind of the main character; for example, when Oedipus resolved to hunt out the guilty person and cleanse the city, he spoke metaphorically, but the chorus invoked the gods of vengeance and danced a wild pursuit.

Three Great Tragic Dramatists

The three great writers of Greek tragedy had different visions of the destiny of man. Aeschylus, the earliest, caught the heroic mood of an Athens that had just defeated the invading Persians and was reshaping old institutions and loyalties for a new age of responsible public life. Sophocles reflected the ideals of the golden time of Pericles, when men of intelligence and reason were striving for a well-balanced life in a world where blind chance and old political loyalties were constant sources of danger. And Euripides wrote at a time when the old ideals were fading, as Athens was drawn deeper and deeper into war with Sparta. In a world of torture, madness, and violence, he denounced old superstitions and offered a deep compassion for the suffering of defeated mankind. While Aeschylus' characters are superhuman—Titans, gods, and primeval kings struggling to bring order out of primitive darkness—Sophocles' characters are very human, searching for private identities in the midst of public duties, and Euripides' characters are neurotic individuals, bursting into uncontrolled violence in response to the evil around them.

Of Aeschylus' characters, the most memorable is the great Titan Prometheus, bound and tortured on a mountain peak. Seeing into the future, he shouts his defiance to the upstart Olympian god, Zeus. He knows that raw power must eventually be reconciled with wisdom or it will breed upstart power forever. Though we do not have the last play of the trilogy, we know that it showed the reconciliation of power and wisdom and that, like a number of Greek tragedies, it had a triumphant ending. While Oriental philosophers taught that man is bound to the endlessly turning wheel of desire and pain and that his only hope is to escape from the wheel, Aeschylus believed that by thought and heroic effort the wheel itself could be changed, that even the gods could grow and learn.

Where Prometheus strove for a new order in heaven to replace crude force, the three plays of Aeschylus' *Oresteia*, the only Greek trilogy that has come down to us, trace the emergence of a new social order on the human plane. After a series of horrible murders in a guilt-ridden royal family, the goddess Athena comes down to help replace private hatreds with public order. In the first play, the *Agamemnon*, the queen, Clytemnestra, and her lover, Aegisthus, conspire to murder the king on his triumphant return from Troy. Clytemnestra has not been able to forget that her husband had sacrificed their daughter Iphigenia in order to get favorable winds when he set sail ten years before. The guilty pair think that after their act of revenge they will have peace, but in the next play, *The Libation Bearers*, Orestes, goaded by his sister Electra, murders his mother and her lover. These avengers, in their turn, find no peace, for the Furies, primitive underground spirits of vengeance, come to punish Orestes. If history is nothing but neurotic violence in answer to violence, what hope is there for mankind? The last play, the *Eumenides*, finds the solution. Orestes flees to the shrine of Apollo, but Apollo cannot free him and he must take his case to Athena, the direct representative of Zeus. Knowing that a solution cannot be imposed from the outside, she establishes a new human institution, trial by jury, to hear the case and consider the motives rather than order punishment by the old rules. Even so, the jury is divided and needs divine guidance. Orestes is acquitted, but the old forces and instincts cannot be suppressed or destroyed—they must be transformed. Athena, goddess of wisdom, persuades the Furies to become *Eumenides*, "beneficent ones," and to dwell in open caves near the city, helping to preserve justice in Athens—a solution at once political, psychological, and metaphysical.

Aeschylus' trilogy is a bloody story of violence and vengeance, but the violence is treated indirectly. The actual murders are never shown on stage; they are revealed only as the characters chant of their dread or as a messenger describes a murder in vivid words or as the murderers stand gloating over the bodies wheeled in on a platform machine called the *eccyclema*. Moreover, all the elements of the performance serve to create an atmosphere of beauty rather than of simple shock—the open-air theatre, the sacred shrine, the marble *skene* with its stately formal doorways, the padded, larger-than-life actors, the large sculptured masks, the musical accompaniment, the chanting of much of the poetry, the formal odes of the chorus, and the constant references to religious and philosophical principles. But most of all, Aeschylus shows how man can move out of the primitive age of violent revenge into a more civilized age of justice and order, with public trials before a jury. In Aeschylus' vision of history man is not a hopeless victim of his primitive emotions but is capable of change, both psychological and social.

At the center of any discussion of Greek tragedy is Sophocles, for he has the clearest vision of man struggling mightily against fate, suffering greatly, and facing defeat with dignity. Though religion is always in the background, it is clear that the decisions and choices are made by man. Sophocles' heroes are kings and leaders whose fate involves the health of the state, but their struggles are the inner conflicts of solitary souls.

In Sophocles' *Antigone*, the heroine has to make a dreadful choice. When her newly crowned uncle issues orders on pain of death that no one is to bury the brother who had attacked the city, while giving all honors to the body of the brother who had defended it, Antigone makes up her mind that she will disobey him. She must perform the religious rites due the dead. Creon, calculating the practical politics of the state, is furious that a member of his own family would defy his orders. But to Antigone, political expediency and even death mean nothing when measured against the spiritual value of love. She cannot see that her action will make any practical difference in the world, but she has faith that the laws of the gods are beyond time. By the end of the play, Creon himself has become a tragic figure. His son and the old soothsayer tell him he is wrong, and the citizens do not uphold him. Relenting at the last minute, he tries to save Antigone, but it is too late: she has already hanged herself in the prison cave. His son kills himself, and then his wife commits suicide. The broken man is finally humbled before the gods, awed by the tragic consequences of his miscalculation. We are perhaps even more touched by the anguish of the man who learns too late than by the heroic will of the religious martyr.

Where Antigone sees everything, makes her choice, and faces her punishment, Oedipus sees nothing. He was the famous problem-solver who guessed the riddle of the Sphinx and delivered the city from that pest. In gratitude, the citizens, who had just lost their king, made him king and married him to the queen. But now they have a new problem for him to solve, a blight on the city that can be cleansed only by discovering the murderer of the old king and driving him out of the city. In one sense the play is an exciting detective story: as prosecutor, the king interrogates each witness, piecing the story together until he realizes that he himself is the guilty one. Each witness has his own personality and gives a different quality to each scene as the series of episodes builds to a tremendous climax. The play is rich in irony as each witness, believing he is reassuring Oedipus, reveals one more bit of evidence leading to the awful certainty that Oedipus had, unknowingly, killed his own father and married his own mother. It does not matter that the audience knows the story already. More terrible than simple surprise is this suspense of watching Oedipus come nearer and nearer to the appalling discovery and then seeing him respond to it.

In the nineteenth century *Oedipus* was regarded as a deterministic play. Malevolent fate had already announced the future in a series of oracles. Oedipus had no chance, waking to suffering that came on him from the past. The Victorians concluded that if Oedipus had any responsibility, it was because his rash temper had led him to kill the old king. To them this was, in Aristotle's phrase, the "tragic flaw" that caused his downfall.

But for the twentieth century the tragedy of Oedipus has new meanings. Above all, it is a study of the search for identity, an agonizing concern of our age. It is the need to find out who he is that drives Oedipus on. His wife begs him not to believe the soothsayer, insisting that the world is chance and nothing can be predicted. Yet what she tells him only proves how right the earlier oracles had been. The man who set out objectively to solve a simple problem is mocked by the facts until he realizes that he himself is involved with the world of unchangeable fact and the metaphysical problems of identity, responsibility, and fate. Freud used the phrase "Oedipus complex" to describe a son's conscious antagonism toward his father and unwholesome dependence on his mother; it is startling to realize that in Sophocles' play Oedipus does not have an Oedipus complex. He has gone all the way to patricide and incest without knowing it, and only by facing his guilt can he make the mature adjustment that Freud prescribed.

Unlike Sophocles, Euripides shocked his first audiences; they considered him too sensational in depicting abnormal states of mind. He used exotic foreign melodies and dwelt on the sordid topics of betrayal, cruelty, murder, and incest. But in later centuries, when audiences got used to him, he became the most popular of all the Greek dramatists, and in modern times he has had the greatest influence. He portrayed the skepticism, rebel-

4-5
Tragic hero enhanced by a large bronze mask, a costume that adds size, and boots that add height. Sophocles' *Oedipus.* Stratford Festival production, directed by Tyrone Guthrie, with costumes and masks by Tanya Moiseiwitsch.

lion, and desperation of an Athens drifting away from the high ideals and the religious devotion of earlier times. The democracy broke down in political corruption as the war with Sparta dragged on, and disease, superstition, and hysteria were rife in the crowded streets of Athens. Some Athenians could joke about the situation; the comic poet Aristophanes lashed out at it in fantastical satires that are as funny now as they were at the end of the fifth century B.C. But Euripides could not laugh. He saw no hope of returning to the religious piety and civic heroism of the past. He called on the individual to liberate himself from the superstitions still clinging to religion. As Athens seemed bent on destroying her young men and trampling on any city or group that opposed her, Euripides was haunted by images of Medea in hatred killing her own children, of Agave in religious ecstasy tearing off the head of her own son, of Phaedra in madness causing the death of her stepson—of women helpless in the grip of violent emotion, goaded by the unforgivable cruelty and injustice of the world. Or in another mood he pictured a king so torn by pity that he rushed out to the battlefield and took in his arms the bodies of the dead and dying, whether friend or foe. Euripides was the master of pity, the poet of the agony of Athens.

Euripides was shocked when Athens killed the men and enslaved the women and children of a small island that wanted to be neutral. Then when he saw Athenians building a fleet to conquer Sicily—an ill-fated expedition that led to the defeat of Athens—he produced a play about ancient victims of Greek aggression, *The Trojan Women.* The military authorities could not keep him from presenting it, since they had no control over the sacred festival. He showed the goddess Athena, angry with her favorite Greeks for their impiety, conniving with Poseidon, god of the sea, to bring punishment to them on their way home from Troy. The women of Troy, in noble anguish, leave their burning city to be slaves to the arrogant conquerors. As the ultimate cruelty, the Greeks kill the little son of Hector and deliver his broken body on a shield to his grandmother, Queen Hecuba. A procession of doom, the play has enough indignation, enough compassion, to hold the stage today. Its different episodes are arranged with strong contrast and variety, from the half-insane Cassandra whirling a torch, gloating over her knowledge of the future of her master, Agamemnon, to the wily Helen, conniving to get back into the good graces of her husband, Menelaus.

The Modern Festival Theatre

The Greek spirit lives most vividly today in the festival theatre, usually a large outdoor structure on a hillside at a sacred or historic spot to which travelers make special pilgrimages. Since the seventeenth century, travelers from around the world have gathered every ten years in the Bavarian mountain village of Oberammergau to witness the passion play put on with religious devotion by the villagers themselves. There are Wagner festivals in Germany and special Mozart performances in Austria. England has a well-established tradition of religious festival plays, usually presented in the great cathedrals. Near Palmyra, New York, Mormons and their friends see the Hill Cumorah come alive with hosts of performers reenacting the visions of Joseph Smith. Outdoor pageant-dramas, or "symphonic dramas," of American history have drawn large audiences of vacation travelers over the last three decades. Of these the best-known are Paul Green's *The Lost Colony*, which has been presented annually since 1937 on the spot of the first English settlement in North America; *Unto These Hills*, the moving story of the Cherokee tribes, presented each year in the town of Cherokee near Asheville, North Carolina; and *Texas*, presented annually near Canyon, Texas. Even more popular in recent years have been numerous Shakespeare summer festivals, of which the most famous are those in the three Stratfords—England, Ontario, and Connecticut—and in Ashland, Oregon. While a few festivals use some element of painted scenery, most go back to the unity and simplicity of the formal architectural structure used by the Greeks.

The Theatre of Exaltation: from Medieval Drama to Modern Tragedy

5

Classic tragedy disappeared with the fall of Rome. In fact, in the lavish days of the Roman Empire both comedy and tragedy had been overwhelmed by spectacular shows—gladiators, animal combats, or sea fights—and by vulgar performances of comic mimes or by elegant danced pantomimes, all produced in the enormous half-circle theatres (see Figure 5-1). The young Christian Church set itself squarely against such vulgar theatre and put an end to it. Actors, along with thieves and other vagabonds, were proscribed. For several centuries Europe had no theatre, except for a few wandering mimes and minstrels. It was a thousand years before Renaissance princes built regular theatres and produced tragedies again, but in the meantime Western Europe produced its own exalted religious drama.

Christian Drama of the Middle Ages

Curiously, it was in the Christian Church itself that the theatre made a new start, some four or five centuries after the ancient theatres had been forced to close. In the ninth century, chanted dialogue and action were added to the most sacred service of the Christian liturgy, the Easter Mass, and drama was reborn. Three priests, their heads covered, enacted the three Marys approaching the sepulchre to look for the body of Christ. Other priests dressed as the angels showed them the empty tomb and told them to go and announce to the disciples that Christ was risen. The choir burst into an anthem of praise, adding the power of choral music to the dramatic re-enactment of the sacred event. Even in this church drama, chanted in Latin, touches of comedy were included, such as the scene of the Marys at the spice-seller's booth and the race of John and Peter to the empty tomb. Soon a dramatic episode was added to the Christmas service as priests put on some suggestion of shepherds' costume to bring to the manger their offerings of gifts and song. The standing audience moved with the actors as the Three Kings approached the simple canopied throne of Herod, then talked together on the way to Bethlehem, then came to adore the Christ Child in

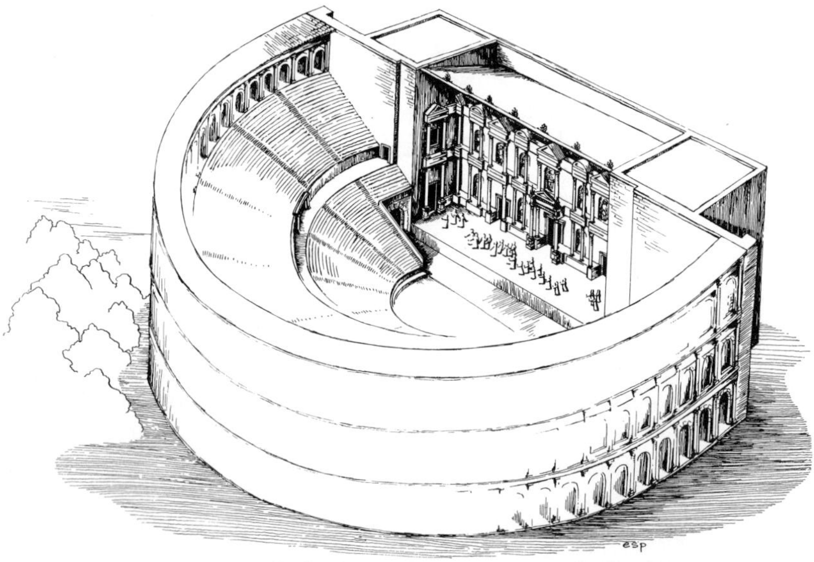

5-1 Roman theatre. Although it developed from the Greek theatre, the Roman theatre differed in that a raised stage and a very high scenic wall continued the structure of the large auditorium. It was used more for clowns, mimes, and spectacular dance shows than for plays. Drawn by Ethelyn Pauley.

a simple crèche. From the ninth and tenth centuries on, the most vivid of all the artistic devices for religious instruction were the church dramas.

Recently, some people have come to realize the power of these old Latin dramas. In 1958 the New York Pro Musica revived a twelfth-century Latin drama, *The Play of Daniel,* first in the Cloisters and then in a New York church, and the public response was amazing. They have since put on many performances in churches in this country and in Europe and have made a good recording of the work. Even in the recording, without the aid of costumes and pageantry, the play is exciting.

In the fourteenth and fifteenth centuries the merchants produced cycles of *mystery plays* during the annual procession and festival that opened the summer trade fair, an important event for every growing city. The plays were presented outdoors, in the language of the people, and were interpreted not just as ancient happenings in Palestine but with much local detail that brought them close to everyday life. From twenty-five to fifty separate plays were required to cover the whole story of the fall and redemption of man. In York some forty-eight plays were given in one long, exhausting day; in Chester the cycle lasted three days; and one cycle in France, not repeated every year, took thirty days to perform. Most of the audience stood in the street, while the rich had special bleachers or raised pavilions. There was no proscenium stage; the action moved from one scenic unit, or *mansion,* to another. Sometimes a row of mansions spread down one long platform made a "simultaneous" stage or setting. Sometimes the audience was in a circle; the important actors would make their entrances from mansions at the outside of the circle but would move to the central playing area for the main action. In most English cities, each episode was played on or around a pageant wagon that was large enough for one or two mansions, with playing room for the actors. The wagon for the first play was drawn to the first playing place, then pulled by men or horses to the second playing place as the second episode came to the first location, and so on until all the plays had been given at the dozen or more chosen stations. In England the separate episodes were usually assigned to different trade guilds, often with some consideration of appropriateness. The shipwrights, for instance, presented the scene of the Flood and the building of the Ark; the goldsmiths, the scene of the Magi bearing jeweled gifts to the Christ Child; and the bakers, the scene of the Last Supper.

This outdoor drama became much more realistic and spectacular than the church drama. Lucifer struts and grabs God's throne. A sinuous devil flatters Eve, and boisterous devils with pots and pans hail Adam and Eve on their road or, in some plays, drive them directly into a monster hell-mouth amidst smoke and flames. Noah's wife refuses to leave her gossip friends and has to be dragged onto the Ark, kicking and scratching. The old Joseph is a blustering comic figure until the angel appears to him, when he becomes

5-2 A pageant wagon showing the play of the Nativity in a medieval street. As each wagon moved to the next playing place, another wagon brought the next episode, until the entire sacred history was presented. Drawn by Ethelyn Pauley.

a devoted attendant to Mary. The shepherds, given local names, tease each other or grumble about their oppressive lords. They offer their caps, toys, and an old horn spoon to the Christ Child. When Herod hears of the child, he bursts into a noisy rage, even moving out among the audience. Shakespeare remembered the Herod of the Coventry cycle as a prime example of unrestrained acting and gave us the phrase "to out-Herod Herod." The women fight back with kitchen spoons and pans at the soldiers who come to slaughter the innocents; then Rachel sings a heartbroken lullaby over the body of her child. Soldiers at the foot of the cross shoot dice for Christ's garments, and Judas was often given a sensational treatment that modern audiences would not endure—when he hanged himself, the entrails of a hog were suddenly let down by means of a trick sack and string, as though his body had burst open, while devils, lifted by wire and pulleys, flew through the air, carrying his soul off to hell. For the burning of a martyr or the damned, not only were real flames seen but animal bones and skin were put on the flames to make the proper stench. At the Last Judgment, Christ sat with his feet on the burning world. We know that in one place four small barrels impregnated with tar were burned, one after the other, as the pageant wagon moved from one part of the town to another. The town ac-

5-3 Medieval simultaneous or multiple settings on a long platform. Each episode had its own mansion, though all the mansions to be used each day were set up from the beginning. Drawn from the manuscript of the Valenciennes production, 1547, by Ethelyn Pauley.

counts list a man who was paid for "setting the world on fire." The mystery plays delighted audiences with these real fires, sudden appearances and disappearances, flights through the air, and other marvels. Yet, despite all their childish details, in many scenes they achieved an exaltation that still has great appeal.

The late Middle Ages and the early Renaissance developed two forms of entertainment that provided a transition to the Elizabethan theatre. The first was the *morality play,* from which playwrights developed the art of creating long plots with sustained conflict and great variety of detail. The second was the street show for a royal procession, from which Elizabethan stage architects learned to combine several scenic symbols into one large structure.

Everyman (c. 1475) is the most impressive of the morality plays. In a single strong plot developed with allegorical characters, God sends Death to summon Everyman. Everyman is terrified of the journey and is not ready to present a reckoning of his life. His earthly friends Fellowship, Kindred, and Goods refuse to go with him, and Beauty, Strength, and Five Wits fall by the wayside. Only Good Deeds can go with him into the grave. *Everyman* is serious throughout, but in the sixteenth century there were many

5-4 The medieval simultaneous principle in a three-part structure for a Shakespearean play. The center section served for the throne, stage left for the tavern scenes, and stage right for the rebels. The battle scenes were played on the forestage and spread across and behind the center section. *Henry IV, Part 1.* University of Arkansas production, directed by George R. Kernodle and designed by Martel Gilbert.

morality plays that included scenes of gaiety and satire on fashions, social life, and politics. One central character would undergo a series of tests as the Virtues contended with the Vices for his soul. Some morality plays included kings and princes as historical examples and, for all their serious moral concern, showed a great deal of humanistic tolerance for fun and revelry.

The street entertainments were occasioned by royal visits to a city. A king's processional entry was welcomed by a number of street shows or tableaux presented along the way on triumphal arches or in front of public buildings. Actors portraying famous kings and heroes would address the king from throne pavilions or from a row of arches in an arcade screen. In a scenic castle or a triumphal arch, a curtain might open to present a tableau on an inner or upper stage.

Tragedy in Renaissance England

The great task of the Renaissance was to organize a compact drama out of the sprawling episodes of the Middle Ages and to create a unified stage by combining the separate mansions of the mystery plays into a single symbol of reality. Two new theatres evolved, at first distinct but later combined in the main tradition of the picture-frame stage. One theatre, in Elizabethan England, put behind an open platform a symbolic structure that combined the various medieval symbols—throne canopy, castle, triumphal arch, and others—into one complex façade with formal doorways, windows, inner stages, and upper balconies. The Italians, as we have seen, created their unified stage by a very different principle, making the medieval mansions more realistic and organizing them as separate houses lining a single street and diminishing into the distance by the laws of perspective. A proscenium frame gave finish and definition to the painted picture and set it off from the audience as an illusion of one real place (see Figures 3-15 and 3-16).

An even greater achievement was the creation of Renaissance drama. The Italian courts, developing both comedies and tragedies in close imitation of the ancients, achieved a great deal. But even more was accomplished in the popular, commercial theatres of Paris, Madrid, and London. In these centers an exalted drama was developed out of the tradition of the sprawling

5-5 Players in an Elizabethan inn yard. The inn yard probably suggested some aspects of the Elizabethan stage. A drawing from C. Walter Hodges, *The Globe Restored.* Courtesy of Coward-McCann, Inc.

religious plays, the popular romances about adventurous knights, and the histories of kings and princes that had impressed the populace in the street shows or tableaux. From the diverse material of these several sources the popular theatres kept the multiple plots, the clowns and servants to accompany the kings, prophets, and saints, the crowd scenes, the spectacular arrival of kings, the trials and council meetings, the battles, sieges, processions, weddings, and coronations. They kept this vivid pageant moving across the platform stage through scene after scene with scarcely an intermission, now by bringing on thrones, beds, or tables, now by using doors, windows, and balconies, now by disclosing arranged tableaux behind curtains.

From this popular sensational drama, like modern movies in many ways, a few poets created an exalted form of art, a romantic tragedy of heroic individuals. The great heroes of history walked out on the Elizabethan platform, defied the limits of medieval society, endured terrible suffering, expanded the bounds of the human spirit, challenged the very heavens, and met their deaths still fighting and striving. The medieval world had taught that unreasoning fortune, like a wheel, raised man to the top and then carried him on to his fall. In the medieval view, it was only by turning away from this world and seeking heaven that man could find meaning. But the Elizabethan hero would accept no such humility. Thomas Kyd's hero in *The Spanish Tragedy* (c. 1589) carries out his revenge though he destroys himself and many others in the carnage. The hero of Christopher Marlowe's *Tamburlaine* (c. 1587), a shepherd who conquers the world, defies every limitation, even mortality. By his determination to control his own fate, he persuades even his enemies to join him. Only in the sequel to the drama does Tamburlaine encounter limitations, and he will not accept them. His love, Zenocrate, dies, and Tamburlaine wants to "wound the earth" and "cleave it in twain." His son chooses a life of peace, and Tamburlaine stabs him and sets out to "march against the powers of heaven and set black streamers to signify the slaughter of the gods," defying fate to his last breath.

Mental aspiration appeals to modern audiences more than an obsession with worldly power; for this reason Marlowe's next play, *Dr. Faustus* (c. 1588), is produced more often than *Tamburlaine.* In a sense *Dr. Faustus* (see Figure 10-18) is merely a highly developed medieval morality play, but here the real experience, the conflict, is in the mind. By selling his soul to the devil in exchange for the removal of all human limitations for twenty-four years, Faustus can explore all experience and search after infinite knowledge. He calls up the image of Helen, the dream of immortal beauty, and sings his paean of praise:

> Was this the face that launch'd a thousand ships,
> And burnt the topless towers of Ilium?
> Sweet Helen, make me immortal with a kiss.
>
> . . .
>
> More lovely than the monarch of the sky
> In wanton Arethusa's azur'd arms;
> And none but thou shalt be my paramour!

At the end the devil exacts the penalty, possession of his soul, and Faustus utters his curses and his remorse as passionately as he had uttered his pride and his determination to explore all knowledge. He cannot exceed God's limits. But the final impression is not of death and defeat but of the magnificent individual who dared.

This is one of the great patterns of Elizabethan tragedy: the daring assertion that expands the limits of the human spirit even as it is defeated. The impact of the deaths of Romeo and Juliet is heightened because they have snatched their moments of ecstasy in the face of the hostility of the old feudal world. Antony and Cleopatra throw away countries and continents, but who would prefer their rival, the practical, successful, calculating Caesar? Othello is another great conqueror who is defeated by the very magnitude of his emotions, who loved "not wisely but too well." Throughout the best of the Elizabethan tragedies there is this great generosity of spirit, this willingness to live and love, even in the face of probable defeat.

It was in his history plays that Shakespeare first worked out his subtle and complex approach to tragedy. During the patriotic years following the defeat of the Spanish Armada in 1588, when plays about English history became popular, Shakespeare wrote four plays about the civil wars among the barons that led to the reign of Richard III, who was regarded in Shakespeare's age as a gloating archvillain, and finally to the accession of Henry VII, the first of the Tudor line, which contemporary historians saw as a strong national dynasty that had replaced the anarchy and confusion of the Wars of the Roses. A few years later Shakespeare wrote four plays about Henry IV and Henry V and the events at the beginning of the fifteenth century that had prepared the way for the later contentions and wars. These eight plays form one of the greatest political epics of all time. While commemorating England's century of struggle to become a united nation, Shakespeare examined the experience that shaped the kings and princes whose private ambitions and guilts so strongly affected their public careers.

The stories of all these royal leaders have tragic undertones. The sense of tragedy is most apparent in the first and last of them, the self-pitying Richard II and the Machiavellian schemer who overreaches himself, Richard III; but it is almost as evident in the guilt-stricken, sleepless Henry IV and in the splendid Hal, who, as Henry V, rationalizes his betrayals, cruelty, and violence in becoming a national hero. We usually call these plays histories rather than tragedies, but they are far more than patriotic pageants. They do portray the sweep of history and the sufferings of a nation when its rulers are wicked or merely foolish and unbending. But there is also a very strong sense of the private ambitions and betrayals, generosities and ideals, of the men who control public affairs.

Tragic Patterns in Hamlet *and* King Lear

Shakespeare's tragic view, suggested in these early history plays, was given its supreme expression in the great tragedies of his later years, especially in *Hamlet* and *King Lear.*

Hamlet was written at a time of bitter disillusionment in the European soul. Renaissance hopes were exhausted, the hopes that had buoyed up so many Italians a century before and so many Englishmen only a decade before: hopes of reconciling Christianity and classic culture, of creating a liberated aristocracy and an enlightened state through humanistic education, and reviving art, literature, and drama for the modern world on classic models. The liberated individual, no longer closely ruled by his trade guild or his parish priest, was free to make money and to lose it, free to rise rapidly in court or market, and free to be lonely and disillusioned. The feudal order was breaking up with the concentration of power in an absolute monarch. The old religious certainties were gone, and wars over religious issues were more frequent and widespread. Individualism, encouraged by humanistic education, ran riot in ruthless murders and court intrigue. Even the heavens lost their old order as the new astronomy first banished the earth from the center of the universe, then traced the earth's course around the sun not as a circle with one center but as an ellipse with two centers, and finally caught glimpses of other planets with their own moons. The feeling of this time of change was expressed in one of John Donne's poems as "all coherence gone."

The complex dramatic form that Kyd and Marlowe had shaped out of medieval traditions served Shakespeare well. While in the comedies several different groups—servants and masters, dukes and villagers, romantic lovers and mischievous revelers—are brought together in harmony at the end, the multiple-plot scheme serves in *Hamlet* to emphasize disruption and disorder. The plots develop displacement by mirror images, where each element reflects and makes an ironic comment on the other element. Hamlet is displaced from the throne. The Elizabethan façade that so richly represents the earthly order of a throne, endorsed by the symbols of heavenly order above, stands as a solid backing of the stage. But Hamlet is out on the open platform, symbol of the free and independent individual, while a usurper king sits on the throne and from either heaven or hell comes the ghost of the dead king. The basic plot is mirrored in two other sons who must avenge their fathers: both Laertes and Fortinbras are reproaches to Hamlet, going to their violent revenges without hesitation or conscience. The immediate plot is what Hamlet calls the mousetrap, a scheme of using the players to catch the king. That plot is mirrored in three analogues as Polonius sets first Ophelia and then the queen as mousetraps to catch Hamlet. It is further echoed in the plot of Polonius to set a spy to watch his own son. Hamlet's mock madness that bursts out of control is mirrored in the real madness of Ophelia. Ophelia, the object of Hamlet's love, is seen reflected in the distorted mirror of the Queen, and Hamlet rejects her with violent disgust and bawdy innuendoes. The multiple images include three kings, three father images, two fools, two madmen, and two women in love. The play-within-a-play is a mirror of both the hidden murder and the nephew's threat of vengeance.

As many students have observed, the imagery throughout the play builds up the sense of disease and corruption. Something is rotten in the state of Denmark, and Hamlet's hope of love is blasted by the cancerous image of his mother's adultery:

> Nay, but to live
> In the rank sweat of an enseamed bed,
> Stew'd in corruption, honeying and making love
> Over the nasty sty.

Yet the mood of the play is not one of total despair. The murky night is shot through with flashes of light. Hamlet himself is keenly aware that the corruption is not normal. He affirms the ideal Renaissance vision of man's nobility in a splendid world even as he notes his own disillusionment:

> What a piece of work is a man! How noble in reason! How infinite in faculty! In form and moving how express and admirable! In action how like an angel! In apprehension how like a god! The beauty of the world! The paragon of animals! And yet, to me, what is this quintessence of dust?

At the end, order is restored after disorder and Fortinbras stands in the center of the throne pavilion, a new king.

Where *Hamlet* is a play about an individual's displacement, *King Lear* is a play about the disruption and agony of a whole age. Where *Hamlet* was the favorite Shakespeare play of the romantic rebels of the nineteenth century and of the individual rebels of the early twentieth, *King Lear* is especially fascinating to those who have watched the global conflicts and revolutionary upheavals of the 1940s, 50s, and 60s. This vision of an old king who turns over his authority to a set of calculating monsters who have

5-6 A permanent setting for Shakespeare's *King Lear*, suggested by the primitive forms of Stonehenge. A design by Norman Bel Geddes.

promised him everything but who are cruel and ruthless beyond belief is amazingly pertinent today. The innocent suffer, the men of good will are exiled or forced to go underground, the world is plunged into a maelstrom of domestic, political, mental, and cosmic disorder. Yet the wicked destroy themselves, and in the end a few survivors establish order and sadly take up the task of rebuilding.

The nineteenth-century poet Swinburne saw nothing but darkness in the play as Lear discovered the enormity of human cruelty, and in 1963 Peter Brook directed the Stratford production with Paul Scofield to emphasize the chaos and despair, as though Shakespeare had written for the wry absurdists of the atomic age. Yet most twentieth-century readers and audiences have found a strong line of development leading to the salvation of Lear. His gradual discovery of love and compassion gives the play a great warmth. Hamlet had only his friend Horatio, an uninvolved observer, as a companion in his suffering. Lear is loved and cared for by a whole band of outcasts—the Fool, the blind Gloucester, the exile Kent, and the mad beggar Edgar. Above all, he discovers that his daughter is as steadfast in her love as she is stubborn in her sincerity.

By studying chaos, by tracing the breakdown of the human personality and the destruction of order, Shakespeare affirms the necessity of order. Chaos leads to a new order, but at the price of an enormous waste of human potential. Macbeth and Othello were men of great deeds and noble character until their judgment was destroyed by ambition and jealousy.

The Elizabethan Stage

To the supreme examples of tragedy created by Shakespeare the modern theatre owes an incalculable debt, but it owes almost as much to the stage on which these dramas were played. In groping for some escape from the everyday detail of the realistic theatre, playwrights, designers, and directors have learned even more from the Elizabethan stage than from the Greek or the Chinese. Though there is not a single completely dependable picture, and though the living tradition was lost in three hundred years of picture-frame scenery, enough is known about the Elizabethan stage for it

5-7 The Elizabethan public theatre, open to the sky. The final scene of *Richard III* as seen from one of the galleries. The crowd of characters, the tents and banners on the forestage, and the trumpeters on the upper stage create an elaborate spectacle. A drawing from C. Walter Hodges, *Shakespeare and the Players.* Courtesy of G. Bell & Sons, Ltd., and Coward-McCann, Inc.

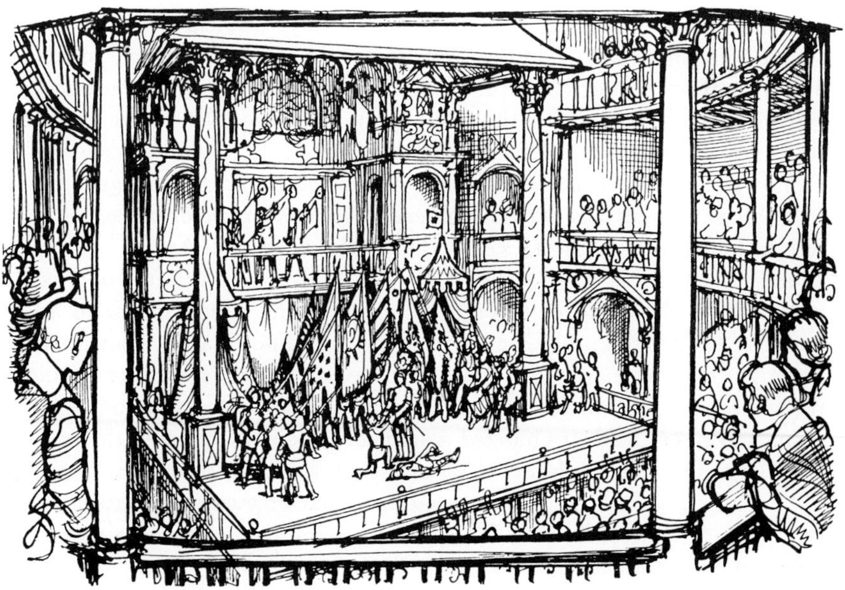

to stand as a beacon for a realistic age. To return to that stage is to enter another theatre world. There was no front curtain and no proscenium frame, no painted scenery, no pretense of creating an illusion of actual place. The action took place in the midst of the audience, on a platform that was open to the sky and to the three rows of galleries that almost completely encircled the stage and the space for standing spectators, or groundlings. The actor enjoyed direct contact with the audience instead of turning away in the strange pretense that it was not there. A splendid façade at the back of the open platform presented at least six openings, either for entrances and exits or for small scenes to be disclosed in doorways or behind small curtains. This arrangement allowed the many scenes of a Shakespeare play to follow one another without interruption for scene changes but with exciting combinations of levels and playing areas. The director could close a scene on the inner stage by means of the curtain and immediately bring another group of actors onto the forestage or the upper stage. With the rediscovery of this flexible stage, Shakespeare's plays can now be put on with the sequence and rhythm of the original productions, without pauses for scene changes, without cutting or combining the smaller scenes, and without the distraction of a different painted setting each time a different group of actors comes on the stage.

Printed versions of the plays have been corrupted since eighteenth-century editors cut them into many separate scenes and inserted indications of place: "a room in the castle," "another part of the forest," "a corridor outside the throne room," and so on. The plays published during Shakespeare's lifetime had no indications of act and scene division, much less any indication of particular place; all Shakespeare wrote was "exeunt" for one group and "enter" for the next. Only since the 1950s have some editions gone back to the Elizabethan practice of letting one scene follow immediately after the other, just as it did on the Elizabethan stage.

If it was necessary for the audience to know an exact place, the playwright had some character say, "This is the Forest of Arden," or "What country, friends, is this?—This is Illyria, Lady," or "What wood is this before us?—The wood of Birnam." Otherwise the action indicated all the audience needed to know. For many scenes it did not matter what the locality might be. There are a few hints that the names of places were visible on the stage, and some historians have supposed that a boy came out for each scene and either held or changed a sign on which was printed the name of the place. The film of *Henry V* shows such a boy with a sign. But other historians consider this nonsense and say that at most a tavern sign was hung out or a heraldic shield with "France" or the name of a castle was changed on the façade.

The most commonly accepted picture of the Elizabethan stage, then,

5-8 The Elizabethan "private" or indoor theatre used during the winter by the professional companies. A reconstruction based on recently discovered evidence. Drawn for this book by C. Walter Hodges.

is of a bare platform strewn with rushes, with a penthouse roof supported by two splendid columns, and backed by an architectural façade, or "tiring house" (where the actors changed their attire). At the stage level of the façade were two doorways and an inner stage with balconies and windows on the upper level. The basic pattern of the Elizabethan stage was apparently derived from the throne pavilion, the arches, and the inner and upper stages of the street shows. But on the Elizabethan stage these were combined into a single formal façade as a backing for the platform of the stage. It was left to the audience to turn that background into field, forest, cave, mountain, room, castle, or city gate.

It has been the fashion since the end of the nineteenth century to build "authentic reproductions" of the Elizabethan stage and to decorate them in the brown and tan half-timber style of many medieval and Elizabethan private cottages. But the contemporary references were to the splendid stage, the gaudy colors, and the painted marble columns. Further study also reveals other sources of splendor. Costumes were elaborate, and actors

5-9 An outdoor festival theatre for Shakespeare. The auditorium is a variant of the Greek theatre, but the stage is based on early twentieth-century reconstructions of the Elizabethan theatre. The Oregon Shakespeare Festival Theatre, Ashland, Oregon, founded by Angus Bowmer. Photo Dwaine Smith.

spent as much as princes for rich garments for the stage. Then, even though there was no painted setting, many properties could be brought on—thrones, tables, beds, shop fronts, altars, tombs, tents, caves, mountains, trees. Add many banners, pennants, and flags, and there is colorful pageantry indeed. A small group of musicians played flourishes for the processions, accompaniment for the many songs and dances, and appropriate background music: quiet, stately tunes for sad and solemn scenes, for example, or "hellish music" for scenes of terror. That plain platform and façade stage, whether decorated in the style of a Tudor cottage or in the classical style, could present a splendid pageant of romantic drama.

Many of the modern Shakespearean festival theatres use some variation of the standard, formal, "authentic" stage (see Figure 5-9), but when only one Shakespearean play is to be produced many designers prefer to make a structure of steps, platforms, shapes, towers, and arches to suit the action of that particular play. With the help of modern selective lighting, they can give a playing area the atmosphere of a corridor, bower, throne, or altar and, when the action moves elsewhere, let that area retire into shadows. Thus the best possibilities of modern, medieval, and Elizabethan staging are combined. The play progresses without interruption, as small changes take place in view of the audience. Such a background creates more atmosphere than the standard "authentic" Elizabethan stage and even permits some symbolism, and the flexible arrangement of levels allows more interesting grouping and movement and more effective use of modern lighting.

Neoclassic Tragedy

The Elizabethan dramatists achieved great vitality in a sprawling, complex form that owed much to the medieval theatre. Half a century later, French dramatists went to the opposite extreme and created a neoclassic tragedy that surpassed that of ancient Greece in compactness, austerity, and polish. The new classicism, in public life as well as in art, was a triumph of simplicity and order over complexity and turbulence. The expansive energies of the Renaissance had led to conflicts and tensions that set Catholics against Protestants and barons against the king. But in the seventeenth century men were tired of religious wars and emotional conflict, and gradually Richelieu brought the turbulent political forces of France under the tight control of a central power. Paris was ready for an age of reason and for a heroic drama in which violent personal forces and conflicting values were brought into controlled harmony.

Neoclassic tragedy was a triumph over the complex, romantic form of drama that was popular in European countries. Like the London of Shakespeare and the Madrid of Lope de Vega, Paris at the beginning of the seventeenth century had a vigorous popular drama. Alexandre Hardy was almost as prolific as Lope de Vega, and year after year he entertained Paris audiences with high adventure, comedy and tragedy, kings and clowns, poetry, and blood and thunder. The Hôtel de Bourgogne, the chief commercial theatre of Paris, continued in a simple form the medieval simultaneous stage, with four or five mansions around a central playing area; the audience identified the place of action by the house from which the main actors entered. Often an entire act was located at one house and the other houses were ignored although they were always in sight. Some French producers, especially in staging operas, imitated the elaborate effects of the Italian opera, with its sliding wings and backdrops, monsters rising from the waves, choirs of angels, and Jupiter descending to restore order.

When in the 1630s critical taste in France demanded a change, classical-minded men rejected both the unconvincing, disunified conventions of the medieval stage and the extravagant display of Italian spectacle. The populace might thrill at the pageantry of the baroque church and the absolute monarchy, and the aristocrats might delight in their splendid masques and operas, but men of taste wanted an austere tragedy that would show man's solitary struggle.

When neoclassic tragedy arrived, with Corneille's *The Cid* in 1637, it was not a direct imitation of Greek or Roman tragedy; it was a distillation or condensation of the popular drama. We can appreciate the compactness of *The Cid* by comparing it with the earlier Spanish play, *The Youth of the Cid*, on which it was based. In his play, Corneille eliminated many incidents found in the earlier play as well as such supernumeraries as giants, hermits, shepherds, princes, and soldiers. Leaving offstage the battle scenes and almost all of the court scenes, he replaced them with scenes between two contending characters and scenes in which a character analyzes his problem of choice. Every motive and every possible decision is carefully debated, and violent emotions are examined with utmost clarity. The Age of Reason produced not a cold debate without passion but a passionate drama of reasoning.

The Cid's choice is not between good and evil but between a private good—his love—and higher, public loyalties—his duty to his father and his king. In the end the loyalties are reconciled. Many a nobleman and merchant who sat in the audience had experienced such a conflict of personal desires and public obligations because of the tightening rule and increasing demands of an absolute monarch. The suppression of one's own desires was painful, but it was bearable because Richelieu was making Louis XIII so splendid a monarch. It was glorious to sacrifice personal inclination in order to follow such a ruler.

Even though the audience was impressed with *The Cid*, some critics thought that the refinement of dramatic material had not gone far enough. The play still contained features that were contrary to classic ideas of unity: more than one climax (though technically the action took place in one day), more than one place represented on the stage (though the different scenes were all near one another at the royal court), and more than one action (though the subplot was closely related to the main theme). The Académie Française, a council instituted by Richelieu to render authoritative judgment on both words and techniques in formal literature, condemned *The Cid* for not adhering to the classic form. In his next plays, Corneille was careful to observe the unities of time, place, and action, to avoid scenes of public spectacle, and to show his characters as abstract, universalized types. The neoclassic ideals of unity and decorum were thus established.

Racine, who began writing plays in the 1660s, found no difficulty in fitting his genius into the neoclassic form. While Corneille stressed the triumph of the will in plays that provoke admiration rather than pity, Racine showed the appalling failure of the will. His heroes—or rather his

5-10 The neoclassic stage of Paris in the middle of the seventeenth century. The characters in their "antique" costumes are copied exactly from an early edition of the play. The setting is a free reconstruction from several sources. Racine's *Andromaque.* Drawn by Martha Sutherland.

heroines, for he specialized in feminine psychology—fall helplessly into evil, finding tortuous justifications and rationalizations until time and their own deeds bring destruction. Racine's first great triumph, *Andromaque* (1667), presents four people, children of the heroes of the Trojan War, involved in conflicts, each torn between two demands. The two offstage deeds, a betrayal and a murder, lead to a series of violent denunciations on stage. Ten years later, in 1677, Racine closed his career in the public theatre with *Phèdre,* which has provided the foremost acting role in classic French theatre, just as Hamlet is the foremost English role. It is an even more terrifying study of tragic destruction than *Andromaque.* Phèdre, in love with her stepson, Hippolytus, is spurned by him. In vengeance, she tells her husband, Theseus, that Hippolytus has attacked her. Theseus calls on the god Neptune, who sends a sea monster to destroy Hippolytus. In clear, careful debate, Phèdre analyzes her own emotions, loathing herself for her degrading passion, seeing herself caught in the fatal net, turning her frustration into destruction. Yet she remains a public figure, a queen of dignity and grandeur. The final effect is one of majestic sadness, for the violent passions

5-11
A neoclassic role as interpreted in the nineteenth century. Elisabeth Rachel wore rather austere Grecian draperies for her most famous part, the title role in Racine's *Phèdre.* Museum of the City of New York.

and convoluted turns of the mind are all expressed in the most polished poetry, the most carefully selected impersonal diction, and the most perfectly proportioned and balanced episodes.

Setting and costume for this neoclassic drama were simple and completely divorced from everyday life. By 1640, after the remnants of simultaneous scenery had been eliminated, the setting was a modification of the perspective set introduced in Italy about 1507, but so simplified that it little resembled the fantastic settings of the opera. Two or three wings at the sides, all painted with dignified columns, led to a back shutter. By modern standards the "antique" costumes seem rather elaborate. The Renaissance had developed a standardized costume for all people of ancient times: the tunic of the Roman soldier with some embroidery added and a wider skirt, and the shepherdess or "nymph" costume of the pastoral plays made a little more courtly. The men, and sometimes the women, wore wigs and plumes. But compared to the elaborate wigs of the audience and the costumes of the opera, these were simple enough. The audience of this period liked all the variety and local color of the contemporary world in its comedy, but the exalted drama had to be set in this uniform, conventionalized world of the ancients.

It is helpful to consider how very different *Hamlet* would be if it had been written in neoclassic form. There would be no comedy, of course, none of Hamlet's bitter wit, no subplot or wide panorama of people, no public scenes, no songs, no players, no gravediggers, no ghost. The action would be concentrated on a few characters—Hamlet, the king and queen, and possibly Ophelia—who would be drained of all individuality and whose amazingly vivid diction would be reduced to a uniform, stately language. All the minor characters would be abstracted into four confidants. Hamlet would have Horatio to talk to—there would be no soliloquies, of course. The king could not have a prime minister, like Polonius, but instead would have a friend-attendant. The scenes of Hamlet refusing to kill the king at prayer, ordering Ophelia to a nunnery, and confronting the queen could all be retained, but each character would have his confidant present—the play would have to be impersonal even in intimate scenes. No throne would be visible, for not the public act but the private decision would be important.

The romantics of the nineteenth century despised neoclassic tragedy as cold and overrefined and compared it to the dead-white plaster casts made from ancient sculpture. But the twentieth century turns back to it with great respect for its ethical concern, its self-examination, its debates on moral issues, its direct scenes of personal conflict. From Ibsen's tight realistic plays, set in one Victorian living room, to Jean-Paul Sartre's *No Exit*, a fantasy about three people confined in one room in hell, to Arthur Miller's *The Price*, a family conflict over the past that takes place in the attic, modern drama has made frequent use of the compact neoclassic form. Far more than the Greeks, who used the elaborate effects of the chorus, the neoclassic playwrights proved that an austere presentation of characters in climactic action, with all preliminary episodes, all physical action, and all public events left offstage, can be very powerful drama.

Modern Tragedy

It is easy to see the magnitude of tragedy in other periods—Greek, Elizabethan, and neoclassic—but can tragedy seem exalted in the twentieth century? Many critics say no, and one of them, George Steiner, has written a book called *The Death of Tragedy*. If tragedy is a heroic vision of man, celebrating the triumph of spiritual nobility over physical defeat and death, how can it exist in an age that finds in man no heroism, but only submission and conformity? In a pragmatic age that emphasizes scientific study of the facts and practical solving of problems, how can there be room for tragedy? What is tragedy but a record of the unsolved problems of the past and a glorification of man's failure to solve them? Instead of brooding about the terrifying gap between the vision and the reality, the practical man will get on with the immediate goal of making the world better and let the infinite—if it exists—take care of itself.

Still, whatever brash front modern man assumes, the need for tragic drama continues to exist. After all the cures of the doctor, there is still disease; after all the prolongations of life, there is still old age and death; after all the sessions with the psychiatrist, anguish and defeat still come to the healthiest minds; and cosmic loneliness finds even the busiest man. Even if man's power were to increase until he could shake the planets from their course, still his achievement would fall far short of his dream. Disappointment, defeat, and death, the inescapable pain and terror, are with us as surely as they were with Sophocles and Shakespeare—two very fortunate, successful, well-adjusted men. The reality can never equal the vision. The truly scientific man will seek some new equation that will accommodate the discrepancy between man's hopes and his reality. He will turn to tragedy.

Three kinds of tragic characters have emerged in the struggle of the naturalists to change the environment, and all three have led their authors beyond the scientific materialism assumed in the naturalistic theory: the hero who is ahead of his time, the heroic little man who salvages a modicum of choice, and the frustrated rebel who turns destructive.

Tragedy was not congenial to the early naturalists. As we have seen, they rejected the easy optimism of the Victorian age, but they felt that in the long run science and reason could build an environment that would be fit for man to live in. They thought that tragedy would only encourage a defeatist attitude. Still, when they looked at the appalling slums of the new industrial cities, they realized that the job of rebuilding would take generations and that in the meantime the individual in such an environment would be defeated no matter how hard he struggled. In this belief they found a modern tragic hero—not a hopeless victim but an individual who sees what is wrong with society and gives his life in the effort to change it. There is no reconciliation or justice in the hero's defeat, as in classic tragedy, but instead the audience takes on the guilt of the injustice and the responsibility for rectifying it. While radical social thinkers have disapproved of classic tragedy, they have accepted the concept of the hero who is ahead of his time.

The greatest hero of this kind is Joan of Shaw's *Saint Joan*, written in 1923, soon after Joan of Arc was made a saint and nearly five hundred years after she was burned at the stake as a heretic. Shaw presents her as the focus of great historical forces that were about to shatter the rigid patterns of the feudal system and to usher in the national state and the Reformation. Joan is crushed by the powerful institutions she had threatened, but Shaw gives her tragic grandeur as she refuses to recant and faces the fire. In the long run what she stood for won out and the church finally canonized her. Shaw adds an epilogue to show that the ghosts of her enemies, come to congratulate her, would still be horrified if she threatened to perform a miracle and come back to life. He believed in the power of the institutionalized environment, and also in the power of the creative individual mind.

Far more deeply tragic, however, are plays that assume that progress will never solve all social problems and that a man must struggle to define his own individuality, even in the midst of unsettled and contradictory social forces. In the mid-twentieth century, the tragic heroes are those who assert their will in a difficult environment. Not Promethean defiance of the ruler of the universe but rather a very modest insistence on choice gives the modern individual heroic stature and raises him above the helpless crowd of naturalistic victims. The shred of heroic goodness discovered by John Proctor at the end of *The Crucible* is "not enough to weave a banner with, but white enough to keep it from such dogs."

Arthur Miller's *Death of a Salesman* (1949) heads the list of plays that achieve tragedy on the modest modern scale by finding dignity in the struggle of the little man. Miller treats Willy Loman, the salesman, with respect. Willy's wife, Linda, says,

> I don't say he's a great man. Willy Loman never made a lot of money. His name was never in the paper. He's not the finest character that ever lived. But he's a human being, and a terrible thing is happening to him. So attention must be paid. He's not to be allowed to fall into his grave like an old dog. Attention, attention must be finally paid to such a person.

As disaster threatens, Willy fights back. He demands some explanation for his failure. He goes over the past to ask whether he was wrong in bringing up his sons to aim for the top, to be "well liked." He talks repeatedly to the image of his long-lost brother Ben, who made a fortune in diamonds and lumber, and wonders whether he himself was right to build his life on sales slips, appointments, and appearances. Willy does more than follow the crowd, and when he fails it is truly tragic.

Most critical discussion has centered on Willy's decision to kill himself in order to make his son Biff "magnificent" with the insurance money. To the end Willy is faithful to his false dream of success. Some critics say that

5-12 Tragedy of the little man. The setting takes its multiple playing areas and its open platform from the Elizabethan stage. Miller's *Death of a Salesman.* New York, 1949. Directed by Elia Kazan and designed by Jo Mielziner. Photo Graphic House.

in a tragedy the main character must arrive at perception. Maxwell Anderson declared that the central experience of tragedy is the main character's discovery of something about himself or about the world that makes him a better person. But Miller thought it more important to show Willy steadfast, ironically happy in his death, than to show him realizing that his whole life had been a mistake. Mistaken or not, Willy is committed to his dream and dies for it. The other characters gain the perception and clarify the issues. In the Requiem at the end, each one has his say. Biff, at last sure of his own identity, declares, "He had the wrong dreams. All, all wrong. . . . He never knew who he was." Curiously enough, Charley, the friend next door who had no patience with Willy's worship of success, is the one who defends Willy's dream: "Nobody dast blame this man. A salesman is got to dream, boy. It comes with the territory." The wife has the final word, and it is a question: "Why?" That question can never be answered because the life of a human being is always a mystery.

In *The Crucible* (1953), social forces are much more important, but Miller is still able to create a drama about the choice and fate of an individual. The play has more of the traditional patterns of tragedy than *Death of a Salesman*, and some critics point to it as clear evidence that tragedy is possible in modern America. Set at the time of the Salem witch trials, the play reflects the irrational fears of the 1950s, when Senator Joe McCarthy led the witch hunt for spies and "reds" that so greatly intimidated Washington officialdom. Investigators, some of them self-appointed, made long lists of "subversives," and anyone who questioned their accusations or their right to make them was under suspicion. Many people found themselves out of jobs because there was some unrevealed question about their "security," and at one time Miller himself could not renew his passport for travel in Europe because his file indicated associations with supposedly left-wing groups.

In this atmosphere of mass hysteria Miller recognized a parallel to the situation in Salem in 1692, when a community was driven by its fears and by the accusations of hysterical adolescent girls to hang more than a score of its citizens. Some few persons were actually trying to commune with Satan, and several young girls danced naked in the woods, but most of the accused were guilty only of the great sin of disagreeing with their neighbors. The play's main couple, John and Elizabeth Proctor, are excellent heroes for a modern tragedy. Not very articulate, not at all interested in rebelling, they only gradually discover the strength to be heroic, to say and do what they must in order to be themselves. John is guilty of more than missing the sermons of a greedy, selfish preacher; Elizabeth has been ailing, cold, and suspicious, and he has taken the maid Abigail to the barn. Now it is Abigail who leads the hysterical girls and includes Elizabeth in her accusations of witchcraft.

Near the end, John cannot face hanging and agrees to confess to witchcraft. Elizabeth, safe from hanging because she is pregnant, admits to John that she was a cold wife and says that she will not blame him if he saves himself. But when it comes to signing his name to the confession, like Shaw's Saint Joan he balks. He will not accuse others and he will not debase his name. He tears up the paper and turns toward the scaffold. Hale, the preacher who had urged him to lie to save his life, is terrified for him and begs Elizabeth to plead with him, but she is at last sure of that which transcends death. As the drum rolls, she turns her face into the dawning sunlight and cries, "He have his goodness now. God forbid I take it from him!"

In some ways, Blanche Du Bois in Tennessee Williams' *A Streetcar Named Desire* (1947) is a restless victim of a difficult environment. She is already badly damaged, a wanderer from the old plantation system. She finds refuge for a moment in the slums of New Orleans, where her sister lives with her apelike husband, Stanley Kowalski, and has adjusted to the life of an animal. But Blanche has visions of finer things, and she tries to rescue her sister and herself. For a moment Blanche hopes to marry Mitch, the gentlest of Stanley's rough friends, and find a secure corner in the cave. But her past finds her out and destroys that dream. If this were all, the play would be an example of the usual naturalistic defeat. But Blanche, refusing her chance for a purely sexual relationship with Mitch, keeps her dream of something finer, fighting to the last, choosing to remain herself and to be carried to the insane asylum rather than to be like her sister.

Stanley Kowalski, especially as sensitively played by the young Marlon Brando, also has a touch of the tragic. He sees his home invaded by a difficult intruder. He suffers under her insults, and in raping and destroying her, his wife's sister, he knows he risks breaking up his own marriage. But he has his own kind of integrity to defend. The intensity of the conflict, with important values involved on both sides, gives the play considerable stature as a tragedy. It involves choice, struggle, questioning, suffering. Many of Williams' characters—Chance in *Sweet Bird of Youth*, Big Daddy in *Cat on a Hot Tin Roof*—refuse to drift on in evasion and ignorance. They wrest identity and meaning even from their pain. As Chance finally stops running away and faces the mob he knows is determined to castrate him, he says, "Something's got to mean something."

Not all modern tragedy centers on the hero who is ahead of his time or the one who clings to his right to choose, to whom "attention must be paid." Some modern tragedies are concerned with the destructive hero. Ibsen's *Hedda Gabler* (1890) is a study of a destructive woman. Hedda's Victorian society offers no outlet for intelligence and energy except complete submission to the desires of men and a smothering motherhood. Even her interference in the life of the young genius who is in love with her turns into a sordid shooting in a brothel, not the magnificent suicide she expected. She is completely in the power of the very "respectable" Judge Brack, but she can still say no. She kills herself. The optimistic naturalist may say that in the new world to come, women like Hedda will find healthy outlets for their creative power, but the fascination of the play is not in the social problem but in the power of destruction.

That love itself, the inspiration of the romantics, could be destructive amazed and fascinated a number of playwrights. In August Strindberg's *The Father* (1887) the mother deliberately destroys her husband, and in his *Miss Julie* (1888) the restless young noblewoman, unable to resist her coachman, gives herself to him and then stabs herself. In Eugene O'Neill's first long play, *Beyond the Horizon* (1920), the romantic ideals of love and aspiration, set against each other, destroy the principal character. A poetic farm boy, about to leave on his uncle's ship to fulfill a lifelong dream of seeing the world "beyond the horizon," confesses his love for a local girl and gives up his dream. But love turns sour, the farm defeats him, and he dies on a hilltop reasserting the dream he had lost. A love that causes a mother to kill her own child is the theme of O'Neill's *Desire Under the Elms* (1924), a melodrama about the violent greeds and lusts seething on a rocky New England farm. Abby kills her own baby to prove that she is not just using her young lover, her stepson, to get possession of the farm. He is furious and sends for the sheriff. Yet at the end he returns to share her fate—an assertion of love and understanding and reconciliation with destiny that has much in common with classic tragedy.

In using the Greek story of Agamemnon in *Mourning Becomes Electra* (1931), set in New England just after the Civil War, O'Neill made a major attempt to recapture the Greek tragic pattern. Instead of a family curse passed on from generation to generation, he used the Freudian concept of the dangers of sexual repression. The trauma of her wedding night has created in General Mannon's wife a neurotic hatred for her husband that eventually leads her to murder him, after taking his cousin as a lover. Then the son and daughter murder the cousin and drive their mother to suicide. The mixture of love and hate, envy and anger, involve the brother and sister too closely with each other and lead to the brother's suicide. Vinnie, the Electra of this play, shuts herself inside the family mansion to live out the rest of her life with her ghosts. In the 1930s the play seemed a profound study of destructive psychological forces, perhaps the greatest play America had produced. When the film was made two decades later, the fourteen acts were compacted into one screen play of ordinary length, and the story became a thin molodrama of no consequence. O'Neill had given the tale a scope that was lost in the condensation. One can understand why Aristotle demanded magnitude for tragedy.

O'Neill's later tragedy about his own family, a labor of love and forgiveness, is one of the finest plays in the tradition of naturalism. Called *Long Day's Journey into Night* (1956), it is a deep, beautiful study of that perverse need of human beings, in their shame, envy, and self-reproach, to destroy those they love.

The vision of destruction indicates a radical change from the attitude of most naturalists, who assumed that reality is good and believed in the great myth of progress. But what if the hope of progress is itself a romantic delusion? What if nature is man's enemy and the scientific pursuit of reality is bound to destroy the old faith in human values?

If this is the case, if truth is inhuman and things of the imagination are lies, then one answer is "Long live the lies." Several dramatists began to talk about life-lies and to defend the illusions even if they were delusions with no relation to the real world. Ibsen, in the middle of his career, reversed his attitude toward the disclosure of truth. In *Ghosts, An Enemy of the People,* and several other plays, he had portrayed stupid, venal people trying to prevent the exposure of the truth; but in *The Wild Duck* (1884) he showed the disastrous results that ensue when a misguided realist insists on telling a happy husband that his wife has been the mistress of her employer and that their daughter is not his own. In Gorki's *The Lower Depths* the truths are hunger, pain, depravity, and death, but the inhabitants of the cellar beguile themselves with impossible dreams of escape, and the compassionate pilgrim, Luka, encourages the dreams. O'Neill enlarged on the pattern in *The Iceman Cometh* (1946), a picture of a large group of derelicts and of the painful failure they experience when someone forces them to try to make their pipe dreams come true. Most of them happily return to their lies, while the few who have acted and tried to face their hidden guilt are destroyed.

The yearning for illusion, for an impossible faith in defiance of reality, is given a romantic treatment in Peter Shaffer's tragedy *The Royal Hunt of the Sun.* Pizarro, the conqueror of Peru, is a disillusioned, cynical old man, yearning for immortality of some kind. An illegitimate peasant, bitter about his struggles to rise in the world, he has little respect for the Church and for the Christians he is leading and feels drawn in sympathy to the Indian emperor Atahuallpa, who believes that his father, the Sun, will resurrect him if he is killed. Pizarro almost believes this too, so strong is his desire to find some faith. But when he is forced to kill the emperor and the Sun does not resurrect the body, Pizarro is left desolate in his grief for the man he had come to love like a son. The objective reality is only death—a dying Spain gorged with gold and a blighted Peru, its men slaughtered or enslaved. Achievement is empty. All faith is a delusion, and only a bitter, compassionate sorrow is left.

Thus, we find Ibsen, Gorki, O'Neill, and Shaffer all caught in the dilemma of scientific naturalism. If the only reality lies in a material, visible world, and if the only way to know that reality is to eliminate all values in order to study and measure the world objectively, then human values are merely subjective—that is, imaginary—and hence not really existent. Man may entertain himself with illusions, but they are really delusions. He may live for a short time by those delusions, but they are lies he tells

5-13 A personal tragedy in epic form. The Spanish conquest of Peru is seen as the tragedy of Pizarro's search for a new faith. Shaffer's *The Royal Hunt of the Sun.* New York, 1965. Directed by John Dexter and designed and costumed by Michael Annals. Photo Friedman-Abeles.

himself—life-lies. In this dilemma the tragic formula is simple: the hero tries to apply his subjective values to objective reality, but that reality destroys him. It is no wonder that many creative thinkers glorify the irrational, the perverse, and the destructive, launching senseless assaults on that inhuman objective reality, or else give up trying to make sense of the outer world and set out to establish meaning only in the subjective life. The latter course is the one taken by the existentialists. If science and history can find no place for myth, purpose, destiny, or tragedy, then obviously science and history have no meaning and can be neglected and the existentialist mind can create its own values.

But existential values are very uncertain and often contradictory. There is pain and anguish in the theatre of the absurd and in the other reflections of modern disruption (see Chapter 7). If the playwright sees only the sharply defined contrast between subjective values and objective reality, he will create a tragic farce, a play exploding with disconnected absurdities. But that concept of total contrast may be wrong. Through the ages tragedy has shown man painfully discovering that his visions, his choices, do have overwhelming consequences in the world. The *reality*, in the tragic view, is not the objective, material world nor a life-lie of the imagination, but the painful process of man's learning to live both in the world and out of it, to be both participant and observer.

The Theatre of Laughter

6

Comedy is far more complex than tragedy and harder to define. The word is used for many different kinds of plays and for a wide range of attitudes toward them, from delight in the broad slapstick of farce to sophisticated enjoyment of high comedy, ambiguous satisfaction in stinging satire, and even enthralled absorption in romantic plays that stir no laughter at all. We see ourselves reflected in a comic character, we come to like him, and then, paradoxically, we rejoice to see him beaten. We project ourselves onto the stage and yet at the same time remain detached, watching from a distance. In some ages, all plays, whether their subject matter was comic or tragic, were simply called comedies. The word "play" itself implies something that is done for sheer pleasure.

The Ways of Comedy

Laughter, that noisy cachinnation, that convulsive expulsion of air and sound so like—and so different from—the barking of a dog, has never been fully explained. It brings sudden relaxation and deep pleasure. It seems involuntary, yet it can be cultivated and stimulated. It seems subjective and individual, yet it most often occurs in social groups. Does it use reactions and reflexes inherited from our animal ancestors, who bared their fangs and barked at what they disapproved of, who snorted to eject from the nose something that tickled or stank? Yet man is the only animal that laughs, and there are many different kinds of laughter. A mother may laugh in delight at her happy baby as freely as a running boy laughs in triumph and scorn at the grown-up who tries to catch him. Will Rogers, the cowboy humorist, said that what makes people laugh is "something funny." When a person suddenly recognizes something left over, something that does not fit into his most careful calculations, he says, "That's funny, it doesn't come out the way it's supposed to." This incongruity is at the heart of comedy—things don't fit, they're not as they're supposed to be. Henri Bergson, in his essays *On Laughter*, tells how we laugh at the conflict between living and the rules we try to impose on it. Whenever the mechanical becomes encrusted on the living, it is thrown off in laughter.

From very early times, festivals and holidays have been special occasions for breaking the normal pattern and returning to a tradition of disorder, freedom, and license. A temporary ruler is crowned in mock pomp to preside over the revels, and at the end of the festival his throne is torn down in wild, destructive glee. Two myths known in various forms in many parts of the world especially influenced the character of the New Year or midwinter festival. According to one myth, the holiday was a time for returning to an earlier age when a trickster god ruled the world, before the later, more serious gods invented hard work and strict rules. In Rome the Saturnalia in December was the reign of the early god Saturn and a time of release from all duties and expectations. Men dressed as women, and servants ordered their masters about. After a holiday of release and reversal, people were able to take up their duties feeling a little less bound by the rigidities of their lives. The other myth gave the New Year festival an even more ancient tie by recognizing an incongruity in the very nature of the creation, since the lunar calendar can be fitted into the solar calendar only if some four days—holidays—are left over. Some mythologies held that creation gave form only to a finite island floating in the waters of chaos. During the new-year gap of four days, more of the surrounding primeval waters flowed into the circle of the year, renewing health and vitality. As people put on outlandish disguises to run, jump, race, dance, and act the

6-1 The spirit of comic acting. The masked actors of the *commedia dell' arte* depended as much on their singing, dancing, acrobatics, and slapstick as on the words that they improvised around an agreed-upon story. Note the platform stage in the background. Redrawn from an engraving by Callot.

holiday roles of revelry, they partook of that vital renewal. Men gave one another impossible tasks, then gave one another beatings when they failed. To make the races more exciting, they added stumbling blocks and pitfalls. In the wild but ordered release of the festival, in singing satiric songs, in beating and cheating a scapegoat, in crowning and deposing a mock king, and in erecting and destroying festive buildings, the revelers found an outlet for the spirit of disorder that can never be eradicated from human nature.

For the civilized man, comedy is the symbolic expression of the ancient festivals. On many levels comedy makes an attack on all forms, rules, and systems, but it is a controlled rebellion. It may point the way to improvement, but it more often shows a way of accepting the world as it is, of living with both order and disorder, rule and rebellion.

The pleasure of comedy is an increase in well-being. If the pleasure is intense and sudden, it bursts out in laughter. Slow smile or quick laugh, it not only relaxes tension but also unites us with the basic sources of life—the release of spring, the surge of the primitive, the triumph of the angel over the beast, of mind over matter, of vitality over calculation. The jack-in-the-box always pops up again, assertive as ever, and the clown comes back with a quip, no matter how severely he is beaten. With Feste in Shakespeare's *Twelfth Night*, the audience is reassured that journeys end in lovers' meeting and that all journeys end. The audience can stand, if not with the gods, at least with Puck in *A Midsummer Night's Dream*, to look down in amusement and delight at the foolishness of men and the perversity of the universe.

> Shall we their fond pageant see?
> Lord, what fools these mortals be!

Puck knows that the delusions of the night can be corrected in time.

> Jack shall have Jill;
> Naught shall go ill;
> The man shall have his mare again, and all shall be well.

Different periods of the past have fostered particular kinds of comedy. In ancient Greece Aristophanes found ready to his artist's hand a festival of spring fertility processions, with songs and dances, competitions and contests, installation of a ruler of the festival, ridicule and expulsion of intruders and obstructors, and a final ritual wedding and feast. Through that time-honored medium, he expressed his bitter anger at the Athenians for allowing their democracy to be controlled by dictators of the war party and for letting their education, law courts, philosophy, and literature be corrupted by irresponsible leaders of cults and fads. The spring festival was a privileged time, and even the war party could not censor the drama. Many Athenians still thought free speech important, and Aristophanes was

6-2 Masked comedians of ancient Greece on a platform stage. On improvised platforms or in open-air theatres, such clowns were popular all over the ancient world. After a vase drawing.

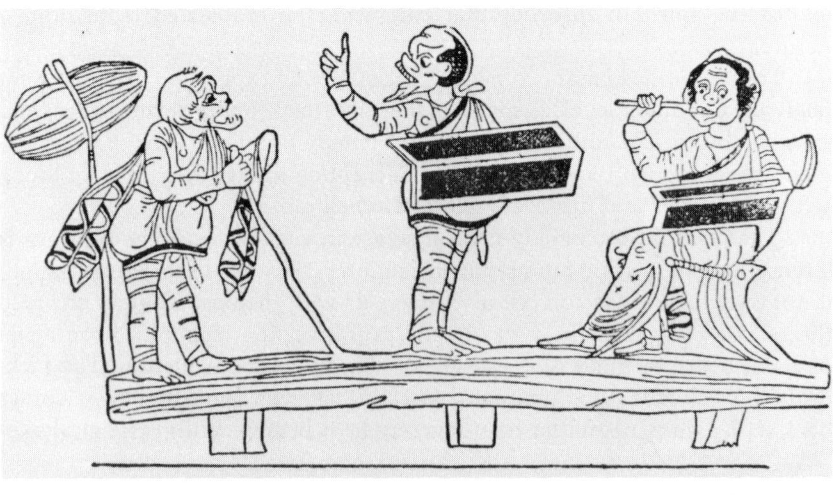

6-3 Comic movements, costumes, and setting for a modern revival of ancient comedy. Aristophanes' *The Frogs.* University of Iowa production, directed by Peter D. Arnott, designed by A. S. Gillette, costumed by Margaret S. Hall, and lighted by David L. Thayer.

not silenced when he wrote the most fantastic, and the sharpest, satires the world has ever known. In *The Knights* he even lampooned the current dictator, Cleon, as an amateur sausage-peddler selling baloney to the public. In *Lysistrata* one woman puts an end to the war by persuading the women on both sides to enforce a sex strike until their husbands make peace. *The Clouds* deals hilariously and sharply with the intellectuals who dwell in the clouds. Although Aristophanes' plays laugh at the struggles of little men faced with difficult public problems, they also carry the assurance that little men can do something about them.

After Athens was overrun by Alexander the Great and then by the Romans, the citizens no longer took an interest in important public questions. The topical satire of Aristophanes gave way to the neat plots of Menander. Later, in Rome, Plautus developed from Menander's situation drama a farcical comedy that has been the standard entertainment for the tired businessman ever since.

The medieval period developed its own little farces, about a clever lawyer tricked by a simple-minded shepherd in *Patelin*, for example, or about wives dominating and cheating their husbands. Such robust tales even intruded into the great religious cycles, as we have seen. Like the sculpture in a medieval cathedral, which included grotesque gargoyles and homely scenes of everyday life, the religious plays included both low and high characters and many elements of comedy. Medieval drama and art made a great contribution to the comic tradition, showing Shakespeare not only how to use comedy in serious plays but how to add the grim, the grotesque, and the demonic to both serious plays and comedies.

The Renaissance saw two great achievements in comedy. The first was a romantic type of comedy in which idealized young ladies and knights, engaged in the loves and intrigues of an aristocratic court, are surrounded by a variety of colorful comic characters. The appreciation of comic characters as enjoyable and even lovable was a result of the new humanistic respect for individuality, explicitly taught at the beginning of the sixteenth century in Erasmus' *Praise of Folly*. Without that attitude, Shakespeare's humorous characters, from jesters, clowns, and bumbling rustics on up to the wise, playful knight, Sir John Falstaff, would never have been conceived; even to this day some overserious moralists cannot love them or indulge them in their foolishness. The second Renaissance achievement in comedy was a realistic, satiric comedy made popular by Shakespeare's young friend, Ben Jonson. Disillusioned and bitter, Jonson attacked men's "humours," or obsessions, with savage anger and took delight in exposing their greed and other vices as well as their gullibility and stupidity. His *Volpone* (1606) and *The Alchemist* (1610) still amaze and delight audiences as dramas of sharp castigation.

The high comedy of the latter part of the seventeenth century took some of the best aspects of both kinds of Renaissance comedy—the sharp, disillusioned view of reality from Jonson, without his bitterness, and the charming, cultivated young lovers and the amiable fools from the romantic comedy. The Restoration gallant, like the Shakespearean prince, is an admirable man, much more mature than the young lovers of farce. Farce, or low comedy, is the comedy of the adolescent boy, energetic, mischievous, impatient of restraint, seeing other people as obstacles to his freedom and desires, making no attempt to understand those who differ from him. But high comedy deals with the relationships of adults who are trying to be civilized. If low comedy liberates the young man from his parents, schoolmasters, and drill sergeants, if romance opens the doors to magic journeys and enchanted castles and offers a sacred sword in the perilous clash with evil, high comedy instructs a grown man in how to get along with his neighbors, his competitors, his passing fancies, and, most difficult of all, his wife. Where tragedy records man's one ultimate clash with the universe and his humble reconciliation with the ways of the gods, high comedy records man's many clashes with his fellow men and his not-so-humble reconciliation with the ways of the world. Tragedy suggests that man's highest achievement is to find his own soul; high comedy suggests that his highest achievement is to laugh at himself, perhaps an even more important way of possessing his soul. Like tragedy, high comedy explores the more mature reconciliations with the outer world, the self, and death. But before we examine this highly developed social type of comedy, we must consider the basic, more universal type—farce.

6-4 Farcical action in a satiric fantasy with music. Mayakovsky's *The Bedbug.* University of Iowa production, directed by Philip A. Benson, designed by A. S. Gillette, costumed by Sandra Williamson under the supervision of Margaret S. Hall, and lighted by David L. Thayer.

Farce Comedy

What this world needs is a good laugh. After a wearing day, the busy man wants a scene of horseplay to relax him, and he turns on the TV to watch a lively comedian. The Romans on their holidays went by the thousands to see a clownish servant in a red wig and a wide-mouthed mask, who would be chased all over the enormous stage and beaten vigorously, yet would always be ready with a clever remark and a new scheme for getting the money or the girl. The Renaissance clown Harlequin made his sword into a "slapstick" of two strips of wood, which gave a maximum of sound with a minimum of damage to the rump. For three centuries, children and adults have screamed with delight as the puppet Punch turns on his nagging wife Judy, on the whining cat, and finally on the devil himself, and gives them such a fast, noisy beating that it seems that the puppet heads will splinter.

Curiously, our loudest laughs are at someone else's pain. A good farce is excruciatingly funny. It provides popular entertainment by turning the difficulties, restrictions, frustrations, and embarrassments of life into laughter. It relaxes the audience by first tying it into new knots of tension, then exploding the tension into guffaws and roars of delight.

To build that tension, a farce must seem completely real. The pain must be completely felt; empathy and identification must be total. As far as farce is concerned, all the old sayings about intellectual and emotional detachment in comedy are utter nonsense. Farce has its own way of making reality ridiculous, but first it must have a strong, serious grasp on that reality. In most productions of Oscar Wilde's *The Importance of Being Earnest,* Jack and Algernon have been portrayed as light, elegant playboys, but in 1939 John Gielgud's extremely *earnest* Jack made it clear how much funnier the play is when the character is dead serious.

With that firm hold on reality, the author and director give the production a treatment that will set it in the right farcical key. Farce acting is not stylized; in one sense, it is the most realistic of all acting. But it is given intensities of volume and speed, mechanical patterns of repetition or interruption, that make it very different from the realistic acting suitable for Chekhov.

Farce is based on a threefold compact between the audience and the play. One term of that compact is the realism; the audience must recognize themselves in farce, whether the actor is Jack Lemmon or Bob Newhart in modern dress, a circus clown in fantastic costume, or Mr. Magoo in a cartoon. The second element is the built-in irony of a false situation as the playwright carefully lets the audience know that it is all a mistake or a lie. The third element is the comic threatment created by the director, the designer, and the actor—the short pants and the glimpse of red underdrawers, the comic gestures and voice of the actor, the speed and noise of the performance, the patterns of incongruity and surprise.

It is the falseness of the situation that makes the pain endurable. The moment may distress the character, but the audience knows it is all a mistake. Someone is in disguise or lying, or it is a case of mistaken identity. Fate may growl like a vicious dog, but it has no teeth to bite. Everything is cleared up in the end because the situation was never real. The playwright carefully lets the audience in on the situation. He shows the putting on of the disguise, the concocting of the lie, or the beginning of the mistaken identity. In actuality, it is painful to see a husband deny his wife and upbraid her, but not in Plautus' *Menaechmi* or Shakespeare's version of the same play, *The Comedy of Errors,* because the audience knows it is not really the husband but his long-lost twin brother.

So it is not lack of empathy and emotion that turns the amazing situation into farce; it is the special comic treatment. The actor himself may contribute some comic qualities: a squeaky or reedy voice, a nasal tone, a peculiar inflection, or a monotone may reinforce the comic quality of a character. In broad farce, actors do not hesitate to use lisping, stuttering, limping, and tics. Madame Arcati's sudden jumps and squeaks are the funniest things in *Blithe Spirit.* The "Laugh-In" TV show depends enormously on exaggerated comic qualities: dozens of characters shown quickly, singly or in small groups, each made more eccentric than the last by an odd coat, hat, mustache, eyebrow, rhythm of movement, or squeaky voice. And, of course, masks of animals and fantastic creatures were used to set ancient comedy into a different realm. With more realistic characters, a floppy hat, an old-fashioned stripe, or a garment a bit too large or too short may give just the needed incongruous touch. Incongruity can make a disguise quite hilarious. The man dressed as Charley's aunt repeatedly forgets and shows his trousers and smokes a cigar, rousing screams of terror in the audience as he almost gets caught by the girls. Moments of undress or threats of exposure cause violent laughter because they come close to breaking our strong taboos. Bright-colored underclothes heighten the effect and at the same time prevent any actual exposure.

More important than the comic qualities are the various kinds of intensities of the performance. Speed is the most obvious farcical intensity. Play anything fast enough and, as long as it carries the audience with it, it will be funny. Charlie Chaplin's Monsieur Verdoux counting money at superhuman speed can never be forgotten. Chase scenes, whether of the couples running around the restaurant tables in *The Matchmaker* or of automobile thieves fleeing over curb and cliff in the silent movies, are high points of delight. Beatings, fights, struggles, pratfalls—all add an enormous amount of energetic action. Of course a good farce scene must be loud. At the end of the first act of *The Matchmaker* the young men are jumping with delight because at last they are to run away from the store. Thornton Wilder adds a whole battery of sounds as the tomato cans in the store below explode and cans and debris fly up through the trap door. Emotions in a farce are exaggerated to the fullest intensity. In a serious play sorrow and pain are suppressed and indicated by half-hidden tensions, but not in farce. It is interesting to note that audiences receive their greatest pleasure from crying on the stage. While their empathy is enlisted, their own tension is released by the sheer intensity of the actors' squalling. The various intensities—speed, energy, loudness, physical action, and exaggerated expression of emotion—all illustrate the basic duality of low comedy. Characters must be convincing, yet played with such single-minded, demoniacal obsession that the audience's empathy spills over into laughter. If a farce character ever stopped one moment to think, the whole situation would vanish. If the actors let the audience stop one moment to think, the whole farce would vanish.

The farce also makes use of many mechanical patterns: duplications, repetitions, sequences, reversals, delays, surprises, interruptions, and sudden breaks in pattern. In the famous nineteenth-century French farce *Le Voyage de M. Perrichon*, for instance, there is a light comic effect when a young lover tries to join M. Perrichon as he is leaving on a trip with his wife and daughter. When another of the daughter's suitors arrives with exactly the same excuse for going, the play moves into farce. Identical twins,

6-5 A climax of farcical surprises at the end of an act of Feydeau's *A Flea in Her Ear.* Wayne University, Hilberry Theatre Repertory Company production, directed by Richard Spear, designed by William Rowe, costumed by Stephanie Schoelzel, and lighted by Gary M. Witt.

two brothers dressed like two servants, or two people who find themselves in the same predicament can be the source of endless amusement as they move in unison, in opposition, or in sequence. Duplication of movement is so funny that in serious plays the director takes great care to see that two actors do not by chance sit, turn, or step in unison. Duplication with variation is a highly entertaining development. Sometimes it is deliberate and derisive, as when one character apes another to make fun of him or express anger. Sometimes the variation depends on incongruity, as when a short and a tall person are made to look alike or act alike. The actor T. D. Rice, whose blackface comic character "Jim Crow" was a great success in the 1830s and 40s, climaxed his program one year by having a young boy, Joe Jefferson, join him dressed and made up as a miniature Jim Crow. It is funny enough when Captain Fisby forgets his army regulations, adopts native costume, and starts building the Teahouse of the August Moon. His colonel is furious and sends a psychiatrist to take over. But the psychiatrist in turn has his weakness—organic gardening—and he settles down like a native, forgetting his own regulations. The colonel reacts to this surprise with a double take and a slow burn and frantically searches in his regulations, saying, "I want to see who I send to analyze an analyst." Sometimes the sequence of repetition is continued with several examples, and it is just a step to a Gilbert and Sullivan chorus, "and so do his sisters and his cousins and his aunts." To see a dozen Keystone Cops tumble out of a car too small to hold them and scramble after a suspect, all falling over the same obstacles, rolling downhill and piling up in a ditch, was one of the delights of moviegoing in the "Golden Age" of film comedy.

The best ending for a sequence is a reversal. Farce and melodrama take great delight in the moment when the worm turns, and it is all the better when he uses the very words the offender has used. Even serious plays often include such moments of farcical retort. When he himself is favored, Shylock praises the young judge as "noble," "wise," and "learned," a "Daniel come to judgment." When the judgment goes against him, he has to listen to his own words in the repeated taunts from the bitter Gratiano. Ibsen allowed Hedda Gabler finally to turn on her fussy husband with his own constant phrase, "Fancy that . . . huh?" The quick reversal is sure to get a laugh as the audience, called on to respond alternately to opposite emotions, cannot change that fast and throws off its confusion in laughter.

The Popularity of Farce

In spite of its enemies, farce has been the most popular of all theatre forms for more than two thousand years. Literary critics have attacked it as trivial and vulgar, and highbrows of all periods have despised it for its use of physical action. Puritans and fanatics have despised it simply because it is funny. Being dead serious is supposed to be more profound, and entertainment is "diversion," a turning away from important things. Yet year after year, night after night, the broad laugh has been as indispensable a part of the lives of millions of people as their food and sleep.

There are at least three reasons why farce continues century after century to delight its audience. In the first place, it is a release of pent-up dormant life, like the arrival of spring. The two boys in *The Matchmaker* break away from the store in Yonkers. They go downtown to the big city; they kiss some girls, take them out to a restaurant, and almost get arrested. The old merchant himself gets into unexpected adventure and brings home a wife and a much more tolerant disposition. It is as important to thaw out his tyranny and stinginess as it is to thaw the frozen ground before new things can grow. In *Mister Roberts* the sailors on the supply ship are finally released from the tight restrictions of their ill-tempered captain. They go into town for a fling, and Mr. Roberts smiles indulgently when he hears that they have wrecked an army officers' club. An unforgettable scene in the film made from the play shows one man returning to the ship on a motorcycle, streaking at top speed down the length of the dock and straight into the ocean. Such release is more important than all the caution and restrictions in the world.

Thus, farce is one version of romance. It shows the youth leaving home to go out and kill the dragon and rescue the enchanted maiden. It also shows the older man trying to slip out and meet the enchanted maiden but running back into the house before the dragon quite gets him. The difference is that farce emphasizes the little realistic details that true romance omits. As the dragon charges with breath of flame your sword sticks in the scabbard. As you lift the veil of enchantment it catches on a nail and rips. As you mount the stairs to her tower you bump your head on a beam. As you slowly move in to kiss her you are interrupted by a sneeze. In true romance such things never happen. Your clothes always fit and look right. You never have to worry about money or weather or law and order. But in farce your friend with the money is late, the rain shrinks your clothes, and the policeman puts handcuffs on you. No one believes you or understands you, least of all when you speak the plain truth. Farce makes the fullest demonstration possible of the breakdown of communication. Romance can soar with poetry into celestial clarity, but farce has to stumble along on the clumsiness of prose. Romance uses the large musical patterns of crescendos and climaxes and sustained anxieties leading to a full issue, then a final completeness and calm. Farce uses much faster crescendos, with interruptions, delayed climaxes, and far more sudden releases—just the pattern of our everyday efforts, irritations, surprises, and anxieties as we push toward the end of the day and the week, with the holiday as our goal. Some of our deceptions are discovered, but the boss is not watching all the time. By putting off this and covering up that, we can often snatch a few moments for our own lives even in a highly organized world. Farce reassures us that if we keep pushing the release will come.

A second reason for man's pleasure in farce is that it brings the great reassurance that all the great clowns have brought, the reassurance that man can take it. The clown takes his beating and survives; by his wisecrack and his comeback he proves his spiritual superiority to his fate. The clown has always been the butt, the victim, the fall guy, the little fellow that something always happens to. He is all of us, unlucky, put upon, mistreated. But he refuses to give up. He never admits defeat. He can always show his indifference to pain, and sometimes, just sometimes, he has a chance to snatch his own victory from his overwhelming enemies.

It is that superb aplomb in the midst of disaster that makes the best moments of the great clowns so memorable. At one moment in the film *A Night at the Opera*, the Marx brothers are frantically fleeing along the galleries high up in the backstage rigging in the opera house. The next moment they are serenely sailing through the air on the tie ropes as the scenery flies up and down around the performers. Or they pretend to be part of the performance, just out of reach of their pursuers. Who can forget the gravity of Charlie Chaplin as a rookie soldier in *Shoulder Arms*, left on the field marking time alone after the rest of the squad has marched away, or his quiet assertion in an early short film, *A Night Out*, when, as he is being dragged away by the collar, he picks a daisy and smells it? It is very painful to keep a bit of individuality in a regimented world, but the clown does it. We may also remember Chaplin's unquestioning absorption in his job on a swaying ladder as he cleans the street sign each time the ladder brings him by, or the same carefree bravery as he walks to the other side of the room to keep the house from toppling over the cliff in *The Gold Rush*. In *The Kid* he is a proud society man refusing to bow down to poverty and rags, twirling his cane, taking off his fingerless gloves with elegance, reaching for his cigarette case (a sardine can), and carefully tapping his choice of the butts he has picked up. Charlie Chaplin in the midst of hostile surroundings can blithely follow the life and logic of his own mind in complete disregard of his enemies. While he is sweeping a pawnshop, a rope on the floor suddenly becomes in his mind a circus tightrope, and he an expert tightrope performer beloved and applauded by the crowd. While fleeing through an enormous house, he suddenly stops before a vast birthday cake to play pool and golf with bits of the frosting, making every shot count. In farce, the world may be reeling and humanity hostile, but the clowns possess what has been called the "incalculable strength of the weak."

Besides giving us strength to free the spirit and to hold the chin up, farce has a third function: It makes an important philosophical synthesis. It is a device for accepting the basic incongruity of everyday living, for spanning the ideal and the real without denying either. Farce accepts the discrepancy between the finite and the infinite; it affirms the infinite as it laughs at man for being bogged down in the finite. In particular, it accepts both the pattern and the impulse to break the pattern. It goes further than the Bergsonian affirmation of the living man throwing off the dead pattern or the springtime release of pent-up energy. It is more than a romantic indulgence for the wild oats of youth or the wayward impulses of old men. Ultimately, farce does not demand revolutionary change. It has no wish to abolish the rules, the officers, the policemen, the parents, the wives, the jobs—the conformity that gives structure to our daily lives. But it does expect to bend the rules, to get around the officer, to vary the conformity. It reaffirms order in the universe as a whole, but it suggests that on the lower levels there may be considerable incongruity. Hence it is not surprising that many famous comic figures have come in contrasting pairs—Don Quixote and Sancho Panza, the young, idealistic Prince Hal and the old, disillusioned Falstaff, the clever slave and the stupid slave of Roman comedy, Pierrot and Harlequin, Mutt and Jeff, Weber and Fields, Amos and Andy, Laurel and Hardy. These are symbols not only of the affinity of different social classes but also of the companionship of incongruous temperaments.

Farce is a means of acceptance and adjustment. It disregards the question of whether the world can or should be changed and is concerned with the world as it is. To many romantic rebels society is an establishment designed to crush the individual. In the world of farce, society is a conglomeration of selfish individuals, clumsy institutions, and foolish customs. In your youth you are hemmed in by parents and policemen, but half the time they are busy or stupid, and you can get around them. When you grow up, your work, your family, and the causes you are committed to would absorb every last minute of your life if you let them. But you can escape. In a universe of incongruity the accidents can work for you as well as against you. If you are stopped in your flight because someone has locked the gate, you find that the demon pursuing you has fallen into an open manhole.

It's a mad world, my masters, and a laugh is the one way of accepting it, better relaxation than wine, women, or song. Without the relaxation of farcical laughter, man would long ago have torn himself and his neighbors apart.

High Comedy

Comedy is not limited to the antics of farce or to the enchanted dreams of romance. It can also create a vision of well-dressed people matching wits and exploring human relations in a world of fashion and sophistication. In this *drawing-room comedy*, or *high comedy*, business deals are made, political intrigues are sketched, plots are foiled, rivals are outdistanced, opponents are won over, friendships are made or lost, secret scandals are revealed, liaisons and marriages are arranged—all kinds of exciting situations develop through the witty conversations and wily maneuvers of urbane, charming people who are enjoying the social games immensely. In actual life, at any social level, conversation is usually one-sided, overweighted with trivia, halting, disconnected, and dull, but in high comedy every line sparkles as it hits the mark precisely in the constant excitement of retort and repartee. Where farce shows a young man bursting the bonds of restraint or a harried secretary scurrying to cover her traces before her little adventures or irregularities are found out, where romantic comedy shows an idealistic young man dedicating himself to his glamorous lady and his distant goal, high comedy shows an experienced adult picking his way skillfully and confidently among the pitfalls of a complex social

6-6 High comedy. Strong conflicts become part of a social game in elegant, upper-class surroundings. Coward's *Present Laughter.* New York, 1946. Photo Vandamm.

world and maintaining his individuality while outwardly conforming to the expectations of the group.

One of man's greatest ambitions, often the reason he works so hard for money or fame, is to be accepted in society, to "arrive," to know the language and manners of the in-group. After the adolescent has freed himself from his parents (the subject of countless farces) and has established his independence, with at least a minimum of financial and professional security, he is ready to find his role in social gatherings where he will hear not only casual gossip but comment on everything from current fashion and human behavior to the latest developments in institutions and ideas. Much high comedy is concerned with the social education of the old as well as the young as both learn, through their mistakes, to deal with the difficulties of human relations and sometimes even to laugh at themselves. It is no wonder that several high comedies have been called "schools"—*School for Husbands, School for Wives, School for Scandal.* Voltaire called the comedy of Molière a "school for civilization." The steps of Eliza's education are carefully drawn in Shaw's *Pygmalion* and even more thoroughly in the musical *My Fair Lady*, as she learns not only the language of society but the subtle art of responding to the expectations of others.

High comedy shows people antagonizing one another, disagreeing, yet somehow coming to terms. *Other* people are impossible. They presume to differ from us, but we must respect them and their right to be different, for they are our neighbors, our parents or brothers and sisters, sometimes our wives and husbands. How can we respect them and still call our souls our own? It would be much easier to follow a romantic hero to some distant crusade where everyone is either for us or against us. Yet in high comedy a few people manage, by wit and contrivance, to gain partial success and, by smiles and patience and some sublimation of anger, to find zest in the game. They learn to be adults.

Society is the basis for high comedy, not only as drama but as point of view. It is assumed not only that man is a gregarious animal but also that his full development is social. Civilized society does not exist until women can freely participate as equals of men. A mixed society adds warmth to intellectual discussion and permits the impersonal appreciation of the opposite sex. In the theatre, high comedy did not develop until women became important as characters, until Molière and Shakespeare brought them in to confront men, outwit them in deception, and stand up to them proudly and independently. Ever since Congreve's women set a classic precedent in laying down the law to their men, playwrights have put a proud, independent woman at the center of nearly every high comedy. Unlike romance, where the woman waits for the man to pursue, high comedy often allows the woman to go after the man.

Attraction, good manners, independence—to keep these three in balance at a proper distance requires a high skill in the social game. In some encounters the game requires a mask, a protective disguise that disarms the opponent by covering hostility with a smile. One of the most famous scenes of charming hostility is the garden scene in Oscar Wilde's *The Importance of Being Earnest* (1895), in which the two girls who think they are engaged to the same man slug it out verbally with more devastating blows than any prizefighter ever landed. They never lose the smile that keeps communication open or the elaborate phrase that keeps it on a generalized level, above the particular or personal. When Gwendolen, the city girl, praises the garden, she adds, "I had no idea there were any flowers in the country." That gives Cecily, the country girl, her chance: "Oh, flowers are as common here, Miss Fairfax, as people are in London." Gwendolen retaliates: "Personally I cannot understand how anybody manages to exist in the country, if anybody who is anybody does. The country always bores me to death." Cecily is ready to answer with, "Ah! This is what the newspapers call agricultural depression, is it not? I believe the aristocracy are suffering very much from it just at present. It is almost an epidemic amongst them, I have been told. May I offer you some tea, Miss Fairfax?"

But the protective disguise is the negative side of high comedy, the necessary but grim discipline of a sense of humor. High comedy also offers positive joys. The hard masks dissolve into live faces as the characters learn to play a game with other people, with themselves, and with the world.

One of the delights of high comedy is to make a game of "the others." Instead of masking hostility, tease the fools, draw them out. It helps them find harmless ways of indulging their foolishness, and they may even begin to see their faults and follies. George Meredith thought that the function of the "Comic Spirit" was to correct the faults of mankind, but through gentle laughter, without the "pain of satiric heat" or the "bitter craving to strike heavy blows." In *An Essay on Comedy*, he wrote of this Comic Spirit as a "sunlight of the mind."

The second joy of high comedy is to laugh at oneself, a very hard thing to do. If the romantic Cyrano had had one touch of humor, the tragedy would have been avoided and he would have had his love. But a romantic cannot laugh at himself, nor can he endure being laughed at. Such acceptance requires the self-knowledge of maturity, the confidence of being an individual able to play a role in society.

The third joy of high comedy depends on disillusionment, a full awareness of the limitations of man's existence. Louis Kronenberger says in *The Thread of Laughter:*

> Comedy is always jarring us with the evidence that we are no better than other people, and always comforting us with the knowledge that most other people are no better than we are. It makes us more critical but it leaves us more tolerant; and to that extent it performs a very notable social function.

In high comedy, disillusionment brings a triumph of balance, spanning the inner and the outer, the self and the others, independence and interaction, self-regard and friendship or love.

Though there were glimpses of it in ancient comedy and in minor scenes in Shakespeare, high comedy was the achievement of the seventeenth century, the first great age that produced a *society*, a class of cultivated people with the time and the inclination to devote themselves to human relations and to the forms and manners that make a society possible. After a century of humanistic education, with its emphasis on classic comedy and on the social graces of good manners, eloquence, and wit, Europe was ready for attitudes of sophistication and maturity. In Paris and London a number of men and women, gathering in the salons, at the royal court, at the coffeehouses of the town, and in the walkways of the parks, set about exploring urbane, subtle, complex, and civilized patterns of human behavior. They created a new concept of ladies and gentlemen and produced a new kind of comedy.

Like the twentieth century, the seventeenth century was trying to achieve a sane, comic view of life in a period of shattering disillusion. For more than a century, religious wars had devastated France, Germany, and England, until everyone was weary of fanaticism and ready to try to achieve toleration and stability.

It was no accident that modern science and the new comedy were born at the same time. Both required a certain detachment, a separation of man as objective observer from man as a subjective holder of values, beliefs, and feelings. Detachment grew out of the painful and disillusioning recognition of increasing complexity in the world: several religions in conflict, many suns in the skies, new continents across the seas. The first reaction to that multiplicity was bitterness and anguish, much like the bitterness and anguish of the twentieth century. We have noted how that anguish found expression in Shakespeare's *Hamlet* and *King Lear*. At the same time, comedy explored gaiety in detachment. Shakespeare's clowns captured that gaiety in a form we can still enjoy, while the masked comedians of the *commedia dell' arte* made Pantalone, Harlequin, and Pulcinella popular in both court and town. By the virtuosity of their singing, dancing, acrobatic acting, broad slapstick, and witty repartee, they taught Europe to laugh at confusion.

It was Shakespeare's friend Ben Jonson who found a literary form for the new laughter. His disillusionment was bitter and cynical, but he took the first steps toward a comedy of acceptance as well as of satire. His *Volpone* presents a monstrous old schemer who bleeds his acquaintances of money and gifts by pretending to be about to die. They deserve their losses because, in trying to curry favor with him in hopes of being named his heir, they are as unscrupulous as he. Jonson created comedy out of wild competition among monsters of viciousness.It was not until the middle of the century that a better balance was achieved. Though not expecting any more of human nature than Jonson, the later generation of playwrights learned to accept the fact that man is an earth-bound creature and to look on fools with indulgent amusement.

The Achievement of Molière

Where Jonson was bitter, Molière was urbane. He showed plenty of fanatics completely devoted to their monstrous obsessions and young people who eventually manage to get around them. Like Jonson, Molière took his plots from Plautus, but what was low-comedy intrigue in Plautus here becomes more complex and subtle. In Plautus the clownish servants had to trick the old fathers, but in Molière the deception, usually played with affection and kindness, becomes a game of juggling with the basic illusions of life. The Miser will have his children marry only for money, the

6-7 Two scenes of comic deception from an early edition of Molière. A servant masquerades as a nobleman in *The Ridiculous Young Ladies,* and a young girl and her suitor deceive the old guardian in *The School for Husbands.*

Bourgeois Gentleman only for title, Orgon in *Tartuffe* only for piety, the Imaginary Invalid only to bring a doctor into the family. Each one is fooled by his own obsession, held rigid in a kind of mask.

Molière brought interesting women into his farcical plays—wily old housekeepers or matchmakers—to trick the old men when necessary and to shake some sense into both old and young when their contentions passed all bounds. The Miser can be teased and indulged and led along by his obsession. The Imaginary Invalid is deceived not by a simple lie but by elaborate indulgence of his concern with his health: His brother and the able housekeeper arrange to have him initiated as a doctor so that he can pre-

6-8 A stylish modern production of Molière. The setting is based on three-dimensional Renaissance wings and painted backdrop. Molière's *The School for Husbands.* New York, 1933. Designed by Lee Simonson. Photo Vandamm.

scribe for himself. They win more freedom not only for the young couple but for the old man by freeing him from his fears and his foolish dependence on doctors.

The young girl also becomes much more important in Molière than she had been in earlier comedy. In Plautus she was merely the prize for the young man or his servant when they had gotten around the old man; sometimes she did not even come on stage. But Molière often told the story from her point of view and made her the active schemer. In *The School for Husbands* (1661) the young girl makes her jealous old guardian carry messages to her young man, and in *The School for Wives* (1662) the ingénue and her sweetheart tell the helpless guardian frankly that they are deceiving him. The scenes are just as funny as any classic farce scenes, but the women provide variety and complexity and add a light touch to the teasing that moves the plays toward high comedy. In several plays Molière set his young couples quarreling; in *Tartuffe* (1664) the quarrel is over how to escape the father's plans to marry the girl to the pious fraud, Tartuffe.

Finally, in *The Misanthrope* (1666), Molière moved fully into high comedy and did not bother to include the low-comedy scenes on which the other plays depend for much of the fun. While his lovers had previously been either grown children still struggling with repressive parents or wives with narrow-minded husbands, in *The Misanthrope* he presents an adult couple, free from all restrictions, exploring their relationships with other free adults. In the decade of the most elegant costumes and wigs, a lively, coquettish young woman, Célimène, is the center of attraction of many beaux, with whom she points out, in malicious character sketches, the shortcomings of their friends. With triumphant, smiling wit, she outdoes her rival in double-edged attack. The overhonest Alceste, who falls in love with her, objects violently to her enjoyment of the social group. Unable to see that his own obsession with sincerity is a fault, he despises flattery and even politeness. The girl refuses, at the age of twenty, to leave society and go off to a desert with him. They separate forever, unable to achieve a workable relationship.

While low comedy since Plautus has shown how easily servants, children, and wives can deceive anyone who tries to control them by force, Molière is also interested in the moments when the dominating character is baffled by that deceit. The audience senses, and the characters sometimes do also, that each person must have absolute trust and respect for the other

6-9 Molière in modern terms. Farcical deception becomes self-deception. *Dr. B. S. Black*, an adaptation of Molière's *The Doctor in Spite of Himself.* Spelman College of Atlanta University production, adapted and directed by Carlton W. Molette II, designed by Louis Maza, costumed by Barbara Molette, and lighted by Charles Walker.

as an independent being or there can be no real human relations, only lies and deception. A century before Jefferson and half a century before Locke, Molière was defining the basic equality of all human beings and the independence of every individual. His plays constitute a social declaration of independence, though his deep skepticism made him realize that full respect for independence is not often achieved.

The Golden Age of High Comedy

Molière was a pioneer in the intricate maneuvers of high comedy, but it remained for the witty playwrights of Restoration London, writing for a small group of sophisticates, to achieve the full realization of high comedy in the union of two proud and independent people. In their plays, the comic crudeness of the unsophisticated characters and the comic silliness of the fops and giddy women are foils for the maturity of one central couple, who learn to play the roles of free, well-adjusted adults, discarding their masks of hostility and caution for the joys of love and partnership.

The characters in Restoration comedy begin where most of Molière's

6-10 Comedy on the Restoration stage. A forestage almost as large as the Elizabethan stage was combined with Italian perspective scenery of wings and backdrop. Candles and oil lamps lit the audience almost as much as the actors. Notice the music box above the proscenium. Drawn by Ethelyn Pauley and Martha Sutherland.

6-11 A painted backdrop for a street scene for the 1936 revival of Wycherley's *The Country Wife.* The actors are on the shallow forestage next to the footlights, with chandeliers above and at the sides. Directed by Tyrone Guthrie and Gilbert Miller and designed by Oliver Messel. Photo Vandamm.

couples end, free from family restraints. They are free from serious political and economic affairs and ready to devote their wit and their leisure to the game of human relations. That game includes gossip, intrigue, flirtation, and a great deal of discussion of social behavior. To most Victorian readers and playgoers these gallants and ladies seemed artificial, if not downright wicked, but a few nineteenth-century writers defended them just because they were free from such important matters as morality and duty. Charles Lamb pictured the characters of Restoration comedy in a "Utopia of gallantry," removed from all responsibility, and William Hazlitt was delighted by their sparkling uselessness:

> Happy age, when kings and nobles led purely ornamental lives; when the utmost stretch of a morning's study went no further than the choice of a sword-knot, or the adjustment of a side curl; when the soul spoke out in all the pleasing elegance of dress; and beaux and belles, enamoured of themselves in one another's follies, fluttered like gilded butterflies in giddy mazes through the walks of St. James's park!

The early twentieth century regarded Restoration society as artificial because it enjoyed dressing up, showing off, and expressing both love and hate with politeness and wit. Presumably it is more natural and honest in the twentieth century to be churlish and ill-mannered. Audiences in the

1920s praised Restoration comedy because it was naughty and disillusioned and made fun of the puritans, taking special delight in the rough escapades of William Wycherley's *The Country Wife* (1675), with its double-entendres and gleeful leers. Present-day audiences are not much disturbed by the naughtiness; on the contrary, they find in the best plays of Etherege, Congreve, and Sheridan important and subtle studies of the complex relationships of men and women. Taking sex for granted as an easy relationship, the best Restoration plays are concerned with the more difficult relations that involve pride and self-respect.

The first fully developed hero of Restoration comedy, Dorimant in Sir George Etherege's *The Man of Mode* (1676), samples the casual relations of sex, insisting on freedom and variety only because he is determined eventually to find someone who is not so casual. When one mistress tries to hold him by his vows of love, he casts her off with indignant irony, saying, "Constancy, at my years! You might as well expect the fruit the autumn ripens in the spring . . . youth has a long journey to go, madam: should I have set up my rest at the first inn I lodged at I should never have arrived at the happiness I now enjoy."

In such an atmosphere there would seem to be little hope of finding a woman of wit and spirit who could interest a man for a lifetime. But the dramatists created a vision of such a woman—rich, independent, proud, sophisticated, but untouched by the shallowness around her. She knows nothing is certain, and still she has faith. William Congreve's Angelica in *Love for Love* (1695) accepts the world as it is and revels in the joy of the game. She insists, "Would anything but a madman complain of uncertainty? Uncertainty and expectation are the joys of life. Security is an insipid thing, and the overtaking and possessing of a wish, discovers the folly of the chase . . . the pleasure of a masquerade is done when we come to show our faces."

Love between two proud, intelligent, independent people is bound to be difficult; and a great many of the best comic scenes between lovers, from Shakespeare's Katherine and Petruchio and Beatrice and Benedict to the couples in *Oklahoma!* and *My Fair Lady*, are built on antagonism that is both exasperating and enjoyable. Congreve gave his most famous couple, Millamant and Mirabell of *The Way of the World* (1700), several encounters where gaiety ripples in the very words and rhythm of the scene. Millamant changes her tactics from the lively to the serious at a moment's notice and leaves Mirabell with a flippant "When you have done thinking of that, think of me," to which he can only reply with a sigh of vexation, "Think of you . . . think of a whirlwind . . . a fellow that lives in a windmill has not a more whimsical dwelling than the heart of a man that is lodged in a woman." But he accepts the fact that she is unpredictable and eventually finds that her follies are "so natural, or so artful, that they become her." Before they will consent to become husband and wife, this couple insist on a clear understanding that they shall keep some self-respect and independence. Their famous "proviso" scene is a Magna Carta of human rights in married life.

The most famous stage duelists in love are Sir Peter and Lady Teazle in Richard Brinsley Sheridan's *The School for Scandal* (1777). For all Lady Teazle's high spirits, she is very fond of her gruff old husband, and for all his anger with her, he finds her irresistible when her fiery temper is up. Though she bests him in battle, he thoroughly enjoys it: "There is great satisfaction in quarreling with her, and I think she never appears to such advantage as when she is doing everything in her power to plague me." Like his high-comedy descendant, Henry Higgins, Sir Peter has much to learn in order to be a better husband. He must learn a little humility and gain a sense of humor. He does finally laugh at himself in one of the funniest scenes in the play. When he discovers his wife behind a screen in the rooms of the young man he had thought perfect, he is outraged. The social gossips, of course, tease him without mercy, and he drives them from the house in a lively low-comedy scene. But when his two close friends begin to laugh at him, he cannot drive them out but must laugh at his own predicament, if grimly. After that he begins to see his wife in a new light, and he forgives her. He realizes that he had expected too much of the young man—untempered idealism is dangerous. He concludes, "Sir Oliver, we live in a damned wicked world, and the fewer we praise the better."

Where the medieval poets had insisted that life must be dominated by love, the Restoration gallants insisted that life, and most of all love, must be a game. In some ways the "game of love" can be compared to the "court of love," since both the troubadours and the Restoration wits demanded major modifications in the relations of men and women. Both shifted the emphasis from the union to the courtship, from the physical to the spiritual, from the family to the person, from blind instinct or moral duty to spontaneity and zest, from habit to choice. Both recognized that it was difficult to combine love with marriage. Both taught that love comes first, even if marriage has to yield a little.

Yet the game of love differs radically from the court of love. Where the medieval knight put his woman on a pedestal—to be worshipped in a shrine, on Juliet's balcony, or in a distant castle window—the Restoration gallant met his woman on the level of everyday life. They were partners and, like partners in a game, also competitors, traders bargaining in an open market. Where the romantic lover is totally transformed by love, giving up his former self to the lady and to the new tasks she orders or inspires, the sophisticated lover expects a partner to enhance his individual life, giving up only enough to avoid the more violent conflicts. His love does not require that he lose his identity, and a sophisticated love must take its place as just one of life's many demands and interests. The romantic attitude that promised everything often led to disillusionment and despair or cynicism. The more modest, practical approach to love expects to outlast the romantic.

Social Comedy in the Twentieth Century

After Sheridan in the eighteenth century, English high comedy was largely superseded by sentimental comedy and made no other notable appearance until the 1890s, when Oscar Wilde shocked and amused the public with his shrewd, witty plays, one of which, *The Importance of Being Earnest*, was mentioned earlier. Following an old theme of comedy, Wilde got his best fun from the contrast between the ideal and the real, especially by using the phrases of idealism to express a practical matter, as when one character describes a widow whose hair had "turned quite gold from grief." Bernard Shaw, too, in play after play showed idealistic people learning to be practical. In *Caesar and Cleopatra* the middle-aged Caesar teaches the young Queen Cleopatra how to manage people. Violet in *Man and Superman* will not let her young man defy his wealthy father by acknowledging her as his wife. "We can't afford it," she says. "You can be as romantic as you please about love, Hector; but you mustn't be romantic about money." We have seen how *Pygmalion* in its musical form, *My Fair Lady*, has its middle-aged bachelor and young flower girl painfully work out all their other relationships before they admit that they are romantically involved. Following Shaw, Somerset Maugham and Noel Coward made drawing-room comedy the characteristic form of drama, usually tracing the difficulties of a husband and wife as they react to a changing society. The pattern was still valid in the movie *Bob and Carol and Ted and Alice* (1969), with its two couples who try to experiment with the new freedom of the "swingers," only to discover that freedom and promiscuity threaten to destroy rather than enhance their marriages. Like Molière's characters, they find that freedom is not enough. There must be mutual respect and considerable self-knowledge.

Shaw's great contribution was to widen the scope of high comedy beyond the personal relationships of lovers, parents, and friends to show characters involved in social, political, and philosophical problems. His *Major Barbara* starts as a drawing-room comedy of family relationships but moves out of the drawing room to a Salvation Army shelter to show Barbara's work in offering food and salvation to the poor, then to her father's factory as she decides that it is more important to offer a purpose in life to those who are no longer poor. In his witty discussions of poverty, wealth, power, and religion, Shaw anticipated by half a century the time when the world would try to use power to abolish poverty and money to help individuals find a higher spiritual life.

After its great period of popularity in the 1920s, sophisticated comedy began to seem out of place in the modern world. Who had the leisure or the security to sit in a drawing room and dispassionately comment on personal adjustments? In the 1930s the two extremes of fascism and communism were threatening by revolution and war to put an end to democracy and the liberal tradition. A fanatical devotion to some great cause seemed to be the order of the day, and those who wanted civilized detachment or independence were lost. In 1934 Robert Emmet Sherwood, who had written delightful high comedies about ancient Rome and postwar Vienna, wrote a very effective play, *The Petrified Forest,* half comedy, half melodrama, about the death of a cultivated English liberal hitchhiking through the petrified forests of Arizona. The liberal, convinced that his urbane world is gone, invites the modern gangster to kill him, leaving his insurance to a young girl who wants to escape to Paris.

S. N. Behrman wrote several drawing-room comedies in the thirties, usually about a sophisticated woman who sadly rejects one or more suitors to keep her independance rather than join the fanatics. When the war came, Behrman tried to dramatize his hope of preserving the values of tolerance and detachment even in difficult times, but his very title, *No Time for Comedy,* shows his dilemma.

Americans have never felt completely at home in the parlor; they are more apt to work out their social problems on the job. Hence American social comedy is often more melodramatic, full of intrigue and action, or more satiric than the London tradition. For four decades American audiences looked to George S. Kaufman and his several collaborators for satiric comment on new fads and interests. Though usually quite ridiculous, the Kaufman characters were treated with sympathy and affection. Most memorable are the lovable American screwballs in *You Can't Take it With You,* first presented in 1936 and revived many times, notably on the New York stage in 1965.

Garson Kanin's *Born Yesterday* (1946) achieved some qualities of high comedy in spite of its satiric sharpness. Its heroine, Billy Dawn, is far removed from the suave upper-class characters of drawing-room comedy. She is a naive and vulgar girl who is living with a gangster junk dealer. Yet she can learn. When a newspaper reporter takes over her education, she discovers Jefferson and Tom Paine and the whole liberal tradition of American thought and becomes a charming adult, with sense enough not only to leave her coarse brute but to trap him in his own game. She gains her independence and marries the crusading liberal reporter. The play has the racy vigor of America and the suspense and action of melodrama. Yet it must be considered as partly high comedy. It even laughs at the heroine. Not quite at home in the vocabulary she has acquired so rapidly, she tells the gangster, "You're just not couth," and in a rousing speech declares that "this country with its institutions belongs to the people who inhibit it." But at the end she is a mature person who has passed gallantly the tests of the wider social world.

A New Age of High Comedy

High comedies were written in the 1950s and 60s and audiences enjoyed them, but to the revolutionary youth they seemed leftovers from a different age. In the midst of racial conflict, antiwar demonstrations, and campus confrontations, what possibility was there for toleration, mutual respect, playful wit, or friendly teasing? The existentialist in his lonely anguish recognized no social world, and the absurdist playwright caused shocked laughter but offered no promise of adjustment to an acceptable world. Yet looking back from the seventies we can see that the elements of a new high comedy have appeared. Like the high comedy of the seventeenth century, the new form is born out of bitter disillusionment, out of the blackest despair. But where the tradition inherited from seventeenth-century London and Paris was reticent, indirect, and polite in its manner, the new American form is frank, cruel, and devastating.

Several of Edward Albee's plays are cases in point. Albee began writing short plays in the absurdist pattern, and there is so much hatred and vituperation in *Who's Afraid of Virginia Woolf?* (1962) that at first its comic aspects were scarcely noticed. The London critic Kenneth Tynan scolded the actors and the audience for the laughter. The movie version, with some of the scenes played in moonlight and with many close-ups, drew less laughter. The movie camera often softens the comic effect by forcing the audience to identify with one character at a time. But in the full lighting of a stage living room, the two, three, or four people playing at bitter games and scoring verbal hits provoke vigorous laughter. The audience is right to laugh; Albee's play is fundamentally a comedy. The characters are painfully learning to make games of their own uncertain relationships. In the course of their games all four characters learn more about themselves and learn to accept their limitations.Because of their failures George and Martha are tormenting themselves and everyone near them. During a very drunken night George kills off their imaginary son and they are left more desolate, but at last free of the drive to hate themselves and torment each other. The younger couple, in the same exorcistic game, are freed of their fear of having children.

Albee's *A Delicate Balance* (1966) is even more obviously a high comedy. It begins like a Pinter melodrama as another couple arrives to stay indefinitely, fleeing a nameless terror that suddenly drove them from their home. But the host and hostess have their own family problems. The wife's alcoholic sister is staying with them, and later their daughter arrives, having failed in her fourth marriage. The house is too crowded, and when conflict bursts out, all are forced to consider the limits of people's demands on one another. The main concern is that of most high comedies: how to relate to other people and still respect both their independence and one's own. As in a Freudian naturalistic play, there is a great deal of exploration of past traumas and unresolved complexes. At the end the problems are not completely resolved, but each person has learned more about himself and has learned to accept relationships that have definite limits.

Love in conflict with power is the theme of James Goldman's *The Lion in Winter* (1966), a play with some elements of high comedy that provided brilliant movie roles for Peter O'Toole and Katharine Hepburn as King Henry II and his queen, Eleanor of Aquitaine. The rivalry and hatred be-

6-12 New patterns of high comedy. Conflicts of love, hatred, and rivalry in a context of important public events. Katharine Hepburn as Eleanor of Aquitaine and Peter O'Toole as Henry II in *The Lion in Winter*, 1968. Avco Embassy Pictures Corp.

tween the two is expressed in the bitter language of a ruthless modern age. Yet equally strong is the love and admiration the two have for each other. The aging king and queen, ashamed of their quarrelsome sons and tired of military warfare, finally gather their strength to accept with some cheer what is left of their separate lives. The film enlarged somewhat on the play's background of coarse twelfth-century life but gave its attention primarily to the problem of preserving a personal identity and a few meaningful personal relations in a world of power and conflict.

Even race relations can occasionally be seen in their comic aspects. Understandably, most race plays have emphasized conflict and have been melodramatic and uncompromising. Jean Genêt's *The Blacks* (1959), a violent play centering in the ritual murder of a white woman, brings into the open the implacable hatred between black and white (see Figure 7-7). A much lighter touch was achieved as some black writers began to write dramas of fantasy: of the first black president, of rich blacks patronizing poor, deprived whites, of the day all the blacks disappeared from a southern city leaving all the work undone. A note of genuine high comedy appeared in Ossie Davis's *Purlie Victorious* (1961), which satirizes the stereotype of old Captain Cotchipee and indulges in the verbal fantasy of bloody retaliation. In the vein of true comedy, it assumes that the two races will somehow learn to get along. While the romantics would try to ignore or obliterate differences, Davis's characters, by acting out their conflicts in play, learn to accept their differences and to regard one another with humor and respect. The musical version of 1970, called *Purlie*, celebrated that wisdom in song (see Figure 3-11).

This new high comedy of the 1960s and 70s, hardly recognized as high comedy because it still contains so much bitterness and hostility, is one of the forms of spiritual reconstruction that will be discussed in the next chapter. To learn to make a game instead of a battle out of differences between people may be of great importance in a world that will have to face racial, national, and personal conflicts for many decades to come.

The Theatre of Disruption and Reconstruction

7

Man has always recognized disruptive elements in his world, but only in the mid-twentieth century has he become so fascinated by lack of order that much of his art is devoted to demonstrating it. Over the ages art has been primarily concerned with order, with tracing the possible paths through areas of apparent disorder. But many twentieth-century artists are so dubious of the old paths and so aware of recent upheavals in the landscape that they are more inclined to prepare the traveler for a rough journey than to try to trace a new path out of the disorder. Yet there are new paths and some fragmentary maps pointing toward possible reconstruction of order.

Plays about disruption, understandably enough, are not easy to classify, but theatre people have been able to discuss most of them under five or six key headings. For the works of the first part of the twentieth century, *symbolism* and *dream* are the important terms, the dream techniques overlapping those of *surrealism* on the one hand and those of *expressionism* on the other. For drama of the 1940s and 50s, *existentialism* and *the theatre of the absurd* are the key terms. The radical explosions of the late sixties have been given many labels: happenings, street theatre, guerrilla theatre, confrontation theatre, political theatre, environmental theatre, and so on. Perhaps the term *open stage* will serve to cover part of what these forms have in common. *Epic drama* deals with the world in fragments and has borrowed much from the symbolists, the expressionists, and even the existentialists. But it tries to piece the fragments together for a real picture of the world we live in. Though a hybrid, it shares the constructive, objective purpose of realism, and it was considered in Chapter 2 as one kind of realism.

Symbolism and the Inner Drama of Strindberg and Pirandello

At the very time when naturalism was getting under way in the nineteenth century, a number of poets were setting themselves against the scientific, rational view. They felt that objective, materialistic art ignored important aspects of the mind and spirit. Such poets as Arthur Rimbaud and Stêphane Mallarmé rejected both nature and reason; instead, they attempted to evoke the eternal beyond the visible by creating suggestive symbols. Like the painters, they were fascinated by symbols of man's alienation—masks and harlequins, tramps and clowns. They cultivated free association of words and images, inducing abnormal states of mind—hallucinations and even hysteria and madness—through the use of drugs and alcohol and through frantic sensuality. To them, love was only a demonic force linked with death.

The symbolist poets had a considerable influence on the theatre. Ibsen used much symbolisn in his later work, even in plays that seemed realistic—the wild duck in the play of that name, the white horses seen before a death in *Rosmersholm*, the tower that was a fatal challenge in *The Master Builder*. The symbols suggested irrational forces driving man, sometimes to fulfillment but more often to destruction. But the chief importance of symbols was as images of the mind in the dream plays and expressionistic plays.

The first great explorer of the new inner geography was August Strindberg. Even Strindberg's great naturalistic plays of the 1880s, such as *Miss Julie* and *The Father*, were far from the objective studies of heredity and environment that Zola, the great champion of naturalism, had called for. *The Father,* in particular, is a turgid study of destructive hate between husband and wife, a torment no one knew better than Strindberg, whose three tempestuous marriages led quickly to angry separation and divorce. For some years after the breakup of his second marriage, Strindberg was on the verge of insanity and put himself into a private hospital for the insane. He wrote several autobiographical novels analyzing his torment and developing his mystical idea that God sends pain to men and lures them with attractive but hateful women in order to purify them. But a more important result of those "inferno" years was a new dramaturgy, a series of plays using many details of his own private life but setting them on the stage with revolutionary techniques. To express man's inner suffering and guilt he invented phantoms and dream images that could appear out of nowhere, dissolve, and change. O'Neill called him "the precursor of all modernity in our present theatre," and he remains one of the great figures of the age.

Two of Strindberg's plays in particular have influenced the later theatre of disruption: *The Ghost Sonata* (1907) and *The Dream Play* (1902). In *The Dream Play,* the daughter of the god Indra sets out to discover whether human life is as bad as human beings say. After each episode she concludes that "human beings are to be pitied." She encounters four variants of the dreamer—the lover who waits in vain for his love, the lawyer whose

7-1 Surrealism as a dreamlike fantasy. Both setting and characters suggest the fantasy and transformations of dreams. Cocteau's *Orphée.* Yale University production, directed by Frank M. Spencer, designed by John Koenig, costumed by Sarah Emily Brown and Frank M. Spencer, and lighted by Charles Elson.

hands are black from contact with the crimes of his clients, the ugly quarantine master who impounds contaminated people, and the poet whose agonized cry for mercy she reads for the heavens to hear. Throughout the play, a castle gradually grows taller out of the muck of the earth. At the end, the castle bursts into flames and a bud at the top opens as a splendid flower. The image suggests that the poet's song has achieved a beautiful blossoming from the pain and struggle of living.

Many strange phantoms are presented briefly by choral groups—monsters, officials, ballet dancers and singers coming from the opera house, the misshapen clients of the lawyer, starving workmen watching the rich pass in the street, and sailors frightened in a storm singing "Christ have mercy." In early productions Strindberg kept the surface appearance of realism, with full changes of settings and costumes, but later productions became frankly theatrical; the choral group, using only suggestive indications of costume and makeup, stayed on stage and shifted from one role to another in sight of the audience. Many later expressionistic plays and many epic plays borrowed the idea of such a group; one example is found in the use of choral groups in half-masks in productions of Brecht's *The Caucasian Chalk Circle.* Strindberg's method was closer to surrealism, in which the dream has the surface appearance of reality, as in Salvador Dali's scrupulously realistic paintings of limp watches and women whose bodies are chests of drawers.

The other great germinal figure in the exploration of the mind was Luigi Pirandello. As steeped in pain as Strindberg, he created a more metaphysical terror in his plays. Perhaps all living is acting before a mirror, he seems to say, a mirror that distorts or gives several different reflections. Must each person keep on acting, since the only reality is in the fleeting reflection? Where writers of high comedy find zest and entertainment in the idea of life as acting a role, Pirandello found only pain. He spent years looking after his insane wife, finding solace neither at home nor in the outside world.

Several of Pirandello's plays written at the end of the First World War made a worldwide impression, and they were probably more influential than Strindberg's dream plays in causing a profound change in the treatment of reality. Some of them are realistic enough on the surface. The husband in *As You Desire Me* is confident that the cabaret singer he has found is the wife he had lost in the war, but she herself is not so sure. A group of sensible neighbors in *Right You Are—If You Think You Are* are determined to learn the truth about the little wife whose husband and mother give quite different accounts of who she is. But the wife herself cannot tell them, and the neighbors find that their intrusion has only increased the pain of people who are trying to sustain the difficult relationships of a family.

7-2 Photographer's impression of a Pirandello play. The characters are caught in the shifting planes of reality. Pirandello's *Six Characters in Search of an Author.* University of Texas production, directed by Francis Hodge, designed by John Rothgeb, costumed by Lucy Barton, and lighted by Neil Whiting.

Two other plays of Pirandello have had even stronger influence. When modern characters appear in the medieval court in *Henry IV* (1922), we learn that servants and relatives of a nobleman have for years kept up the pretense of living in another period because, as the result of an accident while masquerading as the German Emperor Henry IV, the nobleman thinks he really is Henry IV. When the relatives, accompanied by a psychiatrist, stage a shocking surprise in the hope of curing him, he confesses that he is sane but has chosen to remain Henry IV rather than be subjected to the illusive uncertainties of his own life. He chose to live in the past because history, like art, is settled and fixed. But in a fit of anger he kills a cynical friend, and he realizes that he must forever remain Henry IV, though now his attendants know that he is acting. In *Six Characters in Search of an Author* (1921), six people interrupt a rehearsal in a theatre, insisting that the director write a play about them. They show him painful scenes of their story, disagreeing violently over the real relations between the father, mother, stepdaughter, and rejected son. The suicide of the younger son provides a sudden interruption both of the unfinished story of the characters and of the contention between the director and real actors and the real-unreal characters, now never to be fixed in art and never to agree on what their reality was or is.

The image of acting has proved an even more fruitful metaphor of man's uncertain condition than Strindberg's dream images. And Pirandello went further than Strindberg; he implied that there is no systematic reality in the world—that it is not merely a question of a dream as a disarrangement of reality in the twilight zones of the mind, but that the world of thought, undependable and multiple as it may be, is prior to, and basic to, any knowledge of the "facts" of reality.

Expressionism

Strindberg's and Pirandello's disturbing explorations of the mind and of the nature of reality were soon followed by the more positively disruptive movement known as *expressionism.* Where realism and naturalism were sharp rebellions against the cheerful sentimentality of Victorian life, the new threatre forms, beginning with expressionism, have all been rebellions against realism. Realism seemed too dull and quiet, with its muted colors, understated dialogue, restrained acting, and commonplace surroundings. Where naturalism showed a helpless victim determined, or even overwhelmed, by his environment, expressionism showed an angry little man spitting back at a machine-made, fragmented world. Expressionism reveled in sounds, colors, rhythms, and movement, all presented directly to the audience—a style labeled *presentationalism,* as distinct from the *representationalism* of the realistic style.

Expressionism in drama was in keeping with what was happening in the other arts at the end of the First World War. Painters were smearing raw colors on their canvases, using cubistic angles and planes, paying little attention to the appearance of reality. Musicians were breaking away from the muted moods of impressionism, the controlled discords of Debussy and Ravel, to explore the multitonalities, atonalities, and twelve-tone scales, the interruptions, sharp contrasts, complex rhythms, and violent climaxes of postimpressionism. Isadora Duncan and other dancers had broken from the ritualized steps of the ballet to open the way for a freer use of body movement in dance. Why should the theatre disregard the excitement of vivid colors, strange shapes, loud sounds, strong climaxes, and machine rhythms, at once fascinating and terrifying?

The spirit of revolt rejected the bourgeois-imperialistic dominance in Europe. Even during the war, in 1917, a group of disillusioned artists in Zurich started the dada movement which deliberately destroyed patterns and made nonsense of the conventional. It was a negative, partly satiric impulse, but it discovered possibilities of excitement as well as of shock in the juxtaposition of incongruous fragments. Its fur-lined teacups and pasted collages of scraps and objects suggested new ways of using texture even as they defied conventional thinking. If the war was the result of bourgeois conventionality, the dadaists said, then let's destroy the whole tradition—in fact, all tradition, political, cultural, and artistic. Dramatize the insanity of a military-commercial machine age. Explode firecrackers. Paint mustaches on pretty nudes and conventional madonnas. Destroy the institutions and habits that have enslaved and misled mankind. Open the way for a new world, socialist or communist or utopian. By destroying false ideals that had commercialized, mechanized, and militarized bourgeois society they hoped to create the spiritual brotherhood of man.

7-3 Expressionism in the movies. Setting, costumes, and movement are treated as seen in a distorted mind. *The Cabinet of Dr. Caligari*, 1919, directed by Robert Wiene. Museum of Modern Art.

It was out of this postwar spirit of revolt of the 1920s that expressionism was born. Some people have spoken of all revolt against realism as expressionism, but now the word is used primarily for a particular movement that took place mostly in Germany and the United States. One aspect of this movement, which followed the experiments of Strindberg, was a revolt against the objective view of the world in order to show the inner mind, especially in its tortured and distorted states. A second aspect was a reaction to the mechanization and dehumanization of man. Thus the dream and the machine were the two poles of postwar expressionism.

The Techniques of Expressionism

In this time of artistic ferment, almost everything that could be called "experimental" was tried on the stage. Some attempts were silly and ineffective, yet a number of important techniques were invented or adapted from older forms. We can classify these techniques into four groups: first, techniques for dramatizing the inner life; second, the use of sounds, movements, and colors to build to a climax; third, the use of stylized (that is, rhythmic and sustained) voice and movement patterns to suggest the unreality of a dream or the monotony of a machine; and, fourth, generalized, as opposed to individualized, characterization.

The simplest way to dramatize the subjective was to revive the soliloquy and the aside, letting the character put into words his private thoughts, or his "stream of consciousness," an important technique in the modern novel. For soliloquies the spotlight became very useful, allowing one character to speak his thoughts while the background and other characters sank into shadow. The opening scene of Elmer Rice's *The Adding Machine* is a long stream-of-consciousness monologue by Mrs. Zero as she is going to bed; she reveals the resentment she feels at the empty life she has led in twenty-five years of marriage to the little bookkeeper Mr. Zero. In the second scene, the conversation at the office between Zero and his assistant is interspersed with asides telling their hidden thoughts. The most famous use of asides is in O'Neill's nine-act psychological drama, *Strange Interlude,* a fairly realistic play in which the action is suspended and the dialogue interrupted repeatedly as one character at a time utters thoughts he would not speak aloud.

A dream fantasy that actually shows the inner thought is more powerful than words. *Beggar on Horseback,* an expressionistic comedy by George S. Kaufman and Marc Connelly, begins with a realistic scene as the poor composer Neil decides he should marry the rich girl who has just visited him rather than his poor sweetheart. In a dream fantasy he sees the rich girl's family, grotesquely exaggerated. Her mother wears a rocking chair;

her father, a business telephone; and her little brother, who is a baseball fiend, an enormous yellow tie and bat.

The second technique of expressionism is the building of a climax by means other than speech. Something more powerful than the soliloquy of a single actor is needed to show an inner crisis, especially since audiences have come to expect very restrained acting. The Greeks, Shakespeare, and Racine wrote long speeches with slow, rhetorical crescendos, expecting the actor to use a wide range of voice and movement. But a machine-age theatre has other resources. When Rice's Mr. Zero is fired, to be replaced by an adding machine, a crescendo of feeling builds to a climax in which Mr. Zero stabs his boss. First the soft music of a distant merry-go-round is heard, and slowly the part of the floor with the desk and stools starts to revolve. As the boss goes on with his impersonal spiel—"Sorry to lose an employee who's been with me for so many years. . . . I'm sorry—no other alternative—greatly regret—old employee—efficiency—economy—business—business—business—business"—the platform revolves faster and faster, and the sound rises to a tremendous climax.

Stylization, the third technique of expressionism, is a deliberate break with realism. Stylization in stage design immediately indicates unreality by omitting some details and distorting others. Since the emphasis in expressionistic plays is on the insane or abnormal state of the modern world, the distortion is a direct expression of the subjective. Walls lean, posts curve, roofs hang without support, the right angles of normal life become acute angles and sharp points. Objects menace with hands, eyes, pointing fingers. In Georg Kaiser's *From Morn to Midnight*, a tree takes on the appearance of a skeleton. Scenery, usually so static a background, moves before the eyes, falling, leaning in, swinging around, taking an active part in creating the nightmare.

Intensified rhythm is the most conspicuous aspect of expressionistic stylization. The rhythm of a realistic play is always subordinated to the atmosphere of the place, but in the dehumanized megalopolis of the expressionist, rhythm becomes insistent, often dominant. It is usually based on endless repetition of the same movement and sound, such as the monotonous flow of an assembly line or the passage of shiny new automobiles down a highway.

The fourth technique of expressionism is the generalization of character. The central character must represent Everyman, almost as in a medieval morality play. Whether he is the stupid eternal slave Mr. Zero, Yank the Hairy Ape, or just The Young Man or The Poet, he is the dream figure for audience identification, the truth-seeker. That generalized personality moves in a phantom world of even more impersonal characters. We take our name for these machine men from a play by Karel Čapek called *R. U. R.* (Rossum's Universal Robots), in which the few human beings still trying to be human contend with mobs of mechanized robots. The Cashier—the hero of *From Morn to Midnight* who steals money and abandons his dull family so that he can try all the vices that money can buy—finds at the races a chorus of identical attendants, and then, at a cabaret, nameless guests and nameless girls in masks. The Salvation Army Lass leads him to a Salvation Army hall, where nameless penitents make their confessions against a chorus of derisive scoffers. One group of actors, of course, with quick changes of costume, serves for all the nameless mobs in such a play, because they are all part of the same dehumanized nightmare of modern life.

The rapid decline of expressionism—it lasted only from about 1910 to 1925—was due partly to its weaknesses; it was too hysterical and rhapsodic, and its lack of real characters made it too mechanical. But the swift loss of interest in it was due even more, perhaps, to a changing attitude toward the machine and modern life. Where the old heavy machines were noisy and required the monotonous motions of many workers, the later machines are quieter and more nearly automatic. Most people have learned to use the machine as an inconspicuous servant in the background of their lives. The nightmare has lost most of its terror.

The Influence of Expressionism

Although expressionism as a widespread movement is past, it has left traces in realistic plays. One moment in *Death of a Salesman* reminds us that terror of a noisy machine can still be felt. Willy needs human consideration, but the young boss does not listen to him. Instead, he is fascinated by a new mechanical gadget, a tape recorder, on which he has just recorded his young son's recital of the capitals of all the states. When Willy has finally been fired and is left alone, he beats his fists on the desk, accidentally turning on the recorder with its mechanical repetition of a meaningless list. There is a naturalistic explanation of this machine, but the inhuman noise and its terrifying effect on Willy are a vivid moment of expressionism. The flashback scenes in the film *Midnight Cowboy* (1969) are a brilliant expressionistic means of showing the hero's present tension. His confrontation with the religious fanatic, for instance, is cut in with the terrifying stylized memory of his boyhood baptism.

A similar moment of obsessive terror makes the inner life of Blanche Du Bois clear to the audience in *A Streetcar Named Desire*. Any new moment of panic makes her relive in memory her young husband's suicide. The audience hears dance music growing louder and louder, and then the pistol shot. Yet no one thinks of *Streetcar* as anything but a completely realistic play. Both the realistic theatre and the film have so completely

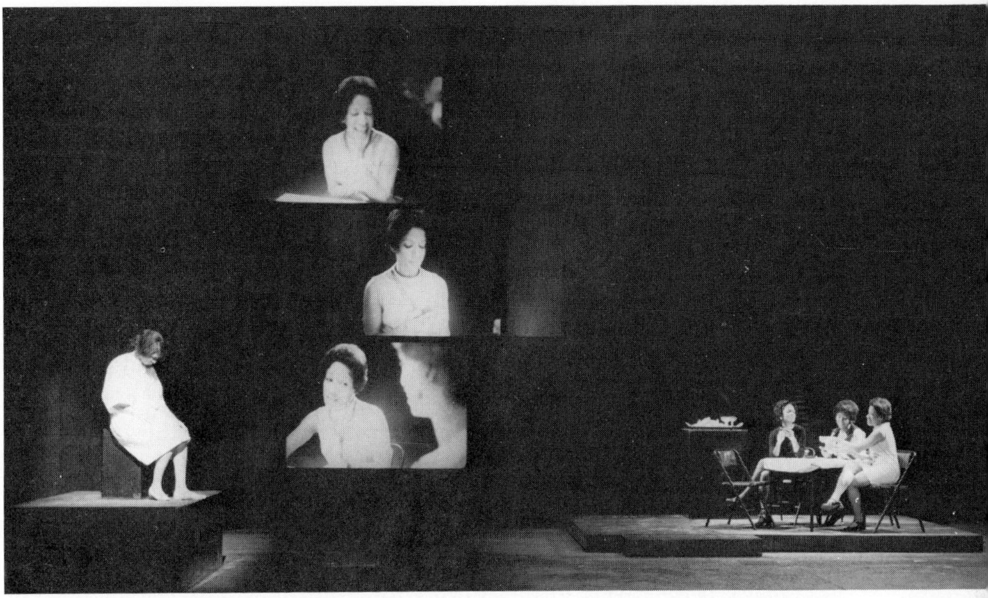

7-4 Multimedia production with expressionistic dream scenes projected on screens and epic scenes of contrast. Carlton and Barbara Molette, *Rosalee Pritchett.* Première production, Spelman College of Atlanta University, directed by Carlton W. Molette II and designed by Louis Maza.

absorbed the incidental expressionistic technique of presenting a subjective experience that no one takes special notice. A dream character like Uncle Ben moves in and out of *Death of a Salesman,* visible to some characters and invisible to others, without disturbing the sense of reality. It is not even necessary to give him artificial or dreamlike rhythms and movements.

Rhythmic group chanting to a mechanical beat reappeared minus the element of terror in the opening scene of the popular musical *The Music Man* (1957). The scene is a railway coach early in the century, and the train sets the rhythm as the salesmen, with jerking movements, chant their conviction that a new age of packaged commodities is coming and that the irregular salesman, Harold Hill, will not fit in. The scene is a clever means of creating interest in an old-fashioned romantic character who resists standardized city life. It is also a strange finale for expressionism: While in the 1920s there had been a real fear that man would lose his identity in the relentless rhythm of the machines, in 1957 an expressionistic machine scene was used in a minor part of a popular musical as a half-charming, half-satiric picture of slightly inflexible but not really mechanized men.

Existentialism in the Theatre

Existentialism, the philosophy that came to dominate much of the thinking of the 1940s and 50s, especially the thinking of the playwrights, grew out of the disillusionment that followed the Second World War. Thoughtful men, despairing of the traditional values formerly found in nature, science, politics, and history, turned inward in the hope of rediscovering a genuine identity, an authentic life of the self. The sense of disruption was far greater than that felt after the First World War. Not only was there a more drastic break with the past, with old buildings destroyed, old institutions discredited, and old patterns of life broken, but now a radically new element had appeared—the atomic bomb. The holocaust at Hiroshima in 1945 seemed to put an end to all that had gone before. If the result of three centuries of science was to be the annihilation of every living thing on the globe, what was to be gained by studying science? Even if destruction could be avoided, the new age of political and economic power that would follow the release of nuclear energy would be so radically different that all traditional values would seem irrelevant.

Many people were disillusioned with political action. The methods of liberalism seemed too slow, its piecemeal gains inadequate. In 1917 the Russians had turned to communism, and in the twenties and thirties the Italians and Germans had turned to fascism and nazism, but it soon became clear that none of these regimes would permit individuality. Yet even in France, England, and America, where liberal institutions survived, the individual felt lost in the masses, a nameless object in a crowd. The impersonality of the city and the constant stream of commercial advertising and political propaganda, a stream that increased with the spread of television after 1946, deprived people of a sense of authentic life; all their experiences were secondhand.

In this depressing spiritual climate, existentialism became the support of many intellectuals. Its great appeal was its rediscovery of the self, an entity with an authentic inner life, a complete being free to choose, free to create values, whether or not the universe supports them. By facing death and nothingness, the individual finds the courage to be; by accepting his isolation and loneliness, he finds strength in his freedom. His anguish and uncertainty are a mark of the authenticity of his experience. Just as his death will be his own and not a statistical abstraction, his choice is his own and he creates himself in making it.

This reaction in favor of the inner life has often gone to the extreme of denying any reality to the external world. Since the seventeenth century, scientists have demanded complete objectivity and have warned against the "prejudices" and "fantasies" of the subjective. The romantic movement was one major protest against this view, reasserting the superiority of the imagination to reason and of the spiritual to the material. Then naturalism reestablished both the worship of the objective and scientific and the dominant power of the environment. But existentialists asked, If scientists persist in defining reality and nature as independent of human values, how can science claim primary importance? Many existentialists wrote as though science and history did not exist and ignored nature as though they had never been outdoors in their lives.

The existentialist mood appeared first in France, where it was especially pertinent during the long, traumatic experience of the German occupation. From 1940 to 1944 each moment seemed one of critical decision—whether and to what extent to collaborate, or whether to say no and face the consequences. Character seemed purely a matter of individual decision, not the result of social forces or natural environment. As thinkers developed this point of view, they discovered that a similar philosophy had been outlined a hundred years earlier by the Danish religious philosopher Søren Kierkegaard, who emphasized man's isolation and uncertainty and the anguish of making choices "in fear and trembling."

The existentialist movement after the Second World War was developed most of all in the plays, novels, and essays of two Frenchmen, Albert Camus and Jean Paul Sartre. Camus' novels made a much stronger impression than his plays, though *Caligula* (1945) interested many people because of its startling hero, who follows the logic of his idea of absolute freedom to the point of killing his friends. Camus' essay *The Myth of Sisyphus* (1942) is one of the classics of existentialism. Sartre's plays were concerned with many problems of guilt and responsibility, from the short *No Exit*, written during the war, to the study of a German's sense of guilt over Hitler, *The Condemned of Altona* (1959). Perhaps more important than his plays are two essays published at the end of the war: *Existentialism Is a Humanism*, probably the most widely read definition of existentialism, and *Forgers of Myths*, which made a radical redefinition of theatre, repudiating the main tenets of naturalism. To Sartre, individual differences of human beings, the qualities due to heredity and environment, were unimportant. A person or a character in a play achieved identity only as he made a decision. Though he was responsible only for his own choice, he knew that other individuals might make his choice their own. At least he could say no. A large number of plays since the war have been designed to say no.

As if to illustrate what Sartre was thinking, Jean Anouilh in 1944 wrote his own version of Sophocles' *Antigone* and actually got permission for a Paris production from the German occupation authorities. It is a political play in which a girl defies a dictator, but Anouilh presented both sides of the dilemma in a way that made his play acceptable even to the Nazis.

7-5 Existentialist isolation of the individual. The costumes are impersonal and are not related to a particular environment, and the abstract setting offers many separate places where characters can take their stand. Anouilh's *Antigone.* Florida Agricultural and Mechanical University production, directed by Randolph Edmonds and designed by Carlton W. Molette II.

Sophocles' Antigone believes that the laws of the gods are more important than the commands of men; the chorus and the prophet Tiresias support her, and finally Creon, the dictator, admits that he was wrong and she was right. Anouilh, on the other hand, completely isolates his Antigone, allowing her no support outside herself. She has no real belief in God, and she finds no validity for her sacrifice in external facts. Still, by saying no to Creon's world she creates a value for herself. At the end, her weak sister Ismene makes the same decision. Choice is contagious; other individuals may be influenced by example.

Anouilh changed the character of Creon even more than that of Antigone from Sophocles' conception. In the Greek play, he is a tragic figure whose pride is humbled, but the modern Creon remains set in his cold, impersonal view to the very end. He compares the state to a storm-tossed ship that he has taken over because somebody has to issue orders. The mob must be led, and anyone who disobeys orders must be shot. He cannot believe that Antigone, or any human being, would go against the herd instinct. "*No* is one of your man-made words. Can you imagine a world in which trees say *no* to the sap? In which beasts say *no* to hunger or to propagation?" But existentialism, as Sartre pointed out, is a humanism. An individual decision raises man above the animals.

The Theatre of the Absurd

Even Sartre derived a strong sense of commitment from his existentialism and worked with the Communists and other groups as he approved of their immediate aims, but the theatre of the absurd, the avant-garde theatre of the 1950s and 60s, discovered no values worthy of commitment. The absurdists even celebrated the breakdown of language and communication, and deliberately baffled the audience. If confusion and chaos are the human condition, then the form of the play itself must make use of interruption, discontinuity, incongruity, and senseless logic and repetition. Eugène Ionesco called his first play, *The Bald Soprano* (1950), an "antiplay." Some absurdists went so far as to write no play at all but to arrange a set of directions for both actors and audience in a "happening." While existentialists like Anouilh, Sartre, and Camus wrote carefully constructed plays that drew the conclusion that the world has no dependable order, the absurdists expressed disorder in the very form of their writing.

7-6
An American play of the absurd. The constructivist setting of different levels is decorated as junk sculpture. Schochen's *The Tiger Rag.* University of Illinois production, directed by Barnard Hewitt, designed by George McKinney, and costumed by Genevieve Richardson.

It is significant that three of the most important absurdist playwrights are exiles by choice, living in Paris and writing in a language other than their native tongue—Samuel Beckett, an Irishman, Eugène Ionesco, a Roumanian, and Arthur Adamov, an Armenian-Russian. A fourth, the Frenchman Jean Genêt, feels that he is set apart from humanity as a criminal and pervert and glories in his defiance of what is lawful and normal. These men have chosen to emphasize the sense of alienation, which Camus has described in a much-quoted paragraph in *The Myth of Sisyphus:*

> . . . in a universe that is suddenly deprived of illusions and light, man feels a stranger. His is an irremediable exile, because he is deprived of memories of a lost homeland as much as he lacks the hope of a promised land to come. This divorce between man and his life, the actor and his setting, truly constitutes the feeling of Absurdity.

The breakdown of conventional language—the use of empty phrases that not only prevent communication but also destroy the sense of identity—was the subject of Ionesco's *The Bald Soprano*. He got the idea from the numerous meaningless phrases in an English phrase book written for foreigners. During a social evening, the Smiths and the Martins courteously and charmingly repeat statements that are not only inane but also contradictory. The Smiths exhaust all the processes of logic in debating whether a ring of the doorbell always or never means there is someone there. The Martins reach the amazing conclusion that since they arrived in the same compartment on the same train and live in the same room, they must, by coincidence, be husband and wife. But after a theatrical climax, the Martins take the place of the Smiths and start the evening over again. While the expressionist hero contended with a depersonalized, nameless crowd, in search of his own identity, here all is inanity. The characters have no hunger, no conscious desires, no identity. They are interchangeable, and everything ends where it started.

As early as the 1920s the significance of man's deeds was brought into question. After the futility of the First World War and peace treaty and the devastating Russian Revolution, who could believe in the value of action? Burlesques of the heroic attitudes and noble gestures of nineteenth-century melodrama were popular. By the 1950s language itself had lost its validity, and audiences today are amused in the absurd theatre, as in pop art, by obsessive repetitions of the banal.

In America infantile regression is made amusing in two of Edward Albee's absurdist plays, in which Mommie and Daddy are lost in baby talk, and the rejected, senile grandmother has to find her own death. In *The Sandbox* she finds a kind angel of death; in *The American Dream*, she finds an emasculated muscle man, an empty dream of vitality.

Things, objects that give meaning and rich texture in naturalistic plays, become in absurdist plays of the 1950s and 60s the grotesque symbols of man's emptiness or even his terror. In *The Caretaker* by the English playwright Harold Pinter, piles of junk fill the rooms of the two insane brothers, who first show kindness to the down-and-out tramp, letting him feel a new security in the promise of becoming caretaker, then turn on him and eject him from his junk-pile paradise. In Ionesco's *The Chairs,* chairs are frantically brought in to fill a large room as an old couple welcome a world of invisible guests invited to hear the old man's great message. When everybody is there, including the emperor, the old couple introduce the orator who is to deliver the old man's message and jump out the windows into the sea. The orator can do nothing but mutter.

In his longer plays, Ionesco has used a typical "little man," called by the common French name Bérenger, as a sympathetic if ineffectual symbol of modern man facing a baffling universe. *The Killer* is a horror story. Bérenger cannot stop the mysterious killer, though he appeals to him with all possible defenses of human values, and he finally submits to his own death. In *Rhinoceros* Bérenger defies the crowd, not entirely convinced as everybody in his town, even his sweetheart, Daisy, turns into a rhinoceros. At least Ionesco's little man makes an attempt to stop the reversion to the barbaric.

The compulsion to act a role, a role that becomes more real than reality, has been the theme of Jean Genêt, whose play-acting scenes conjure up more grotesque images than Pirandello ever created. Genêt follows some of the principles set forth by the French dramatic theorist Antonin Artaud in his influential work *The Theatre and Its Double*, which advocates the theatre's return to the intensity of primitive rituals, of cruelty, incantation, and dream. His plays, in various ways, act out rites, whether the social rites of maids pretending to be their mistress in *The Maids* or the ritual violation and murder of a white woman in *The Blacks.* All Genêt's plays include observers watching a performance, recognizing with mixed feelings the Freudian images of their own suppressed desires.

The brothel in which Genêt's *The Balcony* is set is more than an ordinary brothel; it furnishes not only mirrors but costumes, settings, and actors so that the clients may act out their secret desires—to be a bishop hearing the lurid confessions of a young woman, a judge ordering a half-naked executioner to whip a beautiful girl, or a triumphant general riding a horse, played by an almost nude girl wearing a tail. Outside, a revolution is taking place in the town; the chief of police eventually puts it down by presenting the madam as the new queen and getting the clients to act as a real bishop, judge, and general. The chief gets his fulfillment, the achievement of an image, when finally a client comes to the brothel who wants to play the chief of police. Everything returns to normal, and the madam gets ready for the next clients. The indecent rites of role-playing go on in both the

7-7 Theatre of cruelty. Hidden hatreds erupt in a cruel ritual enacted before an audience of Negro actors in white-face masks. Genêt's *The Blacks.* New York off-Broadway production, 1961. Photo Martha Swope.

brothel and the real world. As in Pirandello's *Henry IV*, the play-acting becomes more real than the reality outside.

Play-acting as a brave pretense in the face of postwar despair was the theme of John Osborne's *The Entertainer* (1957). The run-down music-hall performer—a vivid role for Laurence Olivier on both stage and screen—was a symbol of postwar England. He is facing bankruptcy and failure, but he refuses to give up his music-hall routines and move to Canada. Osborne makes brilliant use of the banality of the popular tradition of stage songs to express the cheap emptiness of modern life. Archie Rice, the entertainer, treats his father, wife, and daughter with bitter harshness, cynically planning to take a mistress, snarling at his own lack of human feeling. Like modern man, his values are exhausted. He remembers with envy the real feeling of a Negro blues singer he heard once, and when his son is killed in Africa—an event with symbolic overtones—he finds true depth of feeling in singing the same song. But Osborne does not completely fit into the absurdist pattern. Where Harold Pinter in his comedies of menace, from *The Caretaker* to *The Homecoming*, continued to use the well-made-play form to explore the private terror of a few passive people tortured by unaccountable intruders, Osborne moved outward. He used epic techniques to explore historical forces of authority and doubt in *Luther* (1961), the failure of conscience in personal and professional life in *Inadmissible Evidence* (1964), and the interrelation of secret decadence and secret military intrigue in *A Patriot for Me* (1965).

Samuel Beckett seemed haunted by images of confinement and loss of freedom. In *Waiting for Godot* (1952) two tramps are unable to leave the desolate rim of the universe. In *Endgame* the two main characters are shut up in an underground dungeon, one confined to a wheelchair, and a legless old couple reside in two ashcans. The woman in *Happy Days* is buried up to her waist, and later up to her neck. In another play called simply *Play*, the characters are enclosed to their chins in urns.

Beckett's *Waiting for Godot* is the masterpiece of the theatre of the absurd; of all the plays it is the most perfect in its form, the most complete in its desolation, the most comic in its anguish. Two lonely tramps are waiting for Godot, who sends word every day that he will not meet them today but surely tomorrow. The place where they wait is a desolate road,

7-8
Theatre of illusion. Identity is achieved by play-acting in a brothel. One of the clients plays the role of a general with a girl as his horse. Genêt's *The Balcony.* New York off-Broadway production, 1960. Photo Martha Swope.

empty save for a stick of a tree not sturdy enough to hang oneself on. But the tramps are also theatrical clowns, using comic routines of vaudeville days, putting on and off their hats, boots, shirts, coats, and ties, arguing, interrupting, telling anecdotes, munching carrots and turnips, paying mock deference to each other, stumbling and falling, alternating groans with sudden squeals or grimaces. Even the most painful moments are exploded into laughter by the clownish antics.

To the existentialists, freedom is a challenge; to a few people, like William Saroyan, freedom is a delight. But to Beckett's tramps, freedom is hell. They have no inner resources, no friends, no memories, and no orientation in place or time; they do not know where they were last night or indeed if it is the Saturday they were told, they think, to wait for Godot. If the audience wonders why they do not join the activities of the world, the answer appears in the arrival in each act of Pozzo, a fat, active master driving his slave, Lucky, by a rope around his neck—a hideous but comic image of all masters and slaves, all employers and employees.

The play has a remarkably strict form, expressive of its meaning. The form of each act is a series of moments that start with an assertion, a plan, a hope, and quickly dissipate it. Discontinuity is both the theme and the form, deflation the theme and the comic method. The repetition in the second act of the first-act pattern, with a slight development, has a classic perfection that is like mathematics, logic, or music.

Waiting for Godot does not point to any of the known sources of values, yet it is a passionate cry for some new faith, and in that sense it is a very religious play. The problem is certainly metaphysical. No economic improvement, no psychological adjustment, no doctor's pill, but only a new definition of man, a new relation to the universe, will serve these forlorn creatures. In its exploration of the last possibility of emptiness, the play may be considered a turning point. If man has such passionate need for the spiritual plane, he will either renew old definitions of man and God or find new ones.

Reconstruction

Out of the very detachment that has been so painful for the absurdist comes the possibility of reconstruction. The existentialists in the decade that followed the Second World War felt cut off from both history and nature and left in anguished freedom to create new values and social relations. Considering how long the naturalistic thinkers had insisted that man was bound by his environment, it is no wonder the existentialists of the 1940s and

50s rejected this view and insisted on separating man from the tight restrictions of nature. Brecht fought the naturalistic acting of Stanislavsky, insisting that the techniques of alienation, or objectification, be applied to both acting and production methods, in order that the mind of the spectator might be free from unthinking identification and open to active thinking about reality. The same desire to insist on the primacy of the creative mind impels recent radical groups to bring the audience into an active, creative relationship to the play in happenings and other open forms of drama.

We can now see in new perspective the long struggle of the naturalists to find a workable view of man in relation to nature. They put far too much emphasis on the power of nature over man and too little on the power of the human mind. No wonder most of their plays were pessimistic and painful. Strindberg, alternating between objective naturalism and the subjective dream form, saw nothing but pain and cried out to the distant heavens for pity. Pirandello had no hope that the mind could come to terms with an illusive reality. Nature seemed overwhelming in its multiplicity, and he blamed the complexity of existence for the inability of man's limited mind to bring any one view of reality into focus. O'Neill saw that man's life-lies, his "pipe dreams," held all his values, but he thought that external nature was an irreducible reality and that ultimately man must face the inhuman reality of death. Although some writers had glimpsed it earlier, it took two decades of absurdist drama to show us that not the natural world but the human mind is the one primary reality. Man's illusions, his myths, his mathematics, his arts, and his sciences are his views—his ways of seeing the world around him—and all these are products of his creative mind.

The primacy of the creative power of the mind is shown in *Rosencrantz and Guildenstern Are Dead* (1967) by Tom Stoppard, a brilliant young English playwright. Most of the play is an absurdist drama about the two nonentities who are called to the Court of Elsinore to solve the mystery of Hamlet's strange behavior but who wander helplessly, finding out only that they are to be sent to England to be killed without explanation or reason. In their inability to find any purpose in the directions they are given they are very much like the two tramps of *Waiting for Godot*. But this play is not merely another absurdist play. In the first place, their Elsinore is not quite the empty universe of the Beckett play. There seems to be something going on within the court, though they are left at the edge, unable to understand. Most indicative of a new age that has gone beyond the drama of the absurd is the presence in the play of the Players. The Players know they are facing the same death as Rosencrantz and Guildenstern, but they are creative artists, not miserable victims of that elementary knowledge. They have learned all there is to know about death by acting it in its multitudinous forms. As creative artists they also know about life, and hence they are free. They know who they are and what they have to do with their lives.

American existentialists have never been quite so despairing as the Europeans. The world they picture, even in their loneliest anguish, is not completely empty, as is that of Beckett's tramps. There is always some awareness of a deity in the distance waiting for man's creative recognition, and nearer at hand there are memories of men of the past and, significantly, mythical and literary figures who are still with us to cheer us in our desolate night. The heroes of our poetry, novels, and popular myths are as much a part of our past as actual men of history.

One such mythical figure is Kilroy, the popular image of the wandering American soldier. In Tennessee Williams' surrealist and absurdist fantasy, *Camino Real* (1953), Kilroy staggers out of the desert into a walled Latin American village where various fugitives, historical and fictional, are trying to escape. He is beaten, made to put on a clown's nose and a clown costume, cheated by a Gypsy's daughter, and dissected by an anatomy teacher while two laughing street cleaners with a white can wait for his body. Camille, with Casanova's help, tries to get on the one unscheduled plane, and the elegant dandy from the novels of Proust is beaten to death. No image is spared of seediness, deception, exhaustion, and cruelty. Yet these echoes of the past are reminders of the triumphs of the human spirit. The legendary Camille, the courtesan who made the mistake of falling in love, and Casanova, now King of the Cuckolds, find companionship and solace in each other. Lord Byron departs to sail back to Athens, to contemplate the Acropolis with its reminders of an earlier dream of purity and freedom. At the end, Kilroy and Don Quixote go out the high gate to cross the terra incognita toward the mountains. It is not a futile life-lie but an indomitable courage we see in the hearts of Williams' characters. The walled town is not the whole universe but a temporary prison, from which men may escape if they have imagination and faith.

It is faith that supports the characters of William Saroyan, a subjective faith that is stronger than objective "truth." They know the "truth" but are searching for something better. Saroyan is as devoted to the subconscious and the dream as any surrealist, and he starts with a human condition as lonely as any the absurdists have portrayed. But since he reaches exactly opposite conclusions, he is dismissed by many critics as sentimental. When his characters realize and accept loneliness and the primacy of faith over facts, they discover both the love of God and kinship with all other lonely creatures. In *The Time of Your Life* (1939), when Joe assures the truck driver and the streetwalker that he believes in their dream of themselves, they have strength to be what they dream and to love each other. Saroyan's immigrants and rural characters, bringing dialect and a touch of color to the bars, public libraries, or forsaken buildings where they gather, find friendship and a racy variety in American cities. A Saroyan hero, unafraid of the machine, challenges a super-pinball machine and finally wins. Every character in Saroyan has some ability—singing, dancing, reciting, yarn-spinning, or merely believing—a picture that is much too cheerful and lively for some theatregoers. Saroyan accepts a world of contradictions, of life and death, inhale and exhale, comedy and tragedy. Where the existentialists chose Kierkegaard and Kafka as their models, Saroyan resurrected from the same past the energetic affirmation of Walt Whitman and the witty zest in dialectic of Bernard Shaw. A man is free to choose.

Charles Gordone's *No Place to Be Somebody* (1969), the first play by a black author to win the Pulitzer Prize, presents a cross section of lonely humanity looking for friendship and hope at a public bar as in *The Time of Your Life.* But Gordone's picture is more desolate than Saroyan's; the dreams meet sudden defeat, the gangsters are ruthless and deadly, and the relations between whites and blacks are in the end bitter. Yet even as he reflects the urban violence of the 1960s and 70s Gordone shows affection for the outcasts who for a moment find common ground in the public streets and bars of America.

The most characteristic American existentialist play is *J. B.*, the Pulitzer Prize play of 1958-59, by Archibald MacLeish. Its hero is a modern man alone in a baffling universe. But again, as in Saroyan's plays, it is not a completely empty universe. God is there, even if not as close as traditional religion teaches, and there are several human attitudes toward the metaphysical to choose from. In the Book of Job the Voice out of the Whirlwind silences the protesting Job with the overwhelming mystery and majesty of creation. MacLeish's J. B., the modern Job, is not so easily silenced. Even more than Beckett's tramps, he cries out in protest, insisting on working out his own human answer. J. B. is a successful American businessman who sees his children taken from him one by one, through war, accident, and crime. In the last act his wife leaves him after an atomic bomb explosion, and he is alone, in pain, as desolate as any European existentialist hero. He finally realizes that his cry for justice is not answered because there *is* no justice, only the creator of the earth and the sky.

The active functions of God and Satan are represented by two broken-down actors who put on masks as they speak the words of the Bible. They indicate two very finite ways of looking at the metaphysical world. Mr. Zuss is impressed by the might and majesty of the universe; man must accept out of fear of God. Nickles has the bitter, naysaying point of view of postwar disillusionment. He cannot believe that J. B. will once again accept his life after learning how much suffering life contains.

Love, as a symbol of life, of positive commitment, is J. B.'s choice in the end, though he knows that "nothing is certain but the loss of love." Sarah, his wife, comes back to him, carrying a tiny sprig of forsythia in blossom, a symbol of the vitality of nature, the instinctive fertility that to both the romantic poet and the naturalistic playwright meant something more important than man's skepticism. In the revised acting version of the play, MacLeish made the isolation of man more complete. Though he is awed by the Voice out of the Whirlwind, J. B. at the end repudiates it as well as both Zuss and Nickles and finds a phrase from the Book of Job itself that encourages him to rely on himself:

> Deck thyself now with Majesty and Excellency . . . .
> Then will I also confess unto thee
> That thine own right hand can save thee.

While rejecting both the traditional view of God and that of the bitter cynics, J. B. realizes that in his lonely choice of love he has found his own new relationship to the deity.

That some paths are possible even in the insane world of political action is the theme of Peter Weiss's *Marat/Sade,* which was mentioned in Chapter 2 in connection with epic realism. Unlike Beckett, Weiss feels that history is real and important to us, even if we can see little more than its insane cruelties. Weiss outdoes the dream fantasies of Strindberg and the role-playing of Pirandello and Genêt, and his images of violence and cruelty might have shocked even Artaud, who invented the term "theatre of cruelty" and dreamed of a drama as devastating as a plague. Weiss sets his play in an insane asylum in France in 1808 and has the inmates reenact, with their own disordered comments, events of the French Revolution of nearly two decades before. Here are alienation and detachment—the debates of the Revolution shown through several distorting mirrors and the actual events all but lost in the wild revelry of the insane. But in its attempt to understand historical events and historical passions, *Marat/Sade* reaches far beyond the plays of the absurd.

There is one American play, now three decades old, that forecast both the absurdist drama of the 1950s and 60s and the wider historical view that seems possible in the 1970s. In its understanding of both disruption and reconstruction, Thornton Wilder's *The Skin of Our Teeth* (1942) is one of the most important of all modern plays. Its theme is interruption and new beginnings, and its very form carries out this theme. Civilization is interrupted and almost destroyed three times: in the first act by ice, in the second by flood, and in the third by war. The play itself is interrupted several times—when the scenery leans in or flies up in the air, when actors miss cues, and when they drop out of character to speak to the audience

7-9 Wilder's *The Skin of Our Teeth* produced as a theatrical fantasy in the tradition of American musicals. In a New Jersey living room suggested by bright-colored fragments of walls, a mammoth and a dinosaur are family pets. Eastern Illinois University production, directed by E. G. Gabbard, designed by John E. Bielenberg, and costumed by James Koertge. Photo Bertram.

or to other actors. These absurd occurrences are included partly for the fun of it and partly to illustrate the theme of interruption. But they also bring in another theatrical level, like the double level in *The Balcony,* as the actors make their own, often unfavorable, comments on the characters they are playing. The second act, which takes place in Atlantic City, is as much a reenactment of primitive rites as Genêt could wish: in the wild whoopee of the convention city, moral habits are temporarily abandoned and old rites of seduction that almost destroy marriage are enacted.

At first the play may seem to mean that all crises in all ages are the same and that man is caught in an endless cycle; but that is not the ultimate meaning. The first disaster, the Ice Age, is entirely external; it is out of man's control and all he can do is build fires and try to preserve a few of his accomplishments as aids in starting over again. The flood of the second act is not so external. Now men have earned their destruction by living for the moment, falling from their earlier dedication; Mr. Antrobus, relaxing at a convention, is about to abandon his wife and children for another woman. Faced with emergency, he rediscovers his dedication to the human family and herds them and the animal representatives into the Ark waiting at the end of the pier. The third disaster, war, is entirely the responsibility of man. While the first two crises came at the end of their acts, the war comes at the beginning of Act III, and the main concern is how to reestablish human relationships after it is over. Mr. Antrobus faces the surviving enemy, his own son Henry (who is also Cain), and soon the two are at each other's throats. The son resents authority, and the father has been so sure of the importance of past achievement that he has not bothered to consider the son's own thoughts and choices.

But even in moments of the play that have the most serious implications, absurdity reduces the tension. At the end of the first act, as the ice gets closer, the family takes in refugees: Homer, the blind singer; Moses, the judge; a doctor; and the Muse sisters, who all sing around the fire. As Mr. Antrobus is teaching Henry the multiplication table, the lights dim, and Mrs. Antrobus starts reading to Gladys from the Bible—"In the beginning God created the heaven and the earth. . . ." When tears come into the eyes of the audience, the absurd interrupts; the ushers start breaking up chairs and the maid, Sabina, says to the audience, "Will you please start

7-10 Man in creative control of nature. Bottomley's *Culbin Sands.* Yale University production, directed by Georgina Johnson and costumed by Virginia Roediger.

handing up your chairs? We'll need everything for this fire. Save the human race." At the end of the play, after the fight between father and son has been settled and mankind is ready to start over, a parade of actors, representing the hours and the planets passing over the sky, speak passages from the great prophets and philosophers—Spinoza, Plato, Aristotle—and that same beautiful passage from Genesis. At the line "And the Lord said let there be light and there was light," the stage lights go out. When they come on, Sabina is starting the play again.

The interruptions, the theatrical discontinuities, and the ritual play-acting give a full picture of the absurdity of the human condition. Anticipating pop art, banalities of school days, of family life, and of Atlantic City conventions are all there. There is acute awareness that the thread of contact with past values is fragile and also that man is free at every moment to choose his values and create a new world. But if man remembers the dreams and hopes that carried him through the crises of the past, he will cherish every book, every formula, every scientific discovery, and every passage of sacred scripture that has come down to him. Like Mr. Antrobus, he is ready to start over again, and unlike Beckett's tramps, he has a vision to guide him.

The youth rebellion of the late 1960s and early 70s seems much like the rebellion of Henry in *The Skin of Our Teeth.* As long as his independence is threatened, Henry is willing to fight his father and destroy all achievements of the past. Gradually he is persuaded that his father is not his enemy. Both tragedy and comedy have always dealt with such conflicts between traditional wisdom and the individual will. From Prometheus to J. B., the tragic hero has set himself against injustice at the lower level of the gods, in the realm of immediate experience. But out of his struggle he achieves a harmony with the higher levels of order and meaning. He gains both an independent self and a sustaining relationship to that which is sacred and timeless.

Where tragedy faces complexity on the metaphysical level, comedy faces it on the social and institutional level. Complexity is the most baffling problem of the twentieth century. It would be easy if the world were all black or all white, all communist or all capitalist, all long-haired or all short-haired. Some romantics have hoped for a world-wide uniformity. In 1940 Wendell Willkie won the Republican nomination for President on the theme of "one world"; and after the atomic bomb of 1945 it seemed that it must be "one world or none." But a quarter of a century later no one is ready for a uniformity imposed from the outside. The prospect of a standardized "man of the establishment" has been so terrifying that many a youth, in grave moral earnestness, has set out to destroy society. But comedy has always shown that society is not an organized conspiracy but a very anarchic, unpredictable, and therefore flexible bundle of patterns of human relationship. Any quick-witted person can participate in the games of society and still manage to have a private life quite separate from the life on the public square.

The postabsurdist view can be a synthesis of many views, using the theatre of the absurd to free us from the false worship of the objective environmental world; using the existentialists to remind us of the primacy of the human mind, but taking the creative values of the mind and applying them again to the external world; using tragedy to confront the absurdist picture of surface disorder with an age-old recognition of profound order; using comedy to remind us that a limited amount of anarchy may be the safety valve that will make an ordered world both possible and endurable.

The playwrights' views, however, are only one element in the theatre. Stage architects and designers are constantly trying new forms of space. Especially in the past two decades, experiments by directors, actors, dancers, and poets have promised to transform our theatre even more than experiments by professional playwrights. Hence after examining the art of the director, the actor, and the designer, we will consider what synthesis seems possible for the 1970s.

Planning the Production

8

The theatre is a synthesis of all the arts and yet it is a complete art in itself. A play is a composition not merely of story in words (and sometimes there is neither story nor words) but of color, line, space, and light, moving in rhythmic order toward a definite goal. The audience sees primarily the actors, but the actors are only part of a large team of workers bringing many different skills to the theatre. Hence in both stage and film production the director is the central artist, often better known than either playwright or actors. Whether he is using an old play or one in the process of being rewritten by the playwright, or even if he is creating something new out of dance movements and sounds without a playwright, he has to plan carefully to coordinate the work of his complex organization. There must be a central plan, a basic agreed-on idea of what kind of play all the workers want to create, and very careful supervision and coordination during the preparation of the play.

The director became important nearly a century ago as the repertory and stock companies, which were actor-centered, began to give way to long-run, carefully prepared productions. T. W. Robertson in the 1860s was both playwright and director, subordinating his actors to the overall mood of his plays and insisting that every detail of setting, properties, and costumes be right for each particular play. In the 1870s and 80s Europe was impressed by the traveling productions of a minor German prince, the Duke of Saxe-Meiningen, who achieved an ensemble that was carefully controlled, especially in crowd scenes. In the free theatres the naturalistic directors, from Antoine to Stanislavsky, retrained actors and chose properties to bring out the rich subtext of the play.

At the beginning of the twentieth century, while both Gordon Craig and Adolphe Appia preached that one guiding hand, the director's, must give unity to the whole production and that the director should know from experience something of all the arts he was supervising, the great producer-director Max Reinhardt showed the world what it meant to give a particular character to each production. He often chose a different place for each play to be produced—*Oedipus* in a large circus in Vienna, *The Merchant of Venice* in a square along a canal in Venice, *Everyman* before the cathedral in Salzburg, or baroque comedies in the beautiful Redoutensaal, one of the reception rooms in the Imperial Palace in Vienna. In several cities, including London and New York, he rebuilt a large theatre or other building for his pageant-drama, *The Miracle*, so that the audience could imagine they were in a medieval cathedral. Each time, he took an entirely different approach, making sure that actors, scenery, music, and the building itself would contribute to the one idea.

Filmmaking requires an even more complex organization, and it is even more difficult for one artist to leave his mark on a film. In the great days of Hollywood, besides the actors and technicians who carried out orders, dozens of people, from a whole battery of scriptwriters to the public-relations men, had a say on how the film should be made to appeal to the supposed taste of the mass audience. Only occasionally did the creative originality of the artist come through. It is no wonder that, in the rebellion against the big studios during the last two decades, filmmakers have insisted on the *auteur* theory, which holds that even if many people work on a film, they should be carrying out the creative idea of one man, usually the director, who should not only control script and photography but also have "the final cut," that is, the final approval of the editing.

In planning a production for the stage, the director first relates the play to the overall *controls*—the kind of play it is and the conventions and style that are most appropriate to this particular theatre and audience; second, he analyzes the play for the structural values of plot, character, and theme and the textural values of dialogue, mood, and spectacle; and third, he decides on the choice and use of the basic materials and techniques of director, actor, and designer. These three phases of planning can be put in outline form.

PLANNING A PRODUCTION

I. Classification of the play in relation to overall controls
   A. Kind of play
   B. Particular theatre and audience
   C. Conventions
   D. Style
II. Analysis of the play by the six means that create structure and texture
   A. Structure
      1. Plot
      2. Character
      3. Theme
   B. Texture
      1. Dialogue
      2. Music (mood and rhythm)
      3. Spectacle
III. Choice of materials and techniques
   A. For the director
      1. Materials: action, space, time, line, form, color, light
      2. Techniques: composition, picturization of relationship, movement, pantomimic dramatization, rhythm
   B. For the actor
      1. Materials: body, voice, thought, feeling
      2. Techniques: reading lines, movement, pantomimic dramatization, rhythm
   C. For the designer
      1. Materials: space, line, form, color, movement
      2. Techniques: cutting down from realism, building up from action, exploiting qualities of mood and atmosphere, treating scenery as idea or metaphor

The three chief workers—director, actor, and designer—must decide just what variety of entertainment or exaltation, romance or reality, they want to create for the audience. They must agree on how to use the particular stage, what conventions of performance they will set up, and what their overall style will be. They must analyze the play for its elements of structure and texture, knowing that the techniques that create a rich mood may not be the ones to make clear the theme or the action of the plot.

The actor learns lines alone or with others in small groups, tries improvisation both alone and at rehearsal, and continues his lifelong training in body, voice, and imagination outside the theatre, but in the long hours of rehearsal he has the director with him. The designer works separately, completing sketches and work drawings, building structures, and setting lighting instruments, but he checks repeatedly with the director at the critical stages, even though he does not expect to bring all parts of his contribution together until the later rehearsals. In an art theatre with control of its own space, the designer often has the main platforms and ramps and steps, and at least practice properties and sometimes practice costumes, available for rehearsal for several weeks before the opening.

Convention and Style

Convention and style were no problem when a standard repertory of plays was presented by a company performing in one house season after season for a faithful audience. But today, when audiences are seeing plays in many different kinds of theatres or in club rooms and churches without the regular theatre arrangements, when playwrights are trying many new forms and directors are reviving old plays in mixtures of old conventions and new, when drama is overlapping with opera, the musical, and dance, it is very important that for each production one set of conventions and one consistent style be agreed on by all.

Convention

Conventions are the theatrical customs, the accepted rules of the game, that define the relationship between the audience and the performance. At a night club the audience expects a master of ceremonies to talk directly to them, even to recognize particular people, and to introduce a series of separate acts. But in a small theatre for a realistic play, the audience ordinarily expects the dimming of the house lights and the opening of the curtain to begin a scene in which the actors talk to one another but never make direct contact with the audience. By the convention of the fourth wall, the furniture is arranged around three walls as if the fourth wall and everything on that side of the room had been removed. Such familiar conventions are not noticed at all, but audiences can adjust to any new convention or set of conventions if the unfamiliar methods are made clear near the beginning of the performance and are used consistently throughout. When, for instance, Wilder wanted the actors to break out of character and speak their own feelings at the climax of the third act of *The Skin of Our Teeth,* he created similar breaks in the first and second acts. His method was simpler in *Our Town,* where he used the Stage Manager to tell the audience from the beginning exactly what method to expect.

The more open forms of theatre set out to surprise the audience, to wake them up and invite them into the action by putting actors out in the audience and otherwise breaking expected relationships. In "happenings," a short-lived fad of the mid-sixties, the audience itself had to perform, with a few suggestions to start them off. Such group improvisation does not need a theatre but is better crowded into an old storehouse or some outlandish cave or tunnel. Guerrilla actors like to stage events in a crowd to provoke spontaneous audience reaction.

If the audience is separate from the play, the conventions must enable them to hear and see the actors. In the large theatres of the nineteenth century, when expansive emotions were popular, movements were large, and the sweeping gestures were always made with the upstage hand so that they never covered the speaker's face. Voices were projected with full tone, inflections were wide, and actors practiced long on consonants and vowels. In defending the old style of diction that often broke a word into parts, Bernard Shaw said that at least the old stock-company actor could be heard in the last row of the gallery when he screeched, "My chee-ild!" Even the conventions of realism allowed the furniture to be turned in an "open" position so that the actors would not stand in front of one another or turn their backs completely to the audience. Many details were made large and brightly colored to project to the audience. In costume materials only large, bold patterns were used.

Some conventions have to do with defining the playing area and marking the beginning and end of scenes, and the rising and falling curtain has been the standard convention since the picture stage began in the sixteenth century. Today the blackout or dim-out of a controlled pool of light often replaces the closing curtain. Even the arena stage, which cultivates a sense of intimacy between audience and actor, needs some subtle but clear definition—if nothing more than a rug—to mark the edge of the playing area.

The choice of the means of expression by playwright and director is also a matter of convention. In realism the actor rarely shows eloquence of voice or language, only suggesting, in broken tones, his inner feelings. Yet the theatre must find expressive intensities of some kind. In musical comedy we are not surprised when the actor bursts into song. Brecht and other advocates of total theatre make extensive use of masks, soliloquy, poetry, song, and dance and ask the audience to accept them in plays dealing with reality. *Waiting for Godot* calls for high skill in clowning.

The indication that a scene takes place at night is also a matter of convention, for night scenes are rarely played in total darkness. On the Elizabethan stage a lantern or torch was brought on to indicate that it was night, though the performance took place in broad daylight. Until electric lights came into use, only a slight lowering of stage lights was possible, but the actors' pretense was acceptable to the audience. Today, both on the stage and on the movie screen, night is indicated by leaving the edges of the scene in shadow, and the characters and main part of a night scene are often quite clearly lighted, even when there is no excuse of moon or street lamp. When *Our Town* amazed the audience with its unusual methods, Wilder reminded the public that a convention is "an agreed-on falsehood." In that sense all art is false—that is, different from reality—and even the most realistic acting is carefully contrived, artificial, and unreal. But good actors can make any conventional medium—prose, poetry, song, Shakespearean rhetoric—seem convincing and real if the audience can be made to understand and accept that medium.

Style

Style is the particular manner of expression, the way a writer puts his words and phrases together, the way an artist handles his lines and chooses his colors, the way an actor moves and wears his costume. It is extremely important that one style be used throughout a production to unite words, movements, lines, forms, and colors. Members of an audience may not be able to describe a style or know how it is achieved, but they are aware of incongruity when one actor stands out from the rest of the cast or when the costumes or settings do not fit in with other aspects of the production. The playwright partly determines the style; a play cannot be done in just any style. But every play permits considerable latitude, as director, actor, and designer decide on a style that emphasizes some aspects and subordinates others.

The realists attacked all the old styles and announced that by presenting reality itself on the stage they were creating a theatre without any style or interpretation. When realists identified their restrained, implicit acting with reality, they had to describe any other style as an artificial and useless ornament superimposed on reality and distorting or obscuring it. They labeled the melodramatic style "ham" and delighted in revivals of melodrama that burlesqued the large emotional gestures and frank playing to the audience of the nineteenth-century theatre. Even Shakespeare, if they played him at all, had to be presented through realistic acting in realistic settings. The poetry was lost, but no matter: the realists had no ear for that. Actually, the realists did not abolish style, they merely invented a new style and insisted that all plays be given in their style or be laughed off the stage as burlesque.

Some directors, however, insisted on reviving old plays in styles similar to those of the original productions. Before the end of the nineteenth century, the Elizabethan Stage Society, under William Poel, began a tradition of playing Shakespeare on a replica (as far as scholars could guess) of the Elizabethan stage. Such revivals did not represent reality but did present the characters and speeches directly to the audience. Why limit the stage to the grubby and factual, the *representational?* Why not use a *presentational* style and be frankly theatrical? Until very recently this distinction has been a standard part of theatre theory. Only gradually has it become clear that realism is itself one style among many and that in their individual ways all styles are theatrical. The director needs a finer distinction than the terms *representational* and *presentational* when he discriminates among the numerous styles possible in the theatre.

The term *stylization,* which came into use when the expressionists began distorting scenery and dehumanizing characters with dreamlike and machinelike movements and voice inflections, implied something markedly different from realism; a director might be asked if he planned to stylize a production or play it straight. Stylization is not the same as style; there are a number of stylized—that is, deliberately artificial and unreal—styles. But a definition of style in its broadest sense must include much more than these.

In its broadest sense, style is the expression of an outlook on the world, a philosophy, a point of view. When many people have the same social, political, or philosophical attitudes, they choose similar ways of expressing themselves and create a style for a whole period. Thomas Jefferson and the revolutionaries in France and America wanted Greek Revival public buildings because they wanted to recapture in all aspects of public life the dignified nobility of the Greek republic. The Victorians wanted for their churches and colleges the mysterious gloom of Gothic architecture and stained-glass windows, and something of their point of view can still be felt in the old buildings. Our kitchens, laboratories, and automobiles must not only be clean and efficient, but they must by their very style express newness, precision, power, and speed. When we revive an Elizabethan play, we may want a speed of movement and streamlining of setting that has some suggestion of modern living; usually, however, we also want the rich splendor and dignity that we see too little of in the twentieth century. When we revive an eighteenth-century comedy, we may prefer light, free-standing screens to the picture backdrops of the period, and we may adapt the rococo costumes to twentieth-century fashions, but we seek to achieve, in the curved lines of the setting and the bold stance and bows and curtsies of the actors, an appropriate elegance and a crisp combination of assertion and politeness. Style in play production is usually an adjustment between the vision of the playwright, the expectation of the audience, and the particular tastes and wishes of director, actors, and designer.

It was fashionable in the twenties and thirties to create expressionistic scenes from certain aspects in old plays—the three witches as dream voices that Macbeth hears as he tosses on his bed, Hamlet hearing his father's voice throughout the play and meeting three actors all dressed as the king. Orson Welles, seeing in *Macbeth* the primitive covered over with false elegance, set the play in a nineteenth-century court in Haiti with an all-black cast and the ominous voodoo drums of witch doctors heard repeatedly throughout the play. During the Second World War, Welles staged a brilliant production of *Julius Caesar* with Caesar as a modern fascist dictator. Such daring reinterpretations run a grave risk. In the hope of finding a novel relevance for some parts of the play, the clever director may destroy other aspects that might have been more important. Brecht completely rewrote John Gay's *Beggar's Opera* and the Greek, Chinese, and Elizabethan plays he borrowed. In *Your Own Thing* some parts of the story and even a few of the speeches of *Twelfth Night* were kept, but it was essentially a new play about rock musicians. Grotowski has been the most thoroughgoing in what may be called a "confrontation" style, placing historical heroes in modern insane asylums or gas chambers for ironical effect, with coarse, patched cloth and rusty metal in costumes and decor, like junk sculpture, creating an image of corroded ideals—an effective and appropriate style (see p. 271 and Figure 11-16). In following the fad, directors and designers too often merely add rough texture and other fashionable effects to plays in which they have no relevance.

Style is achieved largely by selection—the choice of certain conventions and techniques, the choice of certain qualities in the medium, and the limitation of the expression to those few qualities. If the colors are limited to a few pastel shades, the production will have a distinctive delicacy and softness, but the actors must then use soft, delicate movements, or they will not be in harmony with the setting. While each play must have its own particular style to express the exact nuances of what the director considers to be the play's meaning, it is useful to set up a half-dozen or so general classifications of common styles. In addition to period styles, there are several widely used styles that playwrights and producers are aware of as they plan. Although the Moscow Art Theatre has been known primarily for the realism of its style, one of the original directors, Nemirovitch-Dantchenko, taught his actors to consider six other styles which he called heroic, Homeric, epochal, comical, farcical, and lyrical. In teaching directing at Yale

University, both Alexander Dean and his successor, Frank McMullan, had their students distinguish six major styles: classicism, romanticism, naturalism, realism, expressionism, and impressionism, with some subclassifications, such as neoclassic for seventeenth-century versions of tragedy.

Style is not something added to a play as decoration; it is the basic manner of expression, and its control is one of the most powerful means of achieving unity in a production.

Structure and Texture

Every play has six possible dramatic values, and all six may help in different ways to give the play organization and unity. Aristotle listed them as plot, character, theme, dialogue, music (interpreted in modern drama to mean "mood" or "rhythm"), and spectacle. The first three values concern the structure of the play, the last three the texture. The *structure* is the form of the play in time. The *texture* is what is directly experienced by the spectator, what comes to him through his senses, what the ear hears (the dialogue), what the eye sees (the spectacle), and what is felt as mood through the entire visual and aural experience.

In examining a play, the director and his staff must choose the values that they wish to emphasize. Some plays are rich in all six of Aristotle's values. Some productions have held an audience with emphasis on one value and only the slightest attention to the other five, but in general the more values a play stresses, the better. Today character portrayal and mood are valued highly; dialogue is often flat and commonplace, and poetry or witty or poetic prose is rare. The director and his staff must note the values most emphasized by the playwright and then consider whether they might make a better production by reinforcing other values, even if that means not fully exploiting all the obvious values.

Plot

The Greek root of the word *drama* means "to do," "to act." In a drama something happens before our eyes; drama portrays the present moment, but that moment is full of promise and threat, pregnant with the future. There is delay, but the critical moment does arrive and a fate is determined, a choice is made, a door is closed forever. The audience is caught up and carried from crisis to crisis in a rhythmic pattern of tension and relaxation, swept to a climax by an irresistible momentum, then left at the end changed and thrilled by the sense of having gone through a great experience.

Dramatic action is not just external movement. Thought and decision are also action, and the confrontation of two minds can create conflict as tense and exciting as a physical fight on the stage. The rebel Titan Prometheus, chained to a rock from the beginning of the play, cannot move around the stage, but each of his visitors makes him all the more determined to defy Zeus.

Plot is the arrangement of the incidents that take place on stage. A drama is therefore all in the present, a present that calls forth the future. Much of the actual story may already have taken place. A complete narrative about Oedipus would begin with his birth and his rescue from the mountain where he had been left to die. It would include his leaving his supposed parents, killing the unknown man who is his real father, and marrying the queen. But Sophocles' play starts after all that; it does not show how Oedipus got where he is but how he finds out who he is and what he has unknowingly done—it is a dramatic plot. The past is retold incidentally, but every piece of the past becomes dramatic as it makes a present impact on those who must hear. Ibsen's characters are also very much concerned with the long-hidden truth about the past. Discoveries explode one by one like carefully placed time bombs, shaking and sometimes destroying those forced to hear. A drama is interaction, with each speech demanding a reaction from another character.

A plot may be a fight to the finish between a good hero and a villain, arousing our basic fighting instincts as well as our moral indignation. It may be a race or a contest between worthy opponents, creating suspense as first one side and then the other gets ahead. It may be an actual or metaphorical journey in which the young hero, like a medieval knight, searches for his Holy Grail, now getting closer, now distracted and delayed. Courtship is a variation of the journey. "Boy meets girl, boy loses girl, boy gets girl"—there is the structure of a three-act play. Another pattern is the invasion of the lives of stay-at-homes; an intruder or a guest in the house may disturb the peaceful equilibrium and cause all kinds of complications before peace is restored. George Abbott has stated the formula "Get the character in hot water, then get him out" in a three-act form: "In the first act get your hero up a tree; in the second throw rocks at him; in the third get him down." A prophecy calls for fulfillment, and reckless behavior creates an expectation of downfall.

The trial is one of the most powerful patterns for a play, concentrating deeds of the past into the suspense of the judgment—the long-awaited destiny. Sometimes it is in the formal setting of a courtroom, but there is much the same excitement when Oedipus serves as his own prosecuting attorney and his own judge, calling up witness after witness to find the murderer of the old king, only to discover that he himself was the murderer and the old king was his own father. Sometimes the conclusion of a play is a sudden revelation of that which was hidden: the discovery of the lost papers, the clearing up of the mistaken identity, the finding of the stolen child, the true heir, the real prince, the unknown benefactor. Many plays follow some pattern of nature—the rhythm of the day or of the seasons or of a stormy night before the dawn.

In making the ground plan for the structure of the play, the director outlines his plot. Sometimes he consciously divides the play into parts, which, for the benefit of his actors, he gives conventional labels. The opening part is the *exposition*, which makes clear to the audience what has gone before and what the present situation is. Then at a certain *point of attack* the *inciting force* appears, followed by *complication* after complication. The tension increases in a *build*, or crescendo, to a *minor climax*, followed by a *let-down*. There is *anticipation* or *foreboding* of future conflict, and with delay or continued threat comes great *suspense*. Each confrontation of opposing forces creates a *crisis*. Usually there will be a point of no return, when the fight comes out in the open in the *major crisis*, which may also be the point of highest tension, or the *major climax*. After that comes the *conclusion* or the *dénouement*, the French term for "untying" the plot. Aristotle gave us such terms as *discovery*, when that which was unknown becomes clear, and *peripeteia*, the reversal of the plot.

The plot is the basis for the overall rhythmic pattern of the play. Whether a play is broken up into acts and scenes by intermissions and scene changes, or whether it flows without interruption like an Elizabethan play or a movie, it is organized in time. Like a symphony, it must have a pattern of tensions and relaxations, of builds, climaxes, and let-downs, of units of different sizes and intensities. Like a river winding through a valley, a plot does not move in a straight line but pushes toward one side until its impulse is exhausted by the mounting resistance and it is turned with new force against the other side.

Character

If the plot is what happens, character is why it happens. The motivation is the basis of the action. Plot may be what gives the play its immediate sense of excitement, but plays are remembered for their characters. Lear on the heath, Lady Macbeth rubbing blood from her hands, Cyrano helping his rival to win Roxane, the undefeated Amanda of *The Glass Menagerie*, the defeated Blanche of *A Streetcar Named Desire*—characters like these can never be forgotten. It is through the creation of character, the evocation of the nuances of personality, the immediate and the deeper motives of the soul, that actors win their audiences. Even the minor characters come to life to give the play variety and vitality as the actors find a distinct personality and an inner meaning for each.

The director, both alone and with the actor, makes a careful study to create each character with a particular tone and quality—not just the recognition traits of age, size, occupation, appearance, dress, tempo, rhythm, roughness or softness, but characteristic attitude. Is he naturally a doubter, a kidder, joyful or morose, ardent or disdainful, playful or serious? Is he conceived according to the conventional idea of his role in society—father, judge, pedantic schoolteacher, or go-getting young executive? Or does the character violate the conventional picture, such as a mother who is an executive and smokes cigars? Perhaps he can be explained by some of the Freudian concepts—repressions that burst out in unpredictable compensations, inferiority complexes, destructive obsessions and neuroses, nervous tics, and compulsive gestures. He may be introverted or extroverted; he may react appropriately or overreact. Most important are the deeper motives—what he will fight for, what he ultimately respects. The actor may bring to the study of character his own observations from life or from research in books, newspapers, and other plays. Within the play itself director and actor note what the author says, what the character does and says, and how the other characters speak of him and react to him. Does he play a different role with each character he meets? Is there a pattern of change as the character develops or discovers himself in the course of the play?

Whether it is conscious choice, as Sartre and the existentialists demand, or unconscious natural bent that gives the outline of the character, that outline is filled in by the actor. He brings to the part his own natural tones and qualities, and, according to the skill and range he has developed, he adds or emphasizes those qualities that he and the director think the character should have. Even murder on the stage is vicious only if the actor brings out a vicious quality: he might be killing with mindless apathy or with agonized reluctance. The director has to decide, as he looks over his possible casting, how much he hopes to indicate by action, how much by the basic qualities of the actor, and how much by the acting itself. In rehearsal he will help the actor enrich his part by finding unexpected moments when a strong character shows weakness and a weak character strength, and by giving an evil character some moments of sympathy and a good character contradictory moments when he seems not so good. People are not all of one piece and are all the more fascinating for their complexity.

In addition to understanding individual characters, the director and actors must see clearly the playwright's scheme of characters. A play is not a solo by one character but a complex composition. Not only do the characters change one another, but each character is defined by comparison and contrast with all the others. The playwright has added other examples to reinforce, to explore variations of, to oppose and contrast with, his central characters.

Theme and variation is as important in theatre as in music. The situation of two brothers who are treated differently and who grow up in different ways was the subject of one of the earliest Greek comedies; it was then dramatized by Terence in *The Brothers* and has been used in hundreds of plays since. Variation on a different level and in a different key is frequent in all kinds of plays, especially in romantic comedy. A comic pair of lovers sets off the serious pair, and obviously it is easier in any class-conscious society to make lower-class characters more comic. The humble characters are funny for seeming to repeat somebody else, but they serve another function in romance. The ancient Hindus regularly set a clownish servant as the companion to the romantic king. The servant could feel fatigue, hunger, fear, and pain—could suffer all the indignities of finite existence—but the king never could because he dwelt in the realm of ideal perfection.

As in all art, contrast is vital in drama. The hero and the villain enlist our interest in their fight because they are so different. Every protagonist is defined by the nature of his antagonist. Hamlet contends in quite different ways with the king, his mother, Ophelia, Polonius, and finally Laertes, and is provoked into a different role with each. Romeo is defined by contrast with his enemy, the hot-tempered, angry Tybalt, but also by contrast with his close friend Mercutio, who is raucous, bawdy, and cynical about love. Prince Hal in *Henry IV* is defined partly by contrast with Hotspur, whose courage goads Hal into proving his valor; but he is defined even more, in his carefree moments, by his friendship with Falstaff.

Sometimes a more elaborate scheme of characters provides one character for each aspect of a problem. In Shaw's *Saint Joan*, each institution—the Church, the Inquisition, the feudal lords, the State of England—has a champion, and some more than one, to bring out the several attitudes in the debate at Joan's trial. To create a kind of epitome of New York as a melting pot, Elmer Rice in *Street Scene* brought into one New York block representatives of all the principal nationalities in that cosmopolitan city, just as O'Neill in several of his plays of the sea brought on shipboard all nationalities from both sides of the Atlantic. The character scheme may be as important for the theme of the play as what happens or what conclusion any of the characters reaches.

The way a character develops and changes may be the major action of a play. Growth, self-discovery, learning, and conversion can be fascinating to watch and very dramatic. *The Male Animal*, by James Thurber and Elliott Nugent, takes on excitement when the little college English teacher decides he has been pushed around enough, discovers his strength, and fights back. We have seen how Billy Dawn in *Born Yesterday* learns to wear glasses and read books and creates a new personality as she learns self-respect. The belief in growth, learning, and self-realization is among the most sacred beliefs of the Western world. Even naturalistic studies of the erosion and defeat of character by environment reaffirm, by ironic contrast, our belief in the value of growth and identity, the basic values of characterization.

Though the Greeks showed little interest in character development, they were interested in revelation, the discovery of true identity. We have seen how Oedipus, through discovery, gained a new dignity and humble strength and Creon, in Sophocles' *Antigone*, a new humility. After two decades of playwriting, Maxwell Anderson came to the conclusion that discovery was the most important element in tragedy—indeed, in all drama. He did not mean the discovery of hidden facts, as Aristotle did, but the discovery by the main character of something about the world or about himself that made him, even as he lost, a better person.

In planning an absurdist drama, the director and the actor need not discard all the concepts of motivation and development that have enriched the drama over the centuries. But for some plays they must be ready to plan a character who suddenly takes on an obsession, without continuity with previous motives. Actually, there is a great deal of continuity in most dramas of the absurd. Sabina is the same character throughout *The Skin of Our Teeth*, though she takes on a slightly different personality as she sets out to seduce Mr. Antrobus in Act II. In Ionesco's *The Lesson*, the Professor has a strong drive to teach the girl. There is no sudden change as the drive gradually becomes more intense and demonic until he attacks and stabs her. An absurdist play may require that the character be conceived as fragmented or distorted, but even in the most dehumanized or mechanized dance drama the theatre deals with an image of the human race, and that image will always deal with some aspect of character.

Theme

The theme of a play—its full underlying meaning—may not be clear until we have thought it over for some time. The theme may be so implicit in the characters, in what happens, in the rich texture of the actors, the setting, and the performance that it cannot be put into words, though we may know that the play stands for certain values of living and that we have learned more about life by seeing it. Sometimes a minor character states the theme, but the impact is stronger if the main character makes his own discovery. Only in a very few plays can the theme be called a moral, for a moral is a neat, external conclusion *about* life, rather than a complex, gradually developed attitude *toward* life.

We must be careful, however, not to mistake a single statement by one character for the meaning of the whole play. At one point in *King Lear*, the blinded Earl of Gloucester comes to the conclusion that "As flies to wanton boys are we to the gods. They kill us for their sport." But that is only the momentary conclusion of one character. Gloucester later finds a new patience and accepts his condition.

Sometimes the theme is indicated when what is said in the dialogue offers an ironical contrast with what actually happens. Soon after Portia in *The Merchant of Venice* delivers a splendid sermon on mercy, she shows something less than mercy when she has Shylock in her power. In *Hedda Gabler*, Judge Brack seems a wise commentator, quietly watching Hedda, sure that he understands her and has her in his control. But he is the most surprised of all when she kills herself. He ends the play with the famous tribute to the unpredictability of human nature, "Good God!—People don't do such things."

Whether brought out by direct statement, by ironical contrast, or by implication, the theme is an essential part of a play. In epic theatre the theme is often the structure of the play. We have seen how both *Our Town* and *The Skin of Our Teeth* are organized by theme. Even the most trivial farce implies certain philosophical attitudes, and the great playwrights from Aeschylus, Sophocles, and Euripides to Shakespeare, Molière, Goethe, Ibsen, and Shaw have made significant contributions to human thought.

Dialogue, Mood, and Rhythm

Plot, character, and theme, as we have seen, are the elements of structure. Equally important are the elements of texture—dialogue, mood, and spectacle. Indeed, modern theatre people, like modern painters and musicians, are particularly interested in texture. The word is derived, like the word *textile*, from the Latin word for "weaving." Our strongest sensation of texture comes from touch, from feeling the difference, for instance, between a ribbed sweater and a silk shirt, but we extend the word to the other senses. In painting texture adds considerable surface interest as the artist achieves depth and vibrancy by interweaving brush strokes, smears, and spots of color in applying his oils or even by adding pieces of cloth, paper, wire screen, or rope to his canvas. In the theatre texture is created by the sounds and images of the language, by the subtle but powerful hold of the mood, and by the materials, color, and movement of setting and costume.

Most modern plays limit poetic language to local dialect and subordinate words to other elements such as background sounds or movements, clothes, and furniture to create a rich composite effect of local color. Lush language is left to romance, wit to high comedy, and poetry to the outdoor festival plays and a few dramas in verse. Even so, the director and the actor must study the dialogue of any play very carefully, for it is chiefly through the sound, and particularly the rhythm, of the dialogue that the playwright indicates the basic mood of the play and the changing moods of the scenes in sequence.

For his fifth dramatic value Aristotle used the term *music*, but most modern plays make little use of music as such. Hence we substitute the words *mood* and *rhythm* for *music*. Mood in the theatre depends upon a blending of many elements, including spectacle and language, but it is created chiefly by rhythm. For modern man, as for primitive man, rhythm is the great coordinating principle, as powerful and indispensable in the theatre as in dance or music. Movement without rhythm is clumsy, jerky. Rhythm creates a relationship between the parts of the body and between one person and another. Sailors pulling a rope or hauling a sail sing a chanty with a strong rhythm, in order to pull together. The coxswain coordinates the crew of a racing shell by calling out the rhythm. Spectators at a play follow the rhythm of the actors as closely as a crew follows the coxswain; the rhythm reverberates through the audience, binding stage and house together under one spell.

The actor directly and instantly communicates the rhythm of the scene to the audience, not merely as an abstract pattern of beats but with subtle feelings and qualities. The director can guide the actor just as directly, controlling the rhythm by his own tone of voice or gesture of the hands, suggesting modification by such simple terms as "quieter," "sharper," "gentle and slow," "both gay and flippant." Often the actor does not need to be conscious of the rhythm if he is thinking of the mood itself. But the director must know exactly what mood he wants and what rhythm will be best able to produce it.

Many scenes in the theatre have as strong and definite a beat as a march or a dance. In *The Emperor Jones,* a driving, relentless rhythm is created by a drumbeat that at first is very slow but gets faster and faster as the natives pursue Jones through the jungle and stops only with the pistol shot that kills him.

Most theatres in history have made rich use of music, at least as background if not in song and dance, and an orchestra was a regular attraction in commercial theatres until the Second World War. Even though the naturalistic directors banished conventional musical instruments, they used many other sounds, from nature, from human activities, or from the mechanized city. In a movie or TV drama the voices are almost as richly supported by background music as the singers in a Wagnerian opera.

If there is no music in the play to build the rhythm and mood, the director often uses music in rehearsals to set the tone and rhythm for a scene and to help the actors get into the right mood. In period plays, this can be as helpful in creating a style and atmosphere as Cavalier boots and capes, eighteenth-century wigs and ruffled shirts, or Victorian ladies' tight bodices and high collars.

Even for the musician, the notes on the staff cannot indicate all aspects of performance. Besides the marking of tempo, of loud and soft, crescendo and diminuendo, composers have developed a vocabulary, mostly in Italian, to indicate the general tone they want, whether broad, gentle, lamenting, impassioned, solemn, majestic, vigorous, lively, with fire, and so on. Still, much has to be left to the performer. Every concert player makes some use of suspension, pause, interruption, bunching and spreading out, speeding and slowing, and strong dynamic contrasts, though far less now than in Victorian times. Director and actor make some use of the musician's vocabulary and techniques.

From dancers, the director learns how to devise practice exercises; for instance, to vary a walking movement by making it heavier as in marching and stamping, or lighter for swinging or lilting, then to go on to prancing, skipping, jumping, and leaping. Then he may add an intention or emotion—responding to the sky and wind of a hilltop, strutting in front of someone in pride or defiance, tiptoeing around while someone else sleeps—or a special quality, tenseness or relaxation, smoothness or jerkiness. Or he may invent practice exercises that illustrate everyday words such as *punch, slash, press, flick, dab, float,* and *wring,* analyzing how to make movements light or heavy, quick or sustained, working against varying outer resistance or inner restraint. A few minutes of dance practice at the beginning of a rehearsal may help the actors get the right rhythm.

But more immediate to the theatre than rhythms suggested by music or dance are those supplied by the playwright, especially the poet-playwright. The rhythm of his phrases, the sounds of his words, and the rich suggestion of his images give the actor a chance to create a mood that may be the most compelling force of the play. Shakespeare's characters, without the help of scenery or lighting, cast a spell over the scene by the power of movement and words. Much of the dark anguish of *Hamlet* is created in the opening scene of the changing of the guard at midnight and the remark of the guard who is being relieved, "'Tis bitter cold and I am sick at heart." The moonlight balcony scene of *Romeo and Juliet* is built up in the phrases of Romeo, who sees Juliet as brighter than sun and moon, her eyes twinkling like stars. He addresses her: "Bright angel . . . thou art / As glorious to this night, being o'er my head / As is a winged messenger of heaven." He speaks of "night's cloak to hide me," of the blessed moon "that tips with silver all these fruit-tree tops," of "how silver-sweet sound lovers' tongues by night," evoking a spell of idealized love in the sustained light rhythms and sounds.

For the violent scene of the fights and deaths, a hot noon atmosphere is quickly created with sharper rhythms and images:

> The day is hot, the Capulets are abroad,
> And if we meet we shall not 'scape a brawl,
> For now these hot days is the mad blood stirring

—a passage in which the air is stabbed by short phrases, monosyllables, and seven accented syllables in the last line. For the storm scenes in the third act of *King Lear*, Shakespeare devotes a whole scene to two minor characters describing their struggle against the wind, rain, and lightning before bringing on Lear and the Fool. Lear answers the thunder with the trumpet tones and slow, heavy rhythms of "Strike flat the thick rotundity of the world." But in the next storm scene the mood is more quiet and eerie as Lear begins to go mad, and the new tone is set by the strange mock madness of the outcast Edgar: "Through the sharp hawthorn blows the cold wind."

Modern directors are keenly aware of the rhythms of different places at particular seasons and times of day. A Mexican village differs from a Scandinavian or an Irish town, a Spanish festival from an American square dance or a court minuet. In directing classes much time is spent on how to set the movement and stage business by which the actors establish the rhythm of place. There can be a wide range in detail as each actor falls into a variation of one basic rhythm. Alexander Dean used to start with evening in a cabin on an old-fashioned southern plantation. He would put the grandmother in a rocking chair to set one slow, straightforward, basic two-four rhythm. After the beat was established, firm and cheerful, he would bring on the mother, who would iron at a beat twice as fast but synchronized with the grandmother's rocking. Then he would bring in the granddaughter bouncing a ball, with four beats to the grandmother's one. All were united in one rhythm, expressive of the place, the time of day, and the attitudes and qualities of the characters. Then, to show the difference between tempo and rhythm, he would ask the actors to increase the tempo, the speed of the basic beat. Either adding a faster variation of the basic rhythm or increasing the tempo will create a build, a sense of rising step by step to a climax.

The intent of the characters may also set the rhythm. Hope has a brighter, lighter rhythm than despair. A character will set different tones when he is dreading, teasing, urging, begging, or threatening, when he is weary, exasperated, suspicious, quizzical, or puzzled.

Spectacle

Spectacle is the most controversial of the six dramatic values; the purists repeatedly attack it, and the intellectuals despise it. We have seen how the neoclassicists and many of the realists cut it down to a few group effects that could be created by the actors themselves, and we remember that three of the greatest theatres in history—the Chinese, the Japanese Noh, and the Elizabethan—while making much use of poetry, dance, and song, had no painted settings and used colors only for splendid costumes and a few portable symbolic indications of place.

Yet spectacle does belong in the theatre. It is important to see Macbeth and Lady Macbeth in splendid robes, sitting on splendid thrones, with attendants, trumpets, banners, tapestries, and canopies—the full panoply of royalty—to mark their triumph. And the banquet scene must be made an impressive spectacle, showing Macbeth in a closed circle of friends and councilors when his hopes are dashed by Banquo's ghost. In order to know the magnitude of the desecration wrought by the Spaniards in Peru as Peter Shaffer conceived it in *The Royal Hunt of the Sun*, the audience must see the sun-king of the Incas splendidly enthroned in a huge sun-medallion and the glittering procession of his subjects bearing the golden treasure that is to fill the royal chamber. Both in such romantic dramas and in naturalistic scenes we expect most characters to be shown in the larger world around them, the world of nature, history, or society.

Spectacle has been important in motion pictures since the very early days, and the introduction of the wide screen in the 1950s gave it even more impetus. The camera can so easily bring in the wide sweep of mountains and valleys, of buildings and streets, of processions and dances, of battles and holocausts, that many a director has let the spectacle overwhelm all other elements. But spectacle can be used more subtly to show how character is shaped by history and geography and can create symbolic overtones for the main action by the use of montage to cut in parallel examples, symbolic objects, or landscapes that invoke a particular mood. There have been a few epic films that made extensive use of spectacle but also had good plots, sound characterization, and a well-developed theme—among them *Gone With the Wind* (1939), *The Bridge on the River Kwai* (1957), *Lawrence of Arabia* (1963), *Becket* (1964), and *The Lion in Winter* (1968).

The overall texture is a blend of many elements: the dialogue, with its rhythmic phrases, suggestive images, and vibrant sounds; the mood, created by the qualities and rhythms of the actors; and the spectacle, with its colorful settings, changing lights, and moving masses of costumes.

Rehearsal and Performance

9

When the director is sure just what attitude of comedy or tragedy he is aiming for, what style he needs, what patterns he wants in plot, character, and theme, and what qualities in dialogue, mood, and spectacle, he starts to put the play on the boards. After he and the designer have worked out the ground plan and know where the doorways, steps, and levels are to be and where the walls and furniture will shape the playing areas, he lets the designer and his assistants go their own way for a time while he concentrates on putting the actors on the stage. In working with the actors, the director makes use of the five techniques of the director listed in the outline of play production in Chapter 8—composition, picturization of relationship, movement, pantomimic dramatization, and rhythm. The first two are techniques for controlling the picture in space, and the last three set the play into movement in time. The director considers how he can make the play clear and meaningful to both eye and ear. In the early rehearsals he looks at each moment of the play as though it were a still photograph, to see that the composition is clear and the relationships in the picture are meaningful; later he watches and listens as the large movements, the reading of lines, and the small reactions propel the play through its rhythmic patterns in time.

Director and Actor

Controlling the Picture in Space

The director's first step in staging the play is to visualize it in space. He is not putting a single orator on a podium or a preacher in a pulpit. He is visualizing an action involving people with other people and with the world they live in. If the actors were left to themselves, they would get in front of one another and muddle the composition, and each would move without regard to what the others were doing. The grouping would be meaningless, and the attention of the audience would be scattered. The composition of the picture and the picturization of relationships must be controlled by someone outside the picture; hence these two techniques belong very logically to the director.

The movie and television director has a camera with which to select and control what is to hold the attention, but the stage director has only the actor and the space of the stage for his picture. In placing and moving his actors in the various areas of the stage, he has many ways of changing the picture to give different meanings and to shift the attention from one character to another. He may subordinate one character by turning him away from the audience while he gives prominence to another by asking him to "open up" (that is, turn more toward the audience), to stand up, to step out from a group, or to move from a weak area of the stage to a stronger one. Or he can throw the emphasis on one character without moving him by moving the characters around him, so that they give him more space and contrast, and by having them turn their "eye-focus" on him. In deploying his actors, the director divides the stage into six areas (sometimes nine) and labels them *up right, up center, up left, down right, down center, down left,* and sometimes *right center, center,* and *left center* (Figure 9-1). Stage left and stage right indicate the sides as viewed by the actor facing the audience; upstage is away from the audience and downstage is toward it. For

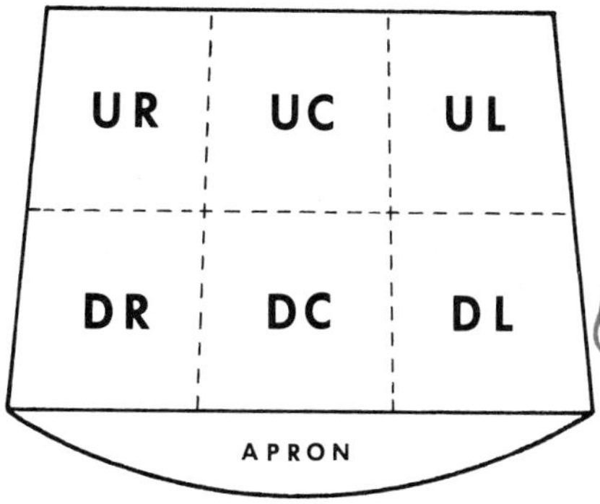

9-1
Stage areas. The director divides the stage into at least six areas, to lend variety and to vary the relative strength from the soft up left or up right to the very emphatic down center.

four centuries—in some places well into this century—upstage was actually higher than downstage, since the old picture stage had a sloping floor to give a forced perspective effect to the wing-and-backdrop setting.

Not only are some areas stronger than others, but different areas have different qualities. The soft, distant areas up left and up right are good for lyric moods, for longing, dreaming, brooding, and for some delicate love scenes. Scenes in those areas are so soft that they do not assure us that action

9-2 Formal versus informal composition. A formal throne scene with many vertical lines is contrasted with a more relaxed, informal scene. A formal duel, symmetrical, vertical, and parallel to the front, is contrasted with a more dynamic fight on a diagonal floor pattern. Drawn by Don Creason.

will follow. For instance, a lonely, isolated person, hearing other people talking unfavorably about him, could smolder up left or up right in pain and anger, but not until he came into the area down left or down right would we believe him capable of taking revenge. Decisions and quarrels often need the strength of the down center position after a climactic move from one of the weaker areas. But scenes of violence are too shocking if brought downstage. A stabbing or strangling is usually played in a weak area; it will be strong enough upstage left, behind a sofa, with other actors covering the body, and more convincing than it would be if the audience could see how the blow is faked. Even a film usually omits the final impact, showing only the arm or the shadow of the murderer or the horrified face of an onlooker.

The director devotes the first rehearsals to *blocking;* that is, he goes through each scene speech by speech, telling the actors when to come in, where to stand or sit, on what lines to move or carry out such "stage business" as handling the properties and how to perform many of the small reactions that go with the lines. As they go through the actions, they write the directions down in their scripts. If a commercial acting edition of the play is used, the director tells them to disregard the printed stage directions. He has usually worked out new movements and actions that will fit the particular stage, the setting, and the dramatic concept he has in mind.

Blocking of the first act may take one three-hour rehearsal or longer, and three or four more rehearsals may be necessary to get the act set before the next act is blocked. Directors vary a great deal in the extent of their blocking, some giving full directions immediately, others leaving much of the detail to be worked out later as the actors try out their lines and their reactions to one another. Almost any director makes adjustments in later rehearsals, modifying the original blocking by adding to it or simplifying it as he and the actors discover better ways of moving and reacting. He must constantly make sure that his picture has clarity, focus, and variety. The form of his composition, its formality or diffuseness, hardness or softness, will add meaning to the play.

A tense moment in a college production of *The Caine Mutiny Court Martial* appears in Figure 9-3. In considering the overall controls, the director has decided that this is a very strong situation play with romantic, even melodramatic, interest in conflict, threats, fears, and concern over justice. With the designer, he decided to bring the action far downstage but not actually to break the fourth-wall convention. Since the concern about justice is abstract and the people are removed from the actual ships and storms where the mutiny took place, the setting and composition can be rather abstract and formal. But since conflict is so important in the play and is not resolved into an unquestioned justice at the end, the ground plan is

9-3 Trial scene with formal lines on a diagonal ground plan. Primary emphasis is on the officer on the stand, and secondary emphasis is on the prosecutor. Wouk's *The Caine Mutiny Court Martial.* Mankato State College production, directed by Ted Paul and designed by Burton E. Meisel.

placed on the diagonal; the court is not square to the front, and the judge is not so dominant as in a civil courtroom. The designer has provided several levels for playing, and in this scene the director is making good use of them to give the prosecutor an uphill handicap in his assault on the witness. The isolation of the two figures at the front, with considerable free space, and their dynamic interaction make them stand out clearly from the seated figures. Of the two, the officer on the stand easily dominates, even without the special lighting, because of his higher position and because his face and body are turned more toward the audience than toward the others. Furthermore, in contrast to everybody else he is relaxed, and contrast, like isolation in space, adds a powerful emphasis. If attention should wander to the judge or his associates, it is sent right back to the officer because they are looking at him. The director constantly uses such eye-focus of the characters on stage to point to the center of interest. If the attention is to go to the judge or one of his seated associates, the director will need to turn several people to look at him and subordinate the forestage men by turning their faces away from the audience.

For a very informal composition, let us consider the scene from *A View from the Bridge* shown in Figure 9-4. Although the space used is fairly shallow, the characters are very much at home, and the environment is important. The play is a naturalistic drama that has strong conflict under the surface, but in this scene the little conflicts and changing interactions are more important than any one thread of action. Character and mood, at least for this scene, are more important than plot. The curved lines of the composition create informality and warmth and bring all the characters into a close circle. Yet the director keeps nearly all of them isolated from one another. All belong to one family, yet they cannot come together. There is a great deal of variety, with two people standing, two seated, and one sitting on the floor; the director has used this variety to create many different relationships. The boy sitting on the floor has one thought—his love for the girl he is with—and both his humble position and his eyes are begging for her love. He is safely enclosed between the two women, but he is isolated from the men, and the line of their faces, with conflict brewing, leads directly to him. The woman standing could easily take the attention—her position gives her a high level; she is near the center of the stage; and she is facing front in contrast with the two seated men. But she subordinates herself by dropping her eyes. At this moment she will not tie herself to anyone, though the lines of the picture tie her closely in three directions. The curved lines and her nearness to the young couple show her sympathy for them; her position at the table ties her to her husband sitting at the table, though she separates herself from what he is saying; her standing shows her implicit sympathy with the young man standing at stage left. The man sitting at the table is obviously the man of the house and all the others are

9-4 Informal scene in naturalistic style. Curved lines hold the compact group together. Though the characters are emotionally isolated, the grouping indicates many potential loyalties and conflicts. Miller's *A View from the Bridge.* University of Oregon production, directed by William R. McGraw and designed by Karl Kaufman.

closely tied to him, but he keeps his isolation and is slightly hostile to the young man at his left. Nobody is completely subordinated, and each could easily be given the center of attention. For instance, if the boy sitting turned his face more toward the audience, he would be stronger, and if one or more of the three other characters turned an eye-focus on him, he would be the center of action.

We see that bringing a character from the side toward the center or from upstage toward the audience will make him stronger. But it is easy to subordinate characters, even in strong areas, by turning the face and body partly away from the audience, for the actor whose face is turned more nearly to the front will hold the greater interest. A higher face will dominate a lower; a character standing will dominate one sitting; one on a step or platform will dominate one on a lower level. Eye-focus of the actors is one of the easiest means of controlling the attention of the audience, since we tend to look at what someone else is looking at. A single figure with space around him can, like a small weight on a long lever, counterbalance a large mass. An element of the scenery that repeats the line of the actor, or a guard or attendant, can give him more importance. Contrast is such a powerful element that it can counteract any of the other methods of controlling attention. One figure sitting, bent over, with his head turned away from the audience, is weaker than a figure standing and facing the audience, but if there are three or four straight standing figures, the weak, bent figure takes the attention by contrast. It is the whole picture that the audience sees, and each actor, each property, each part of the setting must take its place in the controlled context or it will distract the attention and destroy the illusion of the scene.

The audience is seldom aware of the composition in itself, unless it is cluttered or confused. What is seen is the story in the picture, told through the action and interrelation of the characters. Alexander Dean called this story-telling arrangement "picturization," and it may even more precisely be called "picturization of emotional relations." It is a visual language, a medium as powerful as words, by which the director communicates with the audience. It is one means by which a play, so short in comparison with a novel, can make as strong an impression, sometimes even stronger. The actor, the designer, and the director can show the audience at a glance complexities and qualities of relationship that would require many pages of a novel to describe or suggest. In a well-directed scene of an accident in the street, for instance, the audience can tell by the position of the actors which is the wife of the victim, which the mother, the father, the friend, the wife's friend, and which are mere passersby, adding their own groupings and emotional reactions in the background. Characters on stage, as in real life, naturally turn toward and stay near those they like or trust or feel some-

9-5 Formal, balanced composition on an open stage. Characters are evenly spaced for aristocratic stateliness at a wedding that is suddenly turned into a scene of violent accusation. Shakespeare's *Much Ado About Nothing.* The Euclid–Seventy-Seventh Street Theatre of the Cleveland Playhouse production, directed by Kirk Willis and designed by Paul Rodgers.

thing in common with, and keep at a distance or turn away from those they dislike. Many other relationships of characters can be clearly indicated by the stage picture; for instance, one person asking, refusing, suspecting, accusing, protecting, or disdaining another. Farewells are different if someone is leaving for a long or a short absence, for a picnic or for war or for prison. If the director can give the scene a title that describes its basic action, he can see more clearly how to arrange his picture.

Moving the Play in Time

For the director, even more important than the control of the picture in space is the movement of the actors and the progression of the play in time. On the stage people don't just talk, they do something, and as they carry on daily business they are constantly changing their relations with one another. The playwright's dialogue is the surface expression. It is the director's job to find the inner life of the play and see that it, too, is expressed, in the changing moods, the larger movements, and the smaller business and reactions of the actor.

Movement is picturization in action. As relationships and attitudes change, the movements are as important as the words—indeed, often more important, since they can modify or even contradict the words and add other meanings and nuances. Hence the director makes sure that the actor understands the character's motivation and begins his action with the thought; then the movement will express his intention and the words will be part of a total response. It usually takes many rehearsals for the actor to achieve a good integration of intention, speech, and movement, and in the early stages improvisation may be helpful to bring movement and words spontaneously from the thought. The English director Joan Littlewood found that even professional actors needed preparatory exercises to get both the imagination and the muscles limbered up. In the opening scene of *A Taste of Honey*, a weary mother and daughter arrive at their squalid new lodgings. Miss Littlewood had the two actresses spend an hour dragging heavy suitcases around the stage, trying to get on buses, arguing with landladies, struggling with rain, even imagining they were dragging the suitcases down long, dark, filthy tunnels. They learned how to feel worn out and fretful.

No actor on the stage moves alone. Any movement is part of a readjustment that the other characters must at least acknowledge. The actors are all bound in one web of interrelationships as if invisible rubber bands were stretched between them. As they follow curved paths around one another and around the furniture, the actors create a sense of depth in a stage picture that otherwise looks rather flat.

Movement in the group is one of the director's ways of creating a build, sometimes more powerful in increasing tension than the rising speed, volume, and pitch of the dialogue. A long, talky scene needs some "breaking up," even if no great build is required. The first part of a scene will usually carry itself, and the director will conserve his power, adding few movements and only those that are casual and related to the background. As the scene progresses, he will add more and more movements, timing them closer together and increasing their size and intensity, always making sure that they are so placed and motivated as to reinforce the scene and not distract from it. If one character is telling a long story to several others, the director may not want to give any noticeable movement to the teller, but he can gain the needed breaking up or build if some listeners, at first very relaxed, get excited and move in closer, while others interject audible reactions and nod in agreement at one another after vivid moments in the tale.

In the coaching rehearsals, directors differ widely in their ways of stimulating the actor. Those who follow the Stanislavsky or the Actors Studio methods spend a great deal of time discussing the motivation of the character, comparing the character's experience with previous experiences of the actor, becoming almost amateur psychoanalysts in hope of discovering and releasing the actor's inhibitions. Other directors believe there is nothing like simply rehearsing the play itself. Sir Laurence Olivier, director of the National Theatre of England, expressed his impatience with the New York methods in an interview for the *New York Times:*

> I'd rather have run the scene eight times than have wasted that time in chattering away about abstractions. An actor gets the right thing by doing it over and over. Arguing about motivations and so forth is a lot of rot. American directors encourage that sort of thing too much. . . . Instead of doing a scene over again that's giving trouble, they want to discuss . . . discuss . . . discuss. . . .

The final coordinating rehearsals are generally considered to be nightmares, and in the days when amateurs brought everything together—costumes, scenery, properties, and lighting—at one last frantic dress rehearsal, they were just that. The performance could not possibly be as bad as that rehearsal, and the legendary saying was repeated: "A bad dress rehearsal means a good performance." But today school theatres and community theatres are much more serious and usually have from three to five dress rehearsals, besides working out many of the details before the first dress rehearsal. The company of an art theatre with its own building has a great advantage over casts playing in commercial theatres where they cannot get on stage until the last minute. It is a great help to actors to have platforms and steps, doors and windows to practice with and to have scene changes and much of the lighting worked out beforehand. For a period play, practice properties and parts of costume, especially high heels and long practice skirts for the actresses, may be used for weeks. Then just before the dress rehearsal the director and the designer often have a dress parade, bringing all the actors on stage in costume and makeup to try the key moves and see what changes and adjustments are necessary.

After the strenuous coordinating dress rehearsals, it is a good idea to have several full rehearsals that run through without interruption. Most of his suggestions the director makes to the actors after each act or after seeing the play as a whole. He is free to watch the flow of the play, to feel the surges toward the climaxes. He may make many notes, some of them on details that can be improved next time through, but at this point he is chiefly watching the overall effect. Is the style maintained consistently? Is the plot clear? Are the characters believable? Do the important ideas come through in words and actions? Is the texture rich and controlled, not too soft or too harsh? And, finally, do all the elements—setting, lighting, movement, tones, words—move together to carry the play to its big climaxes and give it structure and shape? By this time the actor is free to follow without interruption the secret life of the play in the hundred and one little reactions that give the play vitality. He is ready for the one final spark that will set the performance aflame—direct contact with a live audience.

Actor and Audience

When the audience arrives for opening night, it is the actor it has come to see. They know nothing of the hours of analysis and planning; they care nothing for the long days of rehearsal. Playwright, director, and designer disappear from view, and the backstage workers are mere assistants helping

9-6
Laurette Taylor as Amanda in Tennessee Williams' *The Glass Menagerie,* New York, 1944. She gave the role a combination of stubborn determination and Southern charm. Photo Culver Pictures.

with costume changes, lights, musical instruments, or background sounds—just to enable the actor to create the play.

For all that modern theory calls for the domination of the director, the actor is still the center of the theatre, as he has been from the beginning. For all that modern theory calls for the subordination of the actor to the ensemble and the overall mood of the play, the best actors are remembered even more than the play. One of the greatest appeals of the theatre is the interest in watching a favorite actor in different roles. A good character actor fascinates us as he changes his personality to fit each new character. A "straight" actor may win even more acclaim as, with little variation, he brings a vivid personality, charm, and glamor to a series of roles. It is the actor more than the playwright who creates the dream images by which each age likes to think of itself. There have always been matinee idols, but with the creation of a mass film and TV audience, the popularity of a few stars has been one of the most extraordinary social developments of the twentieth century.

The Actor's Training

Important as the actor is, however, his training has been chaotic and piecemeal since the naturalists repudiated the classical training of the nineteenth century. Some elements of that training have been retained, but with only the vaguest sense that voice and body flexibility might be useful for the naturalistic actor. In America we have put such strong emphasis on the actor's inner feelings and self-analyses that many students are afraid that technical exercises might compromise their sincerity and make them sound artificial. They hope that their inner feelings will be clear to the audience without resort to technique.

Nineteenth-century training of the actor was carefully designed to develop a body and voice to be seen and heard in large theatres, to enable the actor to move in the aristocratic deportment of bows and curtsies, to show skill in singing, dancing, and fencing, and to build long, poetic speeches to ringing climaxes. European and Latin American companies still regularly produce the classics and still have schools to train actors in the classic techniques. Since American college theatres occasionally, and resident and festival theatres regularly, present classic plays, there would seem to be some need in America for the classic techniques. Actually what we have done is to keep a few of the old technical exercises in the hope of giving naturalistic actors some range, expecting that in naturalistic plays they will tone down the "external techniques" and, with the help of the Stanislavsky method of studying the inner text, give their total response a subjective validity.

It takes a great deal of practice to make words come out of a total body response. A single phrase like "I said no" will sound very different when accompanied by a stamp of the foot, or a clenched fist pulled against the body, or a shrug of the shoulders, or an arm being twisted. One reason some opera singers are poor actors is that they learn to produce voice tone without body response, forgetting that in animated conversation people speak with the whole body, and above all with an animated face, raising the eyebrows, thrusting out the chin, tossing the head. The lips and chin are very active in snarling, sneering, disdaining, or mocking, in smiling, savoring, teasing, or laughing, since facial movements reshape and color the tone of the voice. The traditional actor practiced a phrase or speech with different movements, tones of voice, and facial expressions. Some techniques of projection, precision, and clarity are necessary for the actor, since the coordination of the cast and the repetition of a play would be impossible without the precise control that enables each actor to depend on another actor's speaking at a certain spot at a certain time with a certain tone, speed, and emphasis.

And yet, for the realistic actor, time-honored external techniques may seem empty and unimportant, and many students pay little attention to them. While the nineteenth-century actor used elaborate inflection, rich voice tones, and large round gestures, the naturalistic actor uses the central muscles more than the peripheral, the abdomen more than the hands, monotone more than inflection. Such acting requires only a very limited kind of body and voice training, for its power lies in the unconscious mind, which must be stimulated by "psychotechniques." Stanislavsky found that the actor had several ways of calling up his own feelings, of searching for the "inner flow," the "deeper content," the "inner musical score" that lay hidden behind the words of the play. Stanislavsky recognized, as Freud did, that although the subconscious could not be forced to reveal its secrets directly, there might be indirect ways of unlocking its treasures. Most important of the psychotechniques was the appeal to emotional memory. If the actor thought back to an experience of his own that had created a feeling similar to that of his situation in a play—a childhood experience, for example, perhaps trivial in itself but important to him at the time—he might rediscover the tone and texture that had accompanied the original experience. Another psychotechnique was improvisation. Treating the words of the play script as only a surface component of the full experience, the actor might go behind the words, imagining other moments in the life of his character and improvising appropriate actions and words for them. When he returned to the play itself, he would possess the inner flow, the hidden life, of the character and thus could present a whole person.

The actor can usually find some element of the environment, partly re-created in the stage setting and properties, on which to concentrate at each performance and so recapture the feelings and compulsions of his character. Morris Carnovsky tells what a great help he found the properties and business at his first entrance in *An Enemy of the People.* As he came into his brother's house and put down his hat and umbrella, he said to himself, "Here is my hat. It is my hat," and, looking at the room, "Here is the room. There is that lamp, that expensive lamp that my foolish brother bought. Here is a tablecloth. I don't have any such tablecloth in my house. This carpet is probably much finer than anything anybody in town has. What right has he to have a tablecloth and stuff like this around?" Thus, before a word was spoken, Carnovsky had his character established and his hostility to his brother stirred up in his imagination.

Sometimes a picture, a drawing, an anecdote, or a bit of conversation in dialect will give the actor a suggestion for the right mood. Sometimes the actor finds an expressive body stance or movement, a key gesture, that captures the essence of the character. Michael Chekhov, nephew of Anton Chekhov and a follower of Stanislavsky, who for many years acted, taught, and directed in America, provided a useful term, *psychological gesture,* or *P.G.,* for the characteristic gesture or stance that would make the objective of the character more vivid and integrate the inner motives with the outer action. If the character is suggested in condensed form by a grasping or catching gesture of greed, the actor practices the gesture until it involves the whole body in movement. If a character's objective is to dominate, the actor may practice standing wide and strong, his hands pushing downward, until he finds the feel of the body actions that he can carry over into the part. If his character is to fear and dread the dominance of others, he may practice cringing, running, and dodging.

The overall objective, the "spine" of the character, must be clear to the actor, but the audience may be aware of it only in retrospect. The immediate triumphs of naturalistic acting are in the little reactions, the pantomimic dramatizations—the unconscious snarl on the lips, the half-clenched fist, the flinching shoulder—that give color to the spoken phrases and are a visible expression of the inner life of the character.

By the middle of the twentieth century, naturalism seemed to have triumphed in the training of actors in New York and in most American colleges. Yet even in the 1950s not all productions were naturalistic. And as the classics were revived, the superiority of English actors to American actors in plays of the past became evident. The Institute for Advanced Study of Theatre Arts brought directors to New York from European and Asian theatres to teach their traditional techniques and to direct sample productions. The popular musicals, as we have seen, borrowed more and more from ballet and modern dance. Gradually some New York actors began to recognize that there were many other traditions of acting besides the Stanislavsky method. Stanislavsky's insights will of course remain important in any new synthesis that may be achieved, but in the 1970s, actor training is in a fluid state. The radical new developments of the 1960s, which we will discuss in Chapter 11, do not subordinate the actor as naturalistic theatre did. Indeed, several new forms of theatre, like most theatres of the past, demand the highest intensities of voice and movement.

The Actor as Virtuoso Performer

Although the naturalists demanded that the actor give the impression that he was part of a slice of life and not acting at all, the good actors, even as they are playing "to the life," are also virtuoso performers putting on an exhibition for the audience. The actor has much in common with the expert juggler, the concert musician, the auctioneer. He must be a convincing master of his craft, and he must also project with brilliance the role he is playing. As he interprets the words of the playwright, he is creating one of the popular images by which each age, each decade, sees itself.

The playwright may become well known, but it is the skillful actor who holds the audience when the play is first produced. Aeschylus won his prizes as a playwright, but he was equally famous as an actor, and in the next several centuries the actors won all the acclaim. In his time Shakespeare was well paid as a playwright and minor actor, but the leading actor of his company, Richard Burbage, was better known than he. The most popular acting companies of Shakespeare's time had no playwright; they were the Italian *commedia dell' arte* troupes, who in the sixteenth century and for two hundred years afterward entertained Europe both at cultivated courts and at noisy street corners. Each performer was a star, perfecting one role in a lifetime of practice. Yet the troupe took great pride in the way they played together. They made up the words as they went along, following an outline of a plot tacked up behind the scenes by the manager to indicate what episode was to come next. They memorized witty sayings and had at the tip of their tongues clever entrance and exit speeches and riddles and retorts, and the lovers memorized songs and love sonnets and poems of complaint; but the good performers were well-read people who could improvise and adapt their dialogue to the immediate situation, making references to local affairs and taking advantage of any response of the audience or accident on the stage.

The company presented a whole family of stereotypes. The young lovers were constantly interrupted and thwarted by the two old masked fools, Pantalone, the rich *magnifico* from Venice, or the pedantic Doctor from Bologna with a gallimaufry of learned words. The two *zanni,* or comic servants, came to the rescue and at the same time created further complications. Even when the lover sang a charming serenade under his Lucinda's window, Pantalone was around a corner mocking him, waiting to rush out and beat him. Or perhaps it was not Lucinda at all but Harlequin disguised in her cape, showing his black, devil-like half-mask to the audience. Or Pedrolino, the country servant, jumped through a window and interrupted the lovers, or the Spanish captain came strutting and bragging down the street.

Commedia performers were acrobats, mime experts, singers, and jugglers as well as improvising actors, and even in foreign countries they could make their movements and gestures so vivid, their inflections so lively, that nobody needed a translator. Sometimes the plot was serious, but it did not remain so for very long before the comic performers started one of their famous running gags known as *lazzi*. Many of the *lazzi* were so well known that the manager would merely indicate in the scenario that at this point Pulcinella would try to delay the Doctor with the *lazzo* of the broken leg, or of suicide, or of "which would be better," "spill something on his cloak," or "pretend he sees ghosts." Patterns of repetition were set, then broken, reversed, or interrupted. Doubtless some performances did not work—an entrance was made before another actor reached his gag line or the expected lead cues got jumbled. But when the teamwork was right and the comedians were in good form, the *commedia* was one of the highest delights in theatre history. The actor as performer, without playwright or director, has left us a goal and an ideal. Today we get occasional glimpses of that ideal in a few single performers in their top form—Bob Hope, Red Skelton, Woody Allen, Bill Cosby, and others—when there is sheer joy in watching their great skill, their dazzling virtuosity.

Just over a hundred years ago Joseph Jefferson created the title role in *Rip Van Winkle* and held audiences spellbound with it for more than four decades. In an age of Victorian conformity, respectability, and hard work, he gave special meaning to a character who failed to conform. As we read *Rip Van Winkle* it seems a poor play, but theatregoers went to the play over and over again, and they took their small children so that they might tell their envious grandchildren that they had seen the great Joseph Jefferson. The ne'er-do-well Rip, with his Dutch dialect, who accepted his exile, who teased his wife even as she drove him out, who came back years later to find a crumb of domestic happiness at the edge of his daughter's family, seemed the most amusing and lovable man they had ever known. Jefferson must have given a superb technical performance. But the audience did not see the technique. Through their tears and laughter, they saw a fully revealed human being.

Glimpses of some remarkable modern performances can be had in

9-7
The beloved ne'er-do-well Rip Van Winkle as created in the nineteenth century by Joseph Jefferson.

records and films. Shakespeare has been given a new vitality. For the Victorians he was the touchstone, and any important actor had to test his skill in the best-known roles. Sometimes, especially at the end of a season, he would present an evening of favorite scenes from several plays, and he expected to repeat the most dazzling speeches as the audience demanded an encore. The Victorian audience responded to a wide range of acting styles, from the quiet, melancholy gentleman of Edwin Booth's Hamlet to the raving maniac of Tommaso Salvini's Othello, performed in Italian, usually with a local company performing in English. Sir Henry Irving, the first English actor to be knighted, brought acting down to a more respectable subordination of the actor to the production, and after Irving the newer actors, realist or "new school" performers, took the virtuoso dash out of Shakespeare. It is no wonder that Maurice Evans was able to make a sensation of *Richard II* and *Hamlet* in the 1930s when he put a singing tone back into Shakespeare. His recordings may seem too operatic for some tastes, but in live performance it was thrilling to hear the beautiful voice used with superb technical skill. Sir John Gielgud achieved a more balanced reading, adding a wider range of characterization to a rich use of voice tone and poetic rhythms. Besides several early recordings, he made in the

1960s two anthology recordings—"Ages of Man" and "One Man in His Time"—of key passages from a number of Shakespeare's plays.

The triumph of magnificent intensity in acting of the 1940s is captured in the recording of Judith Anderson's Medea; the recording cannot convey the strong, queenly dignity of her movement, but her voice alone enables listeners to sample the range, power, and technical control of a great performer. It is a vivid part for her, a climax to a long career of acting strong, suffering women. But the play hardly matters; such a virtuoso performer is herself a show. As Sir Tyrone Guthrie writes, "In politics, in the pulpit, and above all, in the theatre, the supreme thrill is the thunder and splash of a great personality as, like a wave, it surges over the audience and slaps the back wall of the house."

The screen has given us some idea of the virtuoso acting of Sir Laurence Olivier. Of his Shakespearean film roles, his dashing young Henry V and sly, sarcastic Richard III are perhaps of more lasting interest than his blond, raw-boned, brooding Hamlet. His *Othello*, not produced as a film but recorded electronically as the scenes from the stage production were run in an enlarged studio setting, catches some magnificent glimpses of his power as an actor, though the audience perspective is sometimes all wrong. In many scenes both the camera and the microphone are too close for makeup and acting that were designed for an audience at the distance of a large theatre. Even more astonishing than Olivier's portrayal of Shakespearean characters was his performance as Archie Rice, the seedy music-hall singer in Osborne's *The Entertainer*, which we discussed in Chapter 7. The superb portrayal by a performer of an entertainer who is losing his ability to perform is an extraordinary feat.

Fortunately for present-day audiences, one of the best twentieth-century performers, Charlie Chaplin, after a short career on the music-hall stage in England, came to America to make movies. His films were extremely popular in the twenties, thirties, and early forties, yet many Americans have never seen his major pictures. By the 1940s he had made powerful enemies by satirizing business barons and generals in his films and by speaking too enthusiastically for wartime cooperation with Russia. Finally, the irony of his *Monsieur Verdoux* (1947) cut too deep for some patriotic minds; his debonair hero, who had murdered a half-dozen wives for money, cheerfully went to his execution insisting that in a world that killed millions in war he was not so bad. Patriotic groups hounded him out of the country, and for years he would not allow his major films to be shown in America. As common sense prevails, Americans are now getting a chance to see the greatest of all clowns. There is nothing subversive in his films, unless it is subversive to laugh at pomposity and pretense.

Like the *commedia dell' arte* clowns, Chaplin created his character

9-8
Comedy and sentiment. The elegant tramp as created by Charlie Chaplin in *The Kid*, 1920. Museum of Modern Art.

and his activities as he went along. One day while working on a Mack Sennett comedy, on the spur of the moment he put together his famous tramp costume by combining oddments that were too large and too small—baggy trousers and tight coat, big shoes and small derby hat—with a stiff white wing collar, a small mustache, and a cane for finishing touches. He played some variations as the little tramp met different situations, but, like the *commedia* actors, for the rest of his life he played essentially the same character, elegant and brave in adversity. In all the longer films, in the midst of satiric comment on some aspect of the world—the circus, the army, the Gold Rush, the Depression, the factory, Hitler, or human massacre—there are amazing scenes of clowning while skillfully balancing, miming, or dancing. In *City Lights*, as night watchman in a department store, Chaplin roller-skates through the aisles, a fallen lamp shade over his head blinding him as he boldly skirts the edge of the stairwell with the clown's supreme disregard of danger. As Hitler in *The Great Dictator,* while he dreams of possessing the whole world, he embraces a balloon globe and dances with it. In *The Gold Rush,* as a starving gold prospector boiling and eating an old shoe in the style of a rich epicure, or, in the lonely shack, imagining his dream girl dining with him, performing a dance with forks stuck in two rolls, Chaplin's little fellow bravely carries on the business of living.

When sound came in at the end of the twenties, Chaplin at first refused to let the little tramp speak. He had always used music in making his films, and beginning with *City Lights* in 1931, he himself wrote a superb score for the sound track, not reinforcing the grubbiness of the tramp but providing a romantic lilt of bravery and determination, fitting the melody exactly to the pattern and rhythm of the action. He was fascinated by the Chinese theatre music he heard in Singapore, and of course he was familiar with the use of music in the old melodramas, and he found a similar musical pattern to add a dimension to the action. As late as 1936, when he produced *Modern Times,* he did not use dialogue. In the factory scenes, a full-wall television screen lights up and a tyrannical voice over a loudspeaker orders the workers to speed up. When the salesmen demonstrate the time-saving feeding machine, they bring a phonograph to play their sales spiel. Only near the end of the picture is the tramp's voice heard, singing a song in a night club. Finally, in *The Great Dictator,* Chaplin found one solution, spouting German doubletalk, an amazing farrago of Teutonic syllables that almost made sense. In everything he did Chaplin was a virtuoso, raising his comic image of the little misfit to a high artistic level. He was surprised, when he made a trip from Hollywood to New York, and later around the globe, to discover that he was the most famous, the most worshipped personality in the world, the toast of artists in Paris and the center of adoring mobs from Chicago to Tokyo.

The Star System

Most movie stars have been images of sex appeal and love, but they have usually had some individual quality of personality. Curiously, the first movie producers did not think of advertising particular actors; their names were not even given on the screen. But soon the public demanded the names of their favorites, and of these the list was headed by the Biograph Company girl with the long curls: Mary Pickford. By 1913 she had made 125 one-reel pictures and was one of Hollywood's three or four greatest drawing cards, ready to embark on her career of twenty years as "America's Sweetheart." Her forte was sentimental roles like Pollyanna or Little Lord Fauntleroy, but she was often cast in tomboyish parts in which the show of physical energy was all the more effective because of her delicate features.

The most popular male stars of the twenties were Rudolph Valentino and Douglas Fairbanks. An unknown actor when he was selected for the principal role in *The Four Horsemen of the Apocalypse* (1921), Valentino was an immediate success as a picturesque Argentinean gaucho, and he became one of the greatest screen lovers and romantic figures that Hollywood has ever known. In all his pictures he was an exotic character—bullfighter, sheik, eighteenth-century adventurer, army officer in the Russian court of Catherine the Great—presented in some lavish setting, and if the picture allowed even the slightest excuse, he danced the tango that had first set off his slim figure. Douglas Fairbanks, the most athletic star the screen had known, scaled walls, leaped from parapets, and fought his way through crowds of armed men in one tale of adventure after another—*The Three Musketeers* (1921), *Robin Hood* (1922), *The Thief of Bagdad* (1924), and *The Black Pirate* (1926).

The stars had begun their amazing reign, and Hollywood had become one of the richest and most fabulous of all cities, creating dream images for the whole world. Every clerk in a dime store lived vicariously the glamorous life as she read about the extravagant lives of her favorite stars in her fan magazines and sat at night watching her dreams on the screen. She cared little whether her idols had any acting ability or not. The screen could create the illusion of acting. After the talent scout found a body and a face, the dress designer, the hairdresser, and the makeup artist could add the glamor and the publicity agents could create the emotion.

Some present-day film directors still do not want acting but only a face. The French director Robert Bresson is quoted by John Russell Taylor in *Cinema Eye, Cinema Ear* as saying:

> Acting is for the theatre, which is a bastard art. The film can be a true art because in it the author takes fragments of reality and arranges them in such a way that their juxtaposition transforms them. Art *is* transformation. Each shot is like a word, which means nothing by itself, or rather means so many things that in effect it is meaningless. But a word in a poem is transformed, its meaning made precise and unique, by its placing in relation to the words around it; in the same way a shot in a film is given its meaning by its context, and each shot modifies the meaning of the previous one until with the last shot a total, unparaphrasable meaning has been arrived at. Acting has nothing to do with that, it can only get in the way. Films can be made by by-passing the will of those who appear in them, using not what they do but what they are.

Both the photography and the editing can create the illusion of changing emotional reaction when the actor has done little or no acting. If a strong face is photographed from several different angles, the director may find that one shot has caught just the expression he wants. In soft light, slowly approached by the camera, a face will look quiet and tender. If a close-up of the same face, brightly lighted, is suddenly cut in to the picture, it will look startled, assertive. If a scene that should produce joy is cut in just before it, the assertive face looks joyful; if a scene that should produce anger is cut in, the face looks angry. All the cameraman and director need is a mask, like a Greek or Japanese Noh mask, an Egyptian statue of Nefertiti, or a Gothic statue of the Virgin—a kind of doll endowed with personality that satisfies some deep need of the public: the exotic lure of Theda Bara or Pola Negri or Jean Harlow, the wistfulness of Greta Garbo, the proud imperturbability of Elizabeth Taylor, the vital defiance of Sophia Loren, the tender brashness of Barbra Streisand. Actually, the screen has shown many excellent jobs of acting, but the many brilliant films with little or no acting make us wonder why or how a film actor should be trained.

Cinema experts have repeatedly declared that the star system is gone. Especially in the late 1960s, a huge new generation of young moviegoers showed less interest in films created for established stars than in vivid, fast-cut, unconventional films like *Bonnie and Clyde, The Graduate, Easy Rider,* and *Last Summer,* in which there were bizarre turns of plot, shocking episodes, interesting photography, and mostly unfamiliar faces. Yet the independent young audience often creates its own stars. Dustin Hoffman rose to stardom because of his success in *The Graduate,* and the young audience, enjoying the brilliant short role of the Southern lawyer that Jack Nicholson played in *Easy Rider,* eagerly waited to see him again. The interest in Dustin Hoffman may not be as frantic as the worship of James Dean by an earlier generation, but the need for a dream figure of lonely, misunderstood youth seems as great as ever. The theatre once furnished dream images for a small audience. The group excitement is far greater when a mass medium creates a dream image for a nation-wide audience.

But whether the audience is large or small, seeing a play on a screen or on a stage, the actor is an arresting personality to be enjoyed, admired, and applauded.

Design for the Theatre

10

The design of a production creates an environment for the actor—a pedestal, a showcase, a picture, a machine for acting. It gives the actor form, creating a space in which he can move. It adds color, change, contrast, and mood as it shapes the play in both space and time. As we have seen, the designers of scenery, costume, and lighting must be in on the planning of the production. The locations of entrances and exits and the shaping of playing areas determine the patterns of movement the director can use. The kind of setting and the costume and lighting changes determine how one scene flows into the next and affect the play's rhythmic structure. As much as the playwright or the director, the designers are responsible for the unity of the production.

The Setting

In the nineteenth century, the main function of scenery was to indicate time and place. The painted backdrops, along with the costumes, told the audience they were in ancient, medieval, or modern times, in Spain or China, prince's palace or peasant's kitchen, summer garden or winter snow. No matter whether the mood was comedy or tragedy, satire or fantasy, the designer brought on the stage the results of careful "research." Going to the theatre was as important a way of learning facts as a guided tour through a museum or a social survey of how the other half lived. The historian, the sociologist, the journalist, and the designer were equally interested in presenting local color. The designer used gaily colored landscape backdrops or box sets with realistic detail, according to whether the piece was a romantic opera or a realistic character play. He was glad enough if he created a mood, but mood was a by-product. His first thought was of the actuality of time and place.

The modern designer, in protest, has gone to the other extreme. He insists that design should not be put behind the actors as decoration but should be an integral part of the movement of the play. To indicate time

10-1 Abstract design of platforms and columns. Lunacharski's *Faust and the City.* State Dramatic Theatre, Leningrad.

and place is far less important than to create mood and atmosphere, to shape the movement of the actors, and to give a unifying idea; many modern designs do not indicate place at all but present imaginative, atmospheric abstractions or arrangements of playing ramps, platforms, and steps. In 1899 Adolphe Appia, in one of the most famous theatre books, *Music and the Art of the Theatre*, distinguished the "expressive" from the "symbolizing" functions in a work of art. He said that the symbolizing details that indicate the particular locale should be kept to a minimum—just enough to orient the audience, as a signboard might—in order to allow the expressive functions freer play. By 1919 Kenneth Macgowan had defined the aims of the new stagecraft as simplification, suggestion, and synthesis: simplification to get rid of all Victorian ornament that might distract attention from the actor; suggestion to evoke a mood by simple means—"a single Saracenic arch can do more than a half dozen to summon the passionate background of Spanish *Don Juan*"; and synthesis to create a unity and consistency whereby actor, setting, lights, and action would express the essential inner quality of the play and would change as the play progressed.

In a sense the new ideal means the complete abdication of the designer, for the modern design must not stand out as a beautiful picture. Robert Edmond Jones described the new challenge in an inspired book called *The Dramatic Imagination*.

> A setting is not just a beautiful thing, a collection of beautiful things. It is a presence, a mood, a warm wind fanning the drama to flame. It echoes, it enhances, it animates. It is an expectancy, a foreboding, a tension. It says nothing, but it gives everything. . . . The designer creates an environment in which all noble emotions are possible. Then he retires. The actor enters. If the designer's work has been good, it disappears from our consciousness at that moment. . . . The actor has taken the stage; and the designer's only reward lies in the praise bestowed on the actor.

The Design Format

The first task of the designer is to find a format—a scheme of settings and transitions that will give the play a smooth and meaningful progression from one scene to the next. If, for example, he is to do *Boris Godunov*, an opera of many scenes, he first makes a chart showing which are interior and which exterior scenes; which are Russian and which Polish and what differences the two must show; which are intimate scenes and which crowd scenes; what contrasts must set the palace scenes off from the church and inn scenes; how the crowd can be shown off; how and to what degree the coronation scene should be made a climax to the others. He examines pic-

10-2 Design for unity, mood, and idea. The groups of actors on the steps are dominated by one huge, leaning street lamp. Robert Edmond Jones's drawing of a Berlin production by Leopold Jessner of a play about Napoleon. From Macgowan and Jones, *Continental Stagecraft.*

tures of the architecture and decoration of the period and listens to the music of the opera to catch the mood. He constantly considers how his ideas would work on the stage. If he plans to fly several painted backdrops or sections of wall, he must find out whether the theatre has enough lines to hold these and still leave lines for a few rows of lights. He must decide whether there is enough space at the sides to move more solid structures; whether the same platforms, steps, and ramps can be used in several scenes; whether some small scenes can be set in front of larger scenes that are not moved; whether the format can show a meaningful sequence in the order of the scenes. Should he use a conventional romantic format of painted wings and backdrops or more realistic three-dimensional settings? Or should he borrow a formal structure from some of the classic theatres or use a modern space stage with lights and small movable forms?

The old wing-and-backdrop format was simple. The drops could be lifted up into the flies by ropes and pulleys and the side wings could be slid out in grooves to show another set of drops and wings already in place—a change easily made before the eyes of the audience. The heavy box sets with many realistic details take several minutes to change. Even when the designer has an elevator stage to lift a section or an entire setting up from a lower level or a wagon stage to roll in scenery from the wings, the shift usually means letting the curtain down, a kind of interruption that limits the playwright and the producer to a very few scenes. Most productions with several scenes use some combination of these two formats, making some changes in sight of the audience by raising and lowering drops, turning small turntables, or rolling in small wagon stages and hiding some upstage changes with a curtain or painted drop while another scene is playing in the shallow downstage space. Even so, a change may mean a complete break in the sequence of the show. It is no wonder that designers prefer lighter, more flexible forms that are not only cheaper and easier to construct and to handle than a series of full settings but are also less wearing on the audience.

Epic theatre, as we have seen, demands a format that permits easy flow from one scene to another. Brecht's Mother Courage pulls her ped-

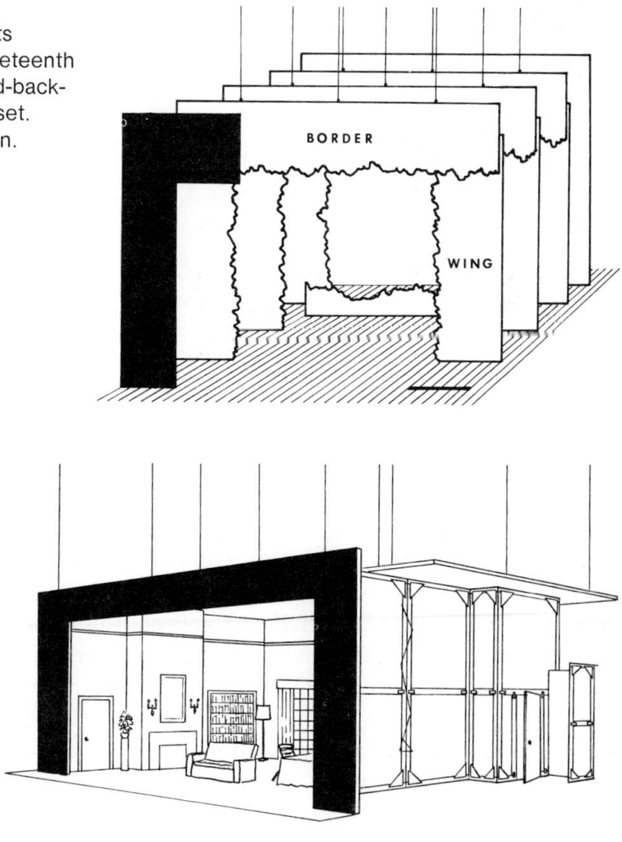

10-3
The two scenic formats inherited from the nineteenth century—the wing-and-back-drop set and the box set. Drawn by Don Creason.

Thunder Rock, 1

Thunder Rock, 2

Thunder Rock, 3

10-4
Three sketches showing the development of a scenic idea from the outside shape to a stage form for actors. Ardrey's *Thunder Rock.* Drawn by Mordecai Gorelik. From John Gassner, *Producing the Play,* rev. ed. Copyright 1941, 1953 by Holt, Rinehart and Winston, Inc. Reproduced by permission.

dler's wagon, like a medieval pageant wagon, on and off the stage as she follows the soldiers of the Thirty Years' War. In *Our Town* the Stage Manager brings on the few suggestive properties needed. For *Death of a Salesman,* Jo Mielziner, the designer, decided not to try to change settings for the thirty-five scenes Miller had written but to borrow from the Elizabethan stage the idea of a permanent symbolic structure at the back, with many small scenes brought onto the forestage. Then he used an expressionistic technique—a painted transparent gauze behind Willy's house and a painted drop behind that, to alternate cool green leaves with threatening brick apartment houses as Willy dreamed of the happy past or felt caught by the ugly present.

Four Methods of Design

There are four ways of creating a design. Sometimes it is obvious which method has been followed, but often a good design looks as if several approaches might have been used at once.

One method is to start with the real place, the full actual scene, and select from it, cut it down, and reshape it for the particular stage, building materials, methods of changing scenery, and moods needed. By leaving off the ceiling and most of the side walls and cutting down the back wall, the designer can suggest a room without overwhelming the actor in naturalistic detail and can create a simple sculptural form that is a welcome change from the splashy backdrops and ponderous box sets inherited from the nineteenth century. A pool of light from spotlights above the stage can concentrate the attention on the actor almost as intensely as a camera close-up. By lighting the cloth or plaster cyclorama at the back of the stage instead of filling out the picture with a painted backdrop or painted walls, the modern designer can show his actor and his streamlined setting against the expanding space and hypnotizing lighting of the sky. As Oliver Smith put it, "Design is principally the elimination of everything which is not absolutely necessary. A beautiful set should be a skeleton allowing air for the other participants of the theatre to breathe in."

A second method is to start with the actors and the few most important events of the play and then add space, platforms, shapes, and voids around them. Mordecai Gorelik tells his students to start with the action of the

10-5 Cut-down setting with wit and fantasy. Hochman's *Margene and the Messiah.* University of Arkansas production, directed by Virgil Baker, designed by Preston Magruder, and costumed by Mary Davis.

play, ignoring locale, season, weather, time of day or night, and time lapses; all that can be put in later. What the actors are doing must come first. He has his students write an outline of the action in two hundred words, then boil the outline down to sixty words, then choose the most important moments of action and draw that action, using stick figures and including props only when they are important—a suitcase if someone is leaving, a boy outside a door with a bouquet of flowers and a box of candy, the girl inside the door. When the student sees clearly what the actors are doing, he can start designing. Norman Bel Geddes was sure that no matter what the nature of the play the designer should disregard any period concept of architecture or locale and think only of abstract "solids and voids." "The voids," he explained, "are spaces where entrances from nowhere to within the sight of the audience can be made," while "the solids are the areas between these voids."

A setting designed with close attention to stage movement is sometimes called a machine for acting. Lee Simonson calls it a plan of action, as important in controlling the movement of the actors as the architect's ground plan for a kitchen or a railway station is in creating and shaping lines of traffic. A design can suggest which relationships are possible and which are not likely to occur. Juliet on her balcony is an object of worship just out of Romeo's reach. Some groups should be completely separated, like a jury set apart by a railing from the others in the courtroom. Other

10-6 Setting as a "machine for acting" in which levels suggest a ship. Coxe and Chapman's *Billy Budd.* University of Minnesota production, directed by David Thompson and designed by Lyle Hendricks.

10-7 Formalism. An architectural screen of large Renaissance arches gives dignity and unity to the play. Slight changes are made behind the arches by letting down simple elements such as leaves for an orchard or a panel for an altar. Shakespeare's *Much Ado About Nothing.* University of Arkansas production, designed and drawn by Don Creason.

groups may be only partly separated, with easy passage up or down steps or between the pieces of furniture that often mark the separation. A row of arches is often used for a ballroom scene to allow small groups to come forward into sharp focus while the dancing continues more quietly behind the arches (Figure 10-7). The Capulets' ball in *Romeo and Juliet* is often staged with such a scene. Or the director may prefer to give full display to the dancers in a large open area, then take most of them offstage or stop the dancing while, in a separate alcove, Romeo whispers his poem to Juliet and takes his kiss.

The ultimate in the machine-for-acting approach was *constructivism,* which was popular among some Russian producers in the 1920s. Using no walls and little or no indication of location, the designer broke the stage floor into different levels with platforms, ramps, steps, and ladders to allow the actors many positions. The supports were frankly exposed, adding the interest of posts, beams, towers, scaffolds, pipes, and guide wires (see Figures 10-8 and 7-6). The constructivist sculptors had led the way in abstract compositions, using wire, string, glass, and metal and borrowing from both mathematics and machine structures. Vsevolod Meierhold, who introduced constructivism into the theatre, brought his lighting instruments into view and even worked out a machinelike, acrobatic approach to acting, which he called biomechanics. He liked to make his props and scenery move, with beds flying through the air and walls sliding, and to have real automobiles and motorcycles run down the aisles, up over the orchestra, and onto the stage. We have Norris Houghton's description in *Moscow Rehearsals* of how a lover expressed his abandonment and joy at a reunion with his love: "Meierhold places the lady at the foot of a tin slide, the lover climbs up a ladder to the top of the slide, zooms down it feet first, knocks the lady off onto the floor, and shouts something that sounds like Russian for 'Whee!'"

Such extremes, useful for satires on the machine age, have not often been seen. Far more popular were the styles called *formalism* and *abstractivism*. Remembering that the Greek, the Elizabethan, and the Chinese classic stages used permanent architectural structures with little or no realistic scenery, designers have turned to modern abstract structures which, with flexible lighting and a few portable cloths and props, can serve for many different scenes. For a number of years Jacques Copeau at the Vieux-Colombier in Paris put on a variety of productions, with slight additions and changes, in a basic architectural form of steps, platform, and upper level. The Festival Theatre in Stratford, Ontario, is now the best-known theatre that uses one architectural structure for all plays.

10-8 Constructivism. A "machine for acting" that emphasizes the machine construction. Setting for Tairov's adaptation of *The Man Who Was Thursday.* From Mordecai Gorelik's *New Theatres for Old.*

10-9 Rugged texture for a revival of a classic. Sophocles' *Electra.* Model of a design by Ming Cho Lee for a production by the Shakespeare Festival Theatre in Central Park, New York City.

A third method of design is to start with the mood of the play, forget the details of actuality, and find the lines, shapes, and colors that will create the mood desired. Of course, both the romantic picture setting and the naturalistic scene sought to create mood, but they did so by borrowing directly the moods of reality—the flowers and clouds of a sunny day, the texture of the slum kitchen. The modern designer wants to make more direct use of the expressive power of line, form, and color.

From the beginning of the century, Gordon Craig called on designers to search for the inner soul of the play. First of all, he wanted a bold shape. It might be a stripped-down abstraction; it might include steps, platforms, and doorways for the actors; it might even include beds, balconies, fountains, and the few properties necessary for the action. But above all, the design must create a single dominant image. In a famous passage in his first book, *On the Art of the Theatre,* he suggested how the designer might go about deciding on a design for *Macbeth:*

> We take *Macbeth*. . . . I see two things. I see a lofty and steep rock, and I see the moist cloud which envelops the head of this rock. That is to say, a place for fierce and warlike men to inhabit, a place for phantoms to nest in. Ultimately this moisture will destroy the rock; ultimately these spirits will destroy the men. Now then, you are quick in your question as to what actually to create for the eye. I answer as swiftly—place there a rock! Let it mount up high. Swiftly I tell you, convey the idea of a mist which hugs the head of this rock. Now, have I departed at all for one eighth of an inch from the vision which I saw in the mind's eye?
>
> But you ask me what form this rock shall take and what color? What are the lines which are the lofty lines, and which are to be seen in any lofty cliff? Go to them, glance but a moment at them: now quickly set them down on your paper; *the lines and their direction*, never mind the cliff. Do not be afraid to let them go high; they cannot go high enough; and remember that on a sheet of paper which is but two inches square you can make a line which seems to tower miles in the air, and you can do the same on the stage, for it is a matter of proportion and nothing to do with actuality.
>
> You ask about the colors? What are the colors that Shakespeare has indicated for us? Do not first look at Nature, but look in the play of the poet. Two; one for the rock, the man; one for the mist, the spirit.

Craig warns of the dangerous attempt to "tell of the moss of the Highlands and of the particular rain which descends in the month of August." But this is no mere picture independent of the actors. He continues, "You have to consider that at the base of this rock swarm the clans of strange earthly forces, and that in the mist hover the spirits innumerable . . . clearly separate from the human and more material beings."

Early in this century, Joseph Urban decided in designing Wagner's *Die Meistersinger* that it was less important to show the whole of Nuremberg with all its Gothic details than to give the impression of joy, of the radiant splendor of sunshine as the people greeted Hans Sachs. The pagan element in *King Lear,* so strong in the imagery and in Lear's oaths and curses, would be reinforced by the setting, designed by Bel Geddes but never used, of an arc of Stonehenge rocks bursting into flames (see Figure 5-6). Different interpretations of Hamlet may be achieved as much by the setting as by the acting. Before dark curtains and shapeless cloths, Hamlet is a lone existentialist wanderer in a nightmare world. Before a throne-tower and a Christian altar, he has ample reason, in his respect for political order and his Christian conscience, for hesitating to murder the king. In the London production of *Waiting for Godot*, the desolate wasteland and the forlorn stick of a tree left the two tramps in an empty universe. In the University of Iowa production, bright-colored puffs of smoke from

10-10 Setting for a mood of brooding conflict. The contrast between the exotic, shadowy foliage and the neat interior creates not only a mood but also a metaphor for the conflict of a princess from Southeast Asia with a New England husband and family. Space-stage forms are enclosed in a proscenium. Anderson's *The Wingless Victory.* University of Illinois production, directed by Ned Donahoe, designed by Warwick Brown, and costumed by Genevieve Richardson.

behind the earth-banks punctuated every pause. That universe was not empty at all: A bright demon was just out of sight, laughing at mankind. Craig, who craved nobility, would not have liked the "confrontation" or "junk sculpture" style of recent years. The rusty stovepipes and wheelbarrow were quite appropriate to Grotowski's production of *Akropolis,* in which old European idealists are confronted with a gas chamber, and musty, decaying, cobweb-covered Gothic arches were effective for the bitter mood of *Rosencrantz and Guildenstern Are Dead;* but some designers like to set up for any play bold structures with the rough textures so sought after by some recent artists, whether or not the play has a bitter or mocking tone.

The fourth method of design is metaphor—scene as idea. The scenic metaphor was an obsession of the expressionists. They not only distorted natural lines to indicate the nightmares of the disturbed mind and to make lines express mood directly, but constantly searched for some symbol, some visual image, to catch the inner meaning of a play. A tree could not just be barren and desolate; it had to look like a skeleton, or, in O'Neill's *Desire Under the Elms,* to let down grasping fingers from brooding heights. For Andreyev's *Life of Man,* Lee Mitchell designed geometrical forms with opening lines for the birth scene and with closing lines for the death scene, while he symbolized the crowning scene of worldly success by a gilt-edged

10-11 Idea and mood in an expressionistic setting. The platform for the confession suggests both a cross and a gallows. The broken fragments of houses suggest anguish and disintegration of personality. The high central figure and the bright light and radiant lines expanding from the center create an exciting release and exaltation. Kaufman's opera *The Scarlet Letter.* Design by C. M. Cristini for an Indiana University production.

screen with a large dollar sign on it. Lee Simonson's *The Stage Is Set* describes two famous productions of *Richard III* in the 1920s.

> I have seen Richard III storm up and down the blood-red stairway provided for him by Jessner and Pirchan at the Berlin State Theatre, but his malignity was as successfully dramatized by Arthur Hopkins and Robert Edmond Jones in New York where a reproduction of the gate at the Bloody Tower backed every scene like a fanged jowl that alternately menaced and devoured. The single background of the prison that was the background of every character's fears and ambitions became as effective a symbol as a single stairway.

Even when the designer does not resort to such an obvious image, he often has some visual metaphor in mind. Albee wanted the setting for *Who's Afraid of Virginia Woolf?* to suggest a cave or a womb, but the designer, William Ritman, created the impression of a cavelike enclosure in a real room. Gorelik describes his own need for a metaphor, whether the audience is conscious of it or not. While telling all the necessary facts of locale and atmosphere, the setting must suggest the essence of the action. Thus, as Gorelik put it:

> The attic bedroom of *The Three Sisters* is not only an attic, not only a bedroom, not only a girls' room, not only a European room, not only a room of the period of 1901, not only a room belonging to the gentlefolk whom Chekhov wrote about. On top of all that, and including all that, it may be, for the designer, the scene of a *raging fever.*

This search for an image of action takes the designer right back to the director's analysis of the basic action of the play. Even when the play requires that the setting and costumes emphasize the period or the local color, the designer can make sure that the appropriate mood is created and the theme clarified. The design becomes much more than a decoration to cover the backstage void or to indicate time and place. It creates mood, style, and metaphor. It must shape the action, reinforce the meaning, and propel the play to its conclusion.

The Costumes

The costumes continue the design into the characterization and movement of the actor. Even if they seem like everyday clothes, they must be given a theatrical flair, a boldness, simplicity, and brightness that can make an impact at a distance. They must create a world of the imagination. Today in the art theatre and the college theatre, the costume shop is a major part of the building, and the design and making of costumes is considered as much a creative art as the writing of the plays or the acting or singing.

The nineteenth-century tradition of costuming, like that of set design, put great emphasis on historical and geographical authenticity. The producer and designer spent great effort in research, and the costume sections of large libraries and of Hollywood studios made large collections of books with pictures and descriptions of the costumes and accessories of all ages and countries. Costume rental houses grew up as every repertory theatre or amateur club or high school production expected to show the audience an authentic costume for King Henry V or for a Palestinian shepherd in the time of Christ. With the same point of view that he held on setting, Craig told us not to try to put a costume museum on the stage but to create imaginative costumes that suggest character. In *On the Art of the Theatre,* he urged:

> Make a barbaric costume for a sly man which has nothing . . . historical and yet is both sly and barbaric. Now make another . . . for a man who is bold and tender. Now make a third for one who is ugly and vindictive . . . it is no easy thing to do. . . . Then go further: attempt to design the clothing for a divine figure and for a demonic figure.

10-12
Theatrical costumes, exaggerated and varied for projection to the audience and for musical-comedy gaiety. *Singing Jailbirds*, New York, 1928. Photo Vandamm.

Even for a historical play like *Henry IV*, Hotspur's costume may tell us that the time is the beginning of the fifteenth century, but still more it must tell us that here is a proud, fiery rebel who despises elegance, subservience, and compromise.

If modern costumes for historical scenes shock us by having too little aesthetic distance, a really authentic costume would distress us by having too much. A good historical costume is a compromise, adapted to the taste of the audience and to their idea of the period. The good designer has always instinctively made that adaptation, and we can tell at a glance whether a medieval dress for the stage was made for an audience that wore bustles or bell-bottoms.

In planning the costumes, the designer is aware of five things costuming can do: It can enhance the actor, create the character, set the style, tie the individual into the scheme of characters, and show the progress of the play.

Just as the scene designer starts with the moving actor and the stage space, creating the areas, levels, and shapes that enhance the action, so the costume designer starts with the moving actor and the costume material, creating new shapes, colors, and movements that enhance the actor. Material may be fitted or draped. Some dancers' costumes are entirely fitted, with color and texture but with nothing added to the shape, allowing the movement of the body to be seen in its simplest form. Most Greek and Roman costumes were entirely draped, as are some ceremonial robes today. But more often the designer combines fitting and draping: a tight bodice leading into a flowing skirt, a tight upper arm leading into a flowing sleeve, a fitted body partly covered by a cape, arms and legs partly seen between the panels of sleeves and skirts. An accent such as a belt, a band, or a ruffle is most interesting at the transition from a fitted to a draped section. Accents sometimes mark the joints of the body, especially the shoulders and sometimes the hips, but, except for comic effects, not the elbows and knees.

Whether fitted or flowing, with accent or accessory, the costume transforms the appearance, the movement, and indeed the soul of the actor. An actor in his underwear or a dancer in a leotard is a very different person from a performer in makeup and costume. A warrior in plumes and war paint and a chieftain in mask and ceremonial decorations take on roles already shaped by the design. In Brecht's *Galileo,* the Pope receives the scientist in his dressing chamber with sympathy and understanding. But as the attendants dress him, adding robe after robe, he is transformed into an official representative of the Church, with a very different attitude.

Psychologically the costume is very important. Looking in a mirror, the actor gets a vision of what he is supposed to be; he must live up to that vision. Some directors say that in many situations no makeup is needed.

10-13
Costume for characterization. A draped ceremonial costume turns the soldier Joan of Arc into a more dignified leader at the coronation, yet the scallops suggest vulnerability. The king's long cloak and fur cape and his sceptre and crown are a little too large, suggesting that he is scarcely equal to the position. Anouilh's *The Lark.* University of Texas production, directed by Francis Hodge, designed by John Rothgeb, and costumed by Lucy Barton.

10-14
Comic costumes using the sturdy, rough texture of canvas as a unifying element throughout the production. Shakespeare's *The Taming of the Shrew.* University of Washington production, designed by John Ashby Conway and costumed by Lucy Barton.

But what actor would be willing to plunge into a role without watching himself transformed into a different being as he puts on his costume and makeup? Dance teachers find that a mask is a stimulation to a dancer, giving him a vision of the character he is to create in movement. In sophisticated society an impersonal mask is worn at a ball to hide the identity, but in primitive societies a mask is the embodiment of identity. Like a primitive tribesman, the actor must put on his *persona,* or mask, before he can become the personality to play his role.

In movement the actor soon learns why the designer gave him a cape or a long sleeve. As he turns his shoulders, lifts his elbow, or raises his arm, the cape or sleeve sweeps on beyond, extending the movement and accenting it. The longer and heavier the cape, the slower the sweep. That extra material is not a hindrance but a tool he can use if he learns its feeling and makes the costume act. At the end of a speech he can swing the cape across his body with an impressive gesture of finality as he turns to walk away. The actress learns to give her full skirt a swing that expresses the character and just what she is thinking. A cane, a pipe, or an umbrella in the hand becomes a telling extension of the personality, and no one has exhausted the possibilities of the fan for indicating changes of thought or feeling.

If the costume makes the actor, it is no less true that the actor makes the costume. No amount of beautiful fabric or dashing style can affect the audience until the actor feels and projects the beauty and the dash.

But the costume designer not only enhances the actor, he creates the character. The costume must tell the audience at a glance if the character is young or old, rich or poor, doctor, beggar, or thief, brassy barmaid or kind old grandmother, if he is arriving from a cold journey or off to play tennis in the sun. It can show character change. The shabby, hard-working clerk of the first act becomes a well-dressed corporation president in the second. The eager girl in her plain school clothes and simple makeup blossoms into an elegant society leader with chic evening clothes and sophisticated hairdo. The dashing young spendthrift becomes a drunkard in untidy clothes. The costume may characterize by not fitting. The king's garments on Macbeth "hang loose about him like a giant's robe upon a dwarfish thief." Not only the traditional insignia—the king's crown, the bishop's mitre, the priest's collar, the scholar's dark-rimmed glasses—but the whole range of caps, canes, fans, gloves, and other accessories indicate immediately who the character is or what impression he is trying to make. The little man in a plain costume bursts forth proudly with a new hat, or Cinderella wears rough, itchy stockings with her unaccustomed new clothes—who can say how much is suggested by costume and how much by the pantomime of the actor?

The third function of costuming is to help establish the spirit and style of the play. Costume can add dignity to tragedy, charm to romance, and playful variety to light comedy. The designer can learn as much about the style of a period from an artist as from a history book—for instance, from Watteau's soft, satin-clad aristocrats in gentle landscapes or from Hogarth's robust, comic caricatures of boorish types.

Selection is a very powerful means of creating style. To limit the color scheme for the entire cast to pastels, to earth colors, to two or three primary colors, or to black and white makes a strong, unified impression. A variety of heavy, dull textures, or of shiny taffetas and satins, creates a particular feeling and style while allowing for considerable adaptation to individual characters.

Sharp contrast is startlingly comic. That is why stripes and bright spots are so often used in comedy. Incongruity is even more comic: the small vertical hat over the big round face, the sleeve or cape that is too small or too large, out of proportion to the rest of the costume, the color or texture that does not match. The costumer may emphasize the peculiarities of the character—the fat stomach of Sir Toby Belch and the thin lines of his companion, Sir Andrew Aguecheek—or he may accent an awkward place, such as an elbow or a knee. Droopy, baggy, and floppy parts of the costume are as comic as a limp wrist, a sagging chin, or a defeated gesture.

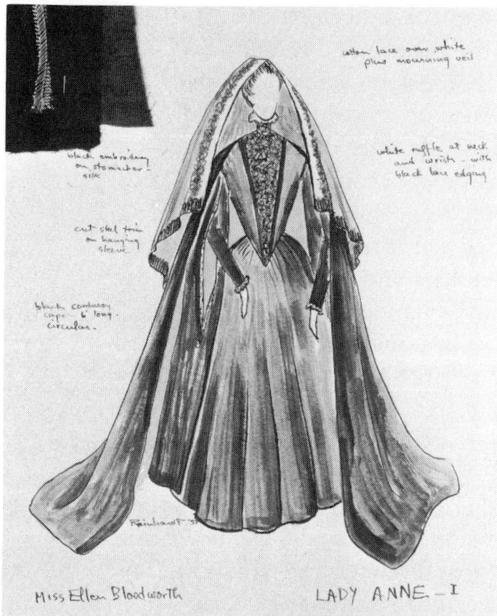

10-15 Two costumes for women in mourning. The costumes are based on the same period, but one is designed for tragedy and one for romantic comedy. Soft flowing lines and heavy corduroy material convey the dignity and sorrow of Lady Anne in Shakespeare's *Richard III,* while the shiny taffeta bodice and skirt, the crisp glittering sleeves, and the low decolletage suggest that bright energy is more important than mourning for Lady Olivia in Shakespeare's *Twelfth Night.* Designs by Paul Reinhardt.

The fourth consideration of the costume designer is the scheme of the characters. The costumes must give harmony to the picture by a unified color scheme and must be closely related to the setting yet stand out from the background. The costumes must look good together, and they must be so planned that in large scenes the colors are well distributed. Yet the costumes must control the spread of attention, indicating which are subordinate characters and which important, and must make many fine distinctions within the overall picture.

The designer can do more than the actor or director in making clear how the characters line up in loyalty or opposition, in similarities and differences. The scheme is simple in *Romeo and Juliet,* where the feud sets two groups apart. The audience should know at a glance who belongs to each group; Mercutio should be in a mixed costume and the friar and the prince should be seen to be completely above the quarrel. Some designers use two quite different colors for the two sides. Similarly, in the back-and-forth fighting in *Macbeth,* it is important to know at a glance who is fighting for Macbeth and who for Macduff. *King Lear* is more complex. Not only are there two families—the king's and Gloucester's—but there are good and bad children in each family. Lear's two wicked, flattering daughters are united against the honest, plain-spoken Cordelia. The costumes can make that clear even if the designer does not go quite as far as a Munich production in which the wicked daughters were in identical scarlet dresses and Cordelia was in pure white. The costumes of the servants reflect the same opposition between flattery and honesty. Lear's plain-speaking servant (Kent in disguise) is plainly dressed and Goneril's sycophantic servant, Oswald, is elegantly dressed. In any play the characters must be vivid enough to stand out from the environment, but those who are at home will be in close harmony with it and with one another, while intruders will be set apart. If a son brings a noisy girl into a dignified home, the costume should signal the conflict as she enters. In the next act the costumes and setting should indicate immediately whether the environment has changed her or she has changed it.

The fifth approach to costume design concerns the progression, the change and development in the course of the play. Katherine in *The Taming of the Shrew* is transformed from a high-tempered, aristocratic girl to a disheveled, almost defeated wife and then to a gracious, compliant wife who is knowing in her gesture of obedience. Her costumes should show the changes; at the end they should be softer and more matronly but still have some lines and colors of assertion and self-reliance. Sometimes the tone of the play must change when it is impossible to change the set. Carnival hats and streamers at a party can quickly add gaiety, while putting on or merely closing and buttoning dark raincoats can cover and dampen the previous brightness.

Like the setting, the costume should be more than charming or spectacular decoration, more than style and mood. As an instrument for each actor to play on, it becomes part of the action. The costuming helps organize and clarify the group on stage.

The Lighting

> Now the dark stage begins to burn and glow under our fingers, burning like the embers of the forge of Vulcan, and shafts of light stab through the darkness, and shadows leap and shudder, and we are in the regions where splendor and terror move.
>
> Robert Edmond Jones, *The Dramatic Imagination*

10-16 Space stage within a proscenium frame. Three beams of light make a light pool on a pyramid of steps. Space is defined by light and actors. A sketch by Robert Edmond Jones of a Berlin production of Toller's *Man and the Masses.* From Macgowan and Jones, *Continental Stagecraft.*

The audience is held spellbound as the house lights go down, the curtain disappears, and the lights bring form out of nothingness. Both the actor and the setting emerge in bold relief, creating highlights and shadows in the controlled, plastic light of the spotlights. Then, as the action moves from one part of the stage to another, the light gets stronger at the point of action and the rest of the stage recedes into the margin of attention. Lighting, even more than setting, shapes the action and exerts a hypnotic control over the interest and emotions of the audience. As Norman Bel Geddes described it, "Good lighting adds space, depth, mood, mystery, parody, contrast, change of emotion, intimacy, fear."

In theatrical lighting, the age of electricity can boast of its superiority to all other ages. While the Greeks and the Elizabethans used the open sky and most medieval performances took place in the daytime, many kings and princes knew the impressive effect of a processional entry into a city at night, with torches and pageants sparkling with lights. When the Renaissance princes created the first modern stages in their palace ballrooms, they started a tradition of bright chandeliers for the well-dressed audiences, bright chandeliers for the actors, and lights behind the scenery for stunning effects of moving clouds and sunrises and sunsets.

Gas lights, introduced at the beginning of the nineteenth century, concentrated much brighter light on the stage and permitted some degree of control because the footlights, the border lights above the actors, and the house lights could be turned down separately. But still stage lighting consisted of the flat general glare from long rows of open flames. Only when the limelight and the carbon electric arc were introduced in the middle of the century was it possible to concentrate a strong light in a narrow space by the use of a lens. When it was discovered that a piece of calcium or lime heated to incandescence in a gas flame produces a very strong, concentrated light,

10-17 The lighting control board under the front of the stage at the Paris opera. The prompter's box is set in the footlights. The border lights are open striplights with bulbs substituted for the earlier gas flames. From *L'Illustration*, June 18, 1887.

in the limelight became a new term in the English language. Even brighter is the light from the spark that arcs between two rods of carbon when a strong electric current is sent across the gap. If a metal box is placed around that arc with a lens at the end, it will send down a bright spot to make one or two actors stand out from all the rest. This "follow spot" is still sometimes used for specialty numbers in a revue, though it is rather crude in comparison with the subtle equipment possible today.

It was with the invention of the incandescent lamp in 1879 that the real development of modern lighting began. The incandescent lamp is safe and noiseless, available in many sizes, and easily controlled by a dimmer. The filament is so concentrated that a spherical or ellipsoidal reflector and a lens create a pool of directional, not diffused, light. It is easy to put a sheet of colored gelatin, acetate, or glass in front of the lens. Today light has shape, direction, and color and can easily be changed from bright to dim.

Light not only gives the actor and setting shape but also gives the picture a new dimension in time. By the end of the century, London and New York were being impressed by the changing moods of twilight, sunset, moonlight, and dawn of Sir Henry Irving's Shakespeare and David Belasco's ultrarealistic, sensational scenes of the Wild West, exotic foreign lands, and city slums. Important developments in the last several decades have provided smaller instruments with more powerful sources of light. In the 1930s the reflector lamp was invented, a light that has the whole spotlight—reflector, lens, and filament—built into the bulb. Too small for the main lighting of a large stage, it is extremely useful in smaller areas, and it is the main instrument for window displays and most architectural and landscape lighting. More recently the quartz lamp, which produces a very intense light from a concentrated source, has increased the flexibility of both stage and outdoor lighting.

The great prophet of the new art of lighting was Adolphe Appia, whose *Music and the Art of the Theatre* has been invaluable to stage designers. He might have called it *The Music of Light*, for light was the new element to express the soul of the drama that was so well created in Wagner's music but impossible to express with the painted backdrops and flat lighting of the nineteenth century. "Light is to production," Appia wrote, "what music is to the score: the expressive element in opposition to the literal signs; and, like music, light can express only what belongs to 'the inner essence of all vision.'" The new use of light meant a radically new approach to the plastic form of the stage. Instead of drawing the third dimension on the backdrop, Appia wanted to set his actor moving in three dimensions on ramps and platforms and to create the third dimension by catching both the actor and the plastic setting in highlights and shadows. That required sculptural forms with very little painted detail and little color; the form, the intensity, and even the color were to be created by the mobile, focused light.

10-18 The same scene in work lights and in stage lights. What is dull and flat in diffused general light takes on life and form under spotlights. Marlowe's *Dr. Faustus.* Indiana University production, designed and costumed by Richard L. Scammon and lighted by Gary Gaiser.

Appia made the first analysis of the kinds of light to be derived from the different instruments. He defined the basic difference between "general" and "specific" lighting, or "diffused light" and "living light," in the four kinds of lights and lighting:

1. The fixed border lights, which light the painted flats, supplemented in the wings and on the stage floor by the movable striplights.
2. The "footlights," that peculiar monstrosity of our theatres, designed to light both the scenery and the actors from in front and below.
3. Spotlights that throw focused beams of light on playing areas or projections on flat screens.
4. Light within the settings, that is, light intended to reveal the transparent parts of the setting by lighting from behind.

The third type, which Appia called "living light," was most important, for it could create form-giving shadows. The first two, giving general or diffused light, could have only a subordinate function, that of softening and blending the sharp contrasts of the living light.

To create and control this dynamic, revealing light, the lighting designer works out a *light plot*, a chart of the placement of all the lights and a list of all the changes. The light plot is actually a complete lighting score comparable to the musical score or the text of the play. This section describes how the lighting is set up for a proscenium stage; the special problems of open-stage forms are considered in Chapter 11.

The spotlights are planned first. Since the general lighting will be only supplementary, consisting of striplights used mainly for blending and for lighting the background and the cyclorama, the main lighting will be by spots—spots from the bridge or from a pipe just behind the curtain and spots from the beams in the auditorium. Since evenly diffused lighting would take away shadows and hence form, the spotlights are not spread everywhere but grouped to form pools of light. The stage is divided into areas, either the six playing areas defined by the director or whatever areas the setting suggests. Usually two spotlights are focused on each area, aimed from the two sides about ninety degrees apart and casting light down at an "angle of throw" of about forty-five degrees. Each side of an actor's face will get some shadowing, but not too much. If one light is stronger than the other, or, better yet, if one is of a warm color and the other cool, the plastic effect will be richer.

Sidelights and backlights are used for special effects. Light from the side or from straight above gives very sharp shadows, far too strong for most realistic scenes unless subtly blended with some front lighting. Back lighting, from above but from upstage of the actors, adds a highlight on head and shoulders, a halo effect frequently used in television lighting to make an actor stand out from a dark background. For most plays only the more

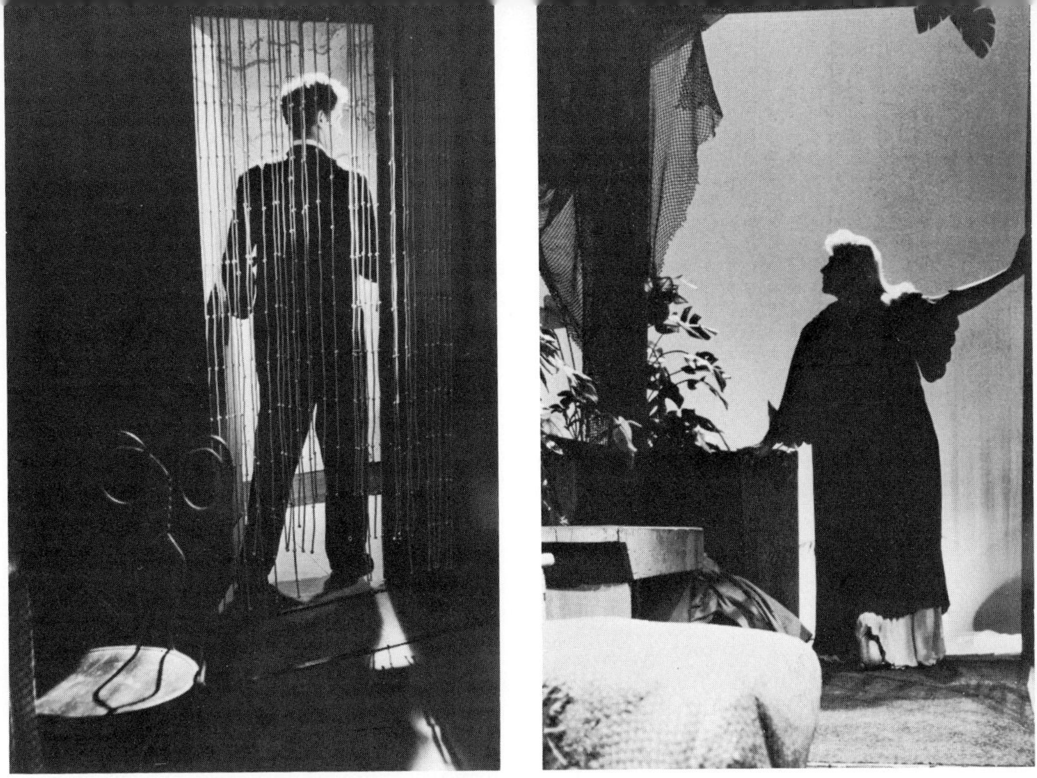

10-19 Back lighting in two consecutive, related scenes. A strong light from above and upstage of the actors catches the top of their heads and shoulders with a halo effect, while they are left dark enough to be silhouetted against a bright background. *Rain*, from a story by Maugham. University of Wyoming production, directed and designed by Richard L. Scammon, lighted by Scammon and Soller, and costumed by Charles Parker.

subtle tints of colors are used: fresh pinks and very light ambers if the scene is warm and sunny, lavender or light blue if a colder mood is needed. But for dance and for less realistic plays, strong colors and sharp angles of throw from the sides, which produce extreme shadows, can give excitement.

General illumination for the cyclorama usually comes from standard strips both above and below, wired in three circuits. In lighting, the three primary colors that mix together to produce other colors are not the red, yellow, and blue of the painter but red, green, and blue. Dimming these three colors up or down will produce almost any sky effect, from night to sunrise to daylight to fire, as well as all the unnatural colors of red and purple.

Appia's fourth kind of lighting, from inside the setting itself, has had very little use in the theatre so far, though it has long been used for commercial signs and juke boxes that glow from within. Architects have begun making use of it to illuminate buildings at night; more exciting than general illumination from floodlights is the effect produced when a building is treated like a piece of sculpture, with sequences of dark and lighted spaces set against the darkness through the use of luminescent panels and alcoves and ledges lighted from hidden sources. The theatre has the same opportunity. Not all the light has to come from far above the stage area. In an age of transistors, of miniature control and illumination units, and of three-dimensional sculptural forms on the stage, a revolutionary, very exciting lighting could be built into the setting.

The nerve center of the lighting is the switchboard that controls the dimmers. The early kind of dimmer was the resistance dimmer, a long handle that pulled the contacts around a heavy plate-shaped coil to put more resistance into the circuit. The early dimmer board might occupy a whole wall and need several strong-armed workers to manipulate, though master handles and large master dimmers were developed so that several circuits could be dimmed together by one handle. Basic and dependable, the resistance dimmer is still used in many places. But many new systems have been invented, each making the last seem old-fashioned and clumsy. The auto-transformer, especially a neat model called the Variac, was the rage in the 1930s. Then electronic systems of control captured the interest of designers. But they now seem enormous, clumsy, and very expensive in comparison to the small silicon-controlled rectifier invented in the late 1950s. Since the designer has available small, sensitive dimmers and small spotlight lamps, each with its own reflector built into the bulb, it has become common practice to supplement the large spotlights with numerous sources of light around the stage, with many circuits, all controlled from one console smaller than an organ console. At this board an expert operator follows the light plot and at each cue moves small levers or punches small buttons that control a number of changes. If the board is even further automated, he puts a punched IBM card in a slot which, at the right cue, may bring one set of lights up fast, one set down fast, and other sets up or down at different speeds. Most lighting designers feel that the human element must never be lost, however, and that the man at the switchboard must make fine, intuitive adjustments as he watches the play, so the switchboard should be located where the operator can see the entire stage.

Like setting and costuming, lighting is an integral part of the play, serving many functions. It highlights the center of action and subordinates the less important areas. It reveals form, giving plasticity to each actor and each background structure and shaping the playing areas to reinforce the composition of the director. It not only suggests local color and time of day but also creates mood through color, intensity, shape, and angle. Perhaps most important of all, dynamic changes of light do as much as the dialogue, the plot, the actors' movement, and the incidental music and sound to propel the play to its goal.

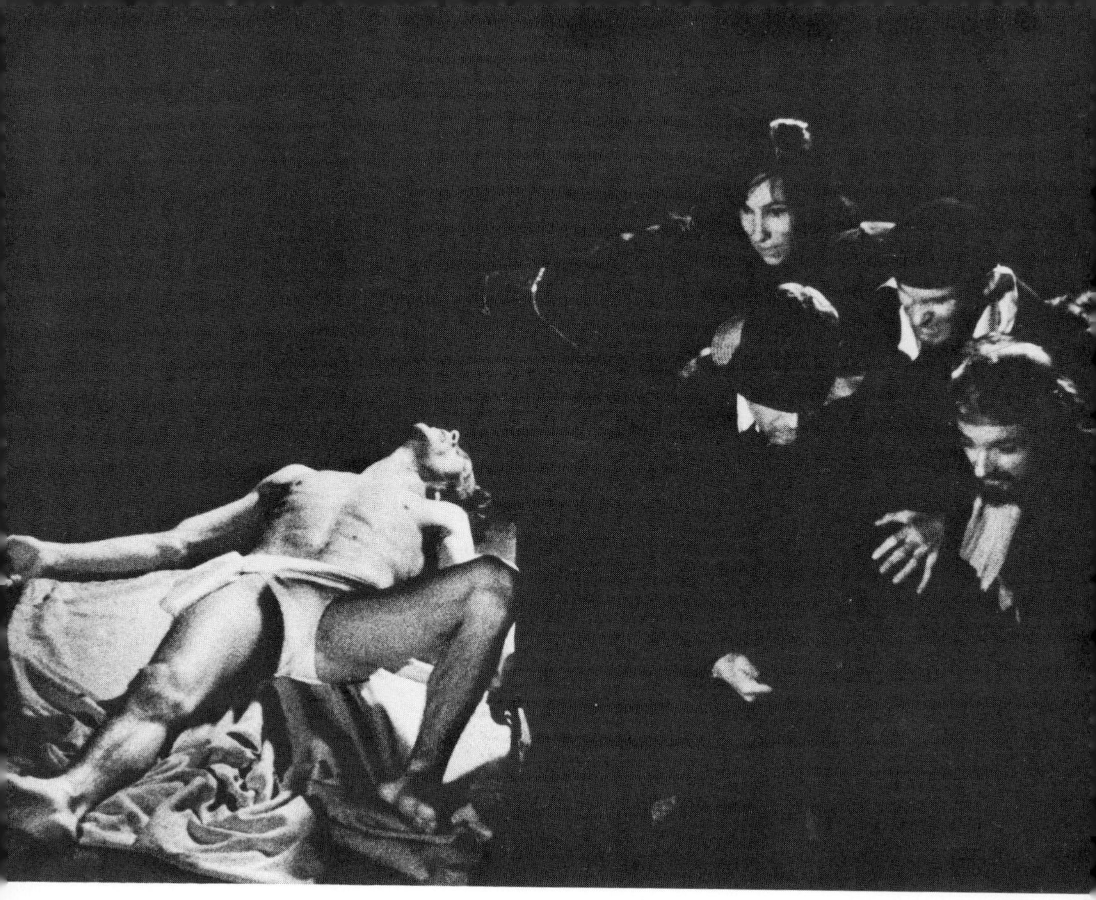

New Forms of Theatre

11

A theatre of controlled light and of carefully designed space was far from the prevailing ideal at the beginning of this century, when the theatre was supposed to reproduce either the objective real world or the romantic dream world. Then scene designers, taking seriously the ideas about space of the two great prophets, Appia and Craig, took the first steps toward a new form of theatre, and a number of other craftsmen of the theatre followed. Appia and Craig also called for new approaches to acting, through dance and music, but their call fell on deaf ears, for realistic acting was new and impressive and not until the 1960s did actors consider any other approach. We have already noted how realism, especially epic realism, and the musical had moved far beyond simple reality and romance by the middle of this century and were approaching a total theatre that could use symbols of reality with Oriental freedom.

In the 1970s it is possible to see how a number of strands that have been created separately are leading toward the same goal of total theatre. So we must trace not only new forms of stage and auditorium but also new forms of poetic drama, religious drama, and dance theatre, and note how separate experiments over several decades can now be brought into closer relationship.

The total theatre we dream of cannot be achieved just by combining poetry, dance, and new space; it involves stripping down old forms in order to get at a core of basic principles. In his reform of acting, Stanislavsky reached the honest feelings and integrity of the actor by stripping away the old techniques of showing off to the audience. But the naturalism Stanislavsky worked for not only omitted a close relationship to the audience, which seems necessary to most theatres, but also omitted poetry, dance, celebration, religion, and metaphysics. The kind of simplification that Craig and Appia called for was as opposed to the realistic acting and absorption in everyday properties of the realistic theatre as it was to the painted backdrops of the romantic stage. The first successful reform was in the use of space, and the new principles were only much later applied to the poetic word and to acting and dance.

New Space

Gordon Craig was the best-known prophet of the new space: He had a flair for publicity and his writings and sketches for stage settings, first published in 1905 and 1911, were soon known in Europe and America. This English dreamer, son of the actress Ellen Terry and for a while an actor with his mother and Henry Irving, promised the birth of a new theatre of simple, noble shapes, of musical movement, of imagination and inspiration, to replace the peephole, literal theatre of the day. He called for design to "create an atmosphere, not a locality," and his sketches showed bold, elementary forms in steps, platforms, towering doors, and sheer cliffs—all simple, stripped of decoration.

The other prophet of new space, the Swiss Adolphe Appia, was known to only a few people, but his writings and creative work have reshaped the modern theatre even more radically than Craig's. An ardent admirer of the music drama of Wagner, he wanted to free the actor from the dead, unchanging, flat painted scenery just as Wagner had freed him from the set series of arias of Italian opera. Appia saw that the actor needed "living" space to move in: a floor broken and varied by platforms, steps, and ramps, and three-dimensional vertical elements—screens, cubes, towers. "Living" light, which was described in Chapter 10, was the blending medium to add color and form to the setting and to make both actor and setting change in intensity. The cyclorama was lighted separately, suggesting the freedom of infinity, but in front of it the sculptural forms and the pools of light defined a new space stage for the drama.

The *space stage* was developed within the traditional proscenium arch, sometimes with a specially designed inner proscenium to frame the cyclorama and hide the equipment that sent down the pools of light. But once the space was established as complete in itself and independent of the proscenium picture, it was easy to accept the idea of a space stage outside the proscenium, in the middle of the audience as an arena stage or theatre-in-the-round or on the stage apron with the audience only partly surrounding it. Light had freed the theatre from its dependence on the proscenium frame—the most radical change in theatre form since the sixteenth century.

A space stage usually has several acting levels, to which may be added simple scenic pieces, either abstract or barely suggestive of reality, that are lightweight enough to be brought on by hand or let down from above. It is seen in its simplest form in the sketch by Robert Edmond Jones of a Berlin production of *Man and the Masses*, which shows a lone woman and the huddled mass caught in pools of light (Figure 10-16). Two other examples can be seen in the pictures of a production of *Lamp at Midnight* at Brigham Young University (Figure 11-1). In one an informal group on several levels is kneeling to authority; a heraldic symbol hanging above them reinforces the theme without reference to a particular place. In the other, the steps are arranged in more formal symmetry while metal grilles, one small arch, and praying figures create the atmosphere of a church. The steps may be thought of either as in the particular church or as somewhere else but suggestive of the church in general.

The space stage is a happy solution for the revival of old plays. In using modern lighting and sculptural forms it is more dynamic than any supposedly authentic reproduction of the stages for which the plays were written, yet not so heavy as a series of realistic settings would be. A space-stage setting for *Antony and Cleopatra* may achieve the panoramic sweep of Elizabethan staging, with several levels and playing areas, but at the same time, in its shape and decoration, suggest Egypt rather than the Elizabethan period and, in its simplicity and dynamic lighting, please modern taste. For *Othello*, Robert Edmond Jones designed a splendid Renaissance screen which, with a few changes, suggested a Venetian throne room, a street, or a bedroom.

11-1 Space stage in a proscenium theatre. Two scenes show how changes are made by rearranging the step units, letting down a heraldic symbol, and bringing on a grille and arch. A large cyclorama for mood lighting is framed by formal elements at the sides and above. Stavis' *Lamp at Midnight.* Brigham Young University production, directed by Harold Hansen, designed by Charles Henson, and costumed by Beverly Warner.

For Molière and Restoration comedy, designers in the early twentieth century liked to use an antiquarian reproduction of the apron-proscenium stage, with footlights and chandeliers, an inner proscenium with formal doors, and, on the inner stage, wings that slid out and a backdrop that rose out of sight to disclose the next setting. But present-day designers have caught as much of the period charm in free-standing screens shaped and decorated to suggest the period, set against the sky or in front of a draped curtain.

The triumph of the space stage is the scenic projection. Instead of lighting the cyclorama to show the vast space of the empty sky, the designer may use the large cyclorama or a smaller reflecting screen as a backing for a projected photograph or image. The projection light, or a simple projection box with a strong light behind a piece of transparent plastic, may be hidden above or below, either in front of the screen or, if the screen is translucent, behind it. The image can fade in or fade out and can be changed as

11-2 Projection of a shadow design as a background for dancers. A lighting demonstration at Yale University.

11-3 Realistic background projected on a screen. *The Dream and the Deed,* a civic pageant-drama of Seattle, designed by John Ashby Conway.

quickly as the piece of plastic on which it is drawn can be slid out or in or the current for another projection box turned on. The image may be a simple, decorative shadow, or it may be a bizarre fantasy. The projection may even be very realistic, as in the Seattle street scene shown in Figure 11-3, where the building seems to be just behind the men on the platform. Yet the projection, by being obviously a picture and not actuality, may easily serve as an ideogram or symbol. Such symbolism is familiar in television; for instance, a picture of the White House may be projected on a screen in the broadcast studio behind a newscaster speaking about White House news. The plain unit setting of the rock musical *Your Own Thing* (1968) had a half-dozen flat surfaces for projection, and all through the play paintings, cartoons, or photographs of well-known people were shown, accompanied by voices or other sounds on a sound track making a comic comment on the action.

Once the space stage has been accepted, the standard theatre seems obsolete. If a pool of light can begin a scene by bringing form out of darkness and end it with a blackout or fade-out, there is no need for a front curtain. If the pool of light can define the edge of the playing area, a box set needs no ceiling and no side walls but only enough of a wall to suggest the place or to provide the doors, pictures, and furniture essential to the action. If there is neither painted landscape nor realistic wall to be lifted out of sight into the flies but only light sculptural pieces, there is no need for vast space above the stage or for elaborate machinery of ropes and pulleys, fly lines and counterweights. Even the cyclorama is changing in form and function. As the action is brought forward in free space, the sky can be indicated by a pool of light on the wall or seen as a free-standing sectioned screen.

It is no wonder that theatres now being built differ widely from the traditional theatre with its picture-frame stage. The advocates of new theatre forms point out that most of the great theatres of the past had open stages, not overwhelmed with scenery, offering the actor an easy relationship with the audience. Even for the first two centuries of the picture stage, the actor came forward on an apron and the scenery was kept back on an inner stage as symbol rather than as enclosing prison.

In the *arena stage*, or *theatre-in-the-round*, the audience sits all around the playing area, almost close enough to touch the actors. Glenn Hughes, who started the movement in college theatres in the early 1930s, planned his arena stage primarily for drawing-room comedy, with only three rows of seats—170 in all—and a playing area little larger than a 12-by-18-foot rug. For most plays he used different arrangements of one specially built set of light-colored, low-backed sofas and chairs. Others have used the form with much larger audiences and with almost all kinds of plays. Margo Jones, who in the 1950s ran a professional theatre-in-the-round in Dallas, thought the only type of drama not suited to it would be scenes of violence and horror that would unnerve an audience sitting so close to the actors. Her theatre seated only 198, with a playing stage of 20-by-24 feet. But the splendid Arena Stage in Washington has a stage 30-by-36 feet and seats 752 in eight steeply banked rows. The Lambertville Music Circus in New Jersey seats 1,300, and Casa Mañana, the music circus in Fort Worth, seats 1,832 under its aluminum dome.

There are special problems in producing in the round. With the audience on all sides, the actor always has his back to one part of the audience. It is as hard for him to project his voice behind him as to project it in the larger, standard theatre. The arena theatre is not a place for whispers. To control attention and make sure that all parts of the audience have either a speaker or an important listener to watch, each actor moves about a great deal, often "making the rounds," going in toward the center on one spoke of an imaginary wheel and out toward the audience on another. In realistic plays it helps to have furniture with usable props both near the center and at the outer edge. For large groups it is useful to have different floor levels on the playing area, with important people stepping to the top.

More scenic decoration is possible in theatre-in-the-round than might be guessed. Columns, arches, pavilions, and other light outline forms can be used in the center and still allow action to be seen. At the corners there may even be rather realistic walls, windows, and doors, if they are indispensable to the action. Built-up levels in the center are possibilities only a few designers have yet explored, and the Arena Stage in Washington has trap doors in the floor for trenches, openings, entrances, or even an orchestra pit. (See Figures 11-4 and 11-5.)

Various methods have been used for opening and closing the scene on the arena stage. To bring actors on in the dark as if by magic and have the lights go up suddenly seemed very important to Glenn Hughes, but others have found that nine times out of ten a little rewriting will make the scene begin with an entrance and end with an exit. Audiences also accept easily the convention of low lighting for the actors to get into position and full lighting for the action to begin.

11-4 Arena staging with the rich texture of local color suggested by fragments of scenery. A small-town yard and back porch are suggested by the flowers and the low board fence built into one corner. The steps and platform give a variety of levels. Inge's *Picnic.* Eastern Illinois University production, directed by E. G. Gabbard and designed by John E. Bielenberg.

11-5 A well-equipped, fairly large arena theatre seating 752 in steeply banked rows. The Arena Stage, Washington, D.C.

The exciting new theatres of the last two decades have used a form somewhere between the arena and the proscenium stage, called variously *thrust, open, apron,* or *three-quarter-round.* Like the arena, the *open stage* can bring a large number of spectators fairly close to the actors, with the acoustical advantage of having the actors and audience in the same room. It too offers the economy of building and operating a stage without heavy scenery, but it permits much more interesting effects of scenery, grouping, and lighting than the arena.

To read Tyrone Guthrie's book, *My Life in the Theatre,* is to follow a prophet who has caught a glimpse of a distant goal. The vision that gradually came to Guthrie was the open stage. In his years as director of the Old Vic in London and as visiting director for many theatres over the world, he was vaguely feeling for a form more open than the proscenium theatre. His crucial experience was the discovery in Edinburgh of the Presbyterian Assembly Hall, a room with seats and balconies on four sides of a central platform, much like the Elizabethan theatre. There he produced a late medieval Scottish morality play, *The Satire of the Three Estates* (Figure 11-7), closing one side of the room for stage entrances and background. The re-

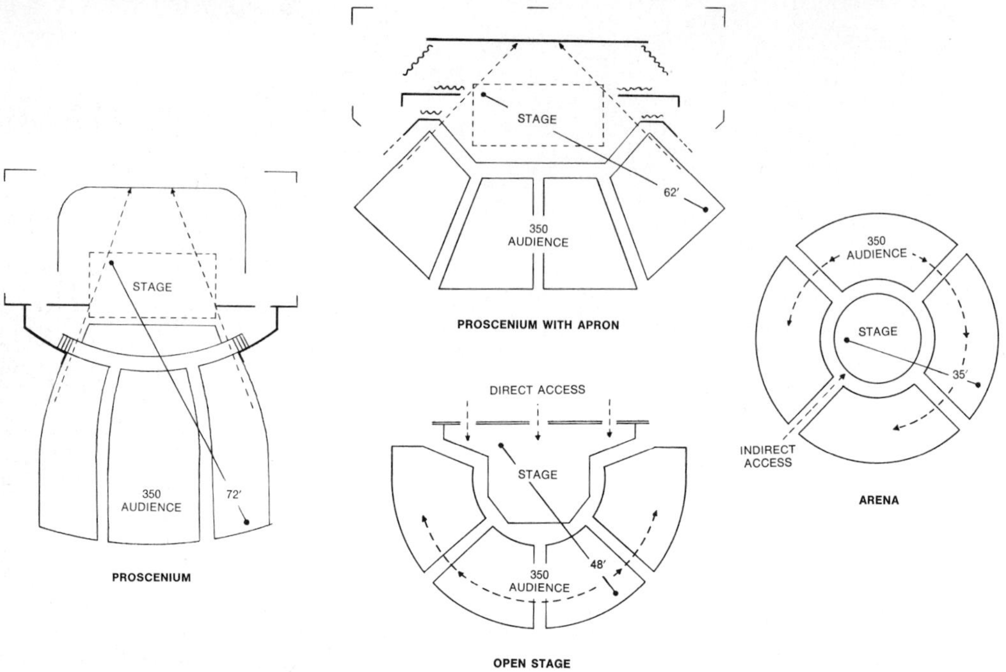

11-6 Ground plans showing the relative distance of the last row of an audience of 350 from the actor in four kinds of theatre—regular proscenium, proscenium with apron, thrust or open stage, and arena. Drawn by Don Creason after a drawing by James Hull Miller.

11-7 Open stage in the Presbyterian Assembly Hall, Edinburgh. Lindsay's *The Satire of the Three Estates.* Edinburgh Festival production, directed by Tyrone Guthrie. Drawn by Richard Leacroft. From Helen and Richard Leacroft, *The Theatre.* Courtesy of Methuen and Co., Ltd., London.

11-8 Realistic scene on the open stage. A strong sense of enclosed reality is created without walls. Chekhov's *The Three Sisters.* The Tyrone Guthrie Theatre, Minneapolis.

sults were exciting. A few years later Guthrie, with the help of Tanya Moiseiwitsch, designed a large Shakespearean theatre for the new festival in Stratford, Ontario, and directed several of their productions. The form has been so well liked that it has inspired the Festival Theatre of Chichester in England and also the new National Theatre in London, designed in this open form after half a century of discussion. When Minneapolis wanted to mark its arrival at maturity as a city, Guthrie was asked to help plan a theatre and become its first director. The Tyrone Guthrie Theatre is built on the model of the Stratford theatre, with a slight concession to the picture stage behind the apron (Figure 11-8).

The theatre at Stratford, Ontario, has no regular place for scenery but offers a dark-colored, formal background of entrances, doors, and steps, with a pavilion and columns supporting a podium above. Color and life are supplied by the actors, who can enter from several directions, even from ramps or steps from below the stage. The auditorium extends in more than a semicircle, like the Greek amphitheatre, and has a balcony above, providing a total of 2,254 seats, the farthest only seventy feet from the stage, closer than the back row of some theatres one-third its size. The

Minneapolis theatre is smaller, seating about 1,400, with no seat more than fifty-four feet from the platform, which is a little off center. It has no formal façade but does have a shallow fly loft, which permits a change of painted backdrops to be combined with movable three-dimensional structures in front. This theatre is planned for a wider range of plays, classic and modern, than the Ontario theatre.

The most daring American advocate of the open stage is James Hull Miller, who has created a number of free-form theatres in a variety of styles. Instead of two rooms, one for audience and one for actors, he thinks of a theatre as a single architectural space, with entranceways for the actors and flat walls or screens for projected backgrounds. The ceiling is an acoustical canopy common to actors and audience and is provided with slots that may be used for lighting or for curtains. Miller believes that decor should be free-standing central accents about which the characters move—scenery not as perimeter but as nucleus. Instead of painted scenery to enclose the actors and fill out the picture up to a frame, he uses scenic islands such as a tower or small platform with properties and a window or doorway, or a fragment of a wall. Instead of a cyclorama, he uses slabs of the theatre wall cut by openings for actors' entrances. Miller's plans have been particularly useful for low-cost public school theatres.

Since there is so much disagreement about the ideal form for the theatre, since some directors prefer a proscenium and some an open stage, since some plays seem better suited to one form and some to another, the best solution might be a *multiform theatre* that could be used in more than one way. There is one obvious difficulty: the side seats of the auditorium, if spread around a thrust stage, will have impossible sight lines when the setting and actors are behind a proscenium. It is not easy to cut the side seats off with screens or curtains, and it is very bad policy to leave them empty—nobody likes to see empty seats. Is some compromise possible? Many suggestions have been offered for a multipurpose building, but most of them have met with loud protests: "An all-purpose theatre is a no-purpose theatre"; "A compromise theatre has no form of its own"; "If you try to please everybody, you please nobody."

The most ingenious solution is to make whole sections of the auditorium mobile. The Loeb Drama Center at Harvard offers such a solution. A large center section of the floor holds seats when the proscenium stage is used. These seats can be rolled to the side and the floor raised to make a thrust stage. When the seats are placed on the proscenium stage, the floor becomes the center of an arena (Figure 11-9). The Vivian Beaumont Theatre at Lincoln Center in New York is likewise convertible. In one arrangement it is a not-quite-semicircular amphitheatre with a balcony, facing a proscenium stage. But it is equipped with a large lift and turntable system

Proscenium Stage

Elizabethan Thrust Stage

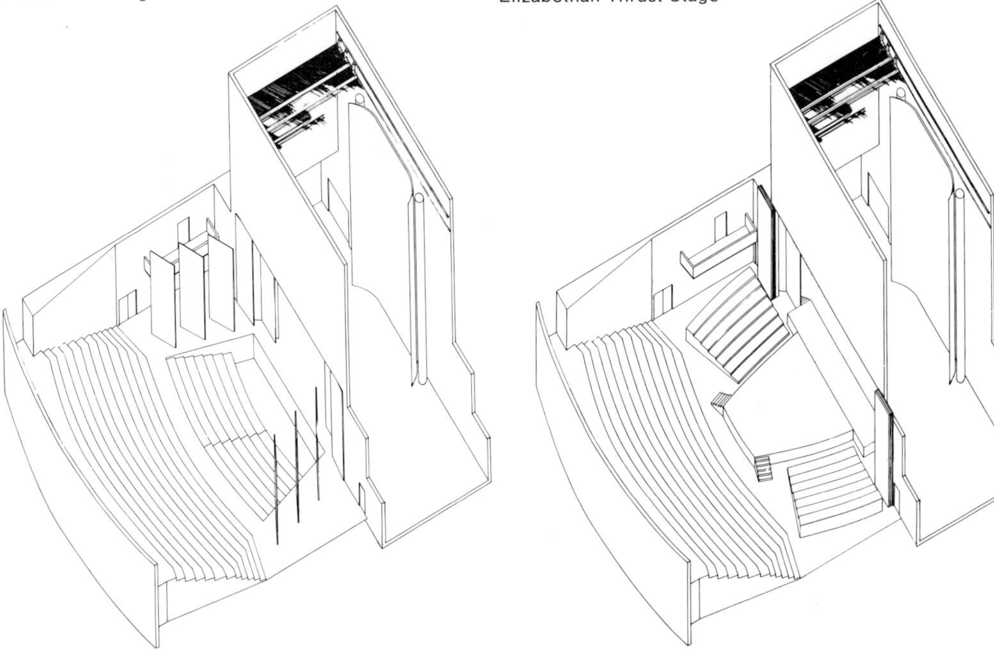

11-9 The convertible theatre, shown first as a proscenium theatre and then as an Elizabethan or thrust stage with the forestage raised and the two sections of seats moved to the side. Loeb Drama Center, Harvard University. Hugh Stubbins Associates, architects. George C. Izenour, theatre consultant.

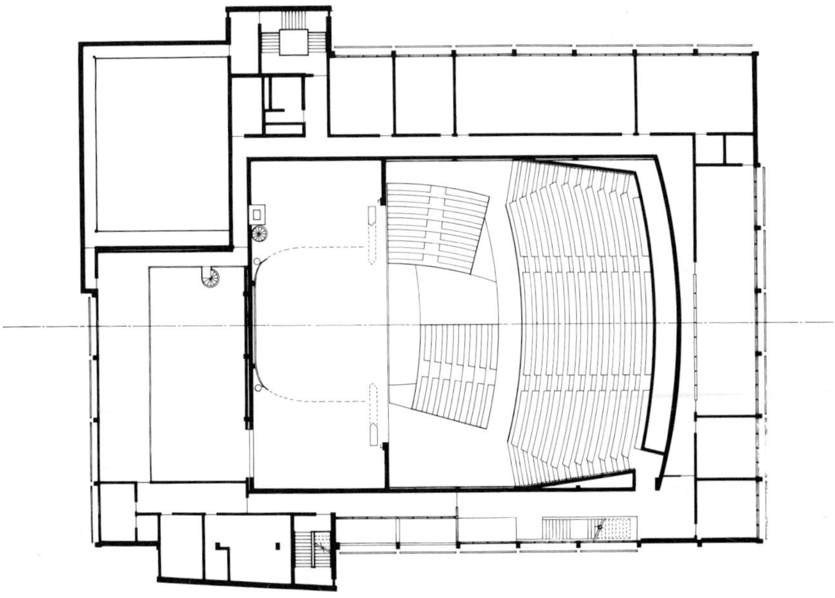

Plan

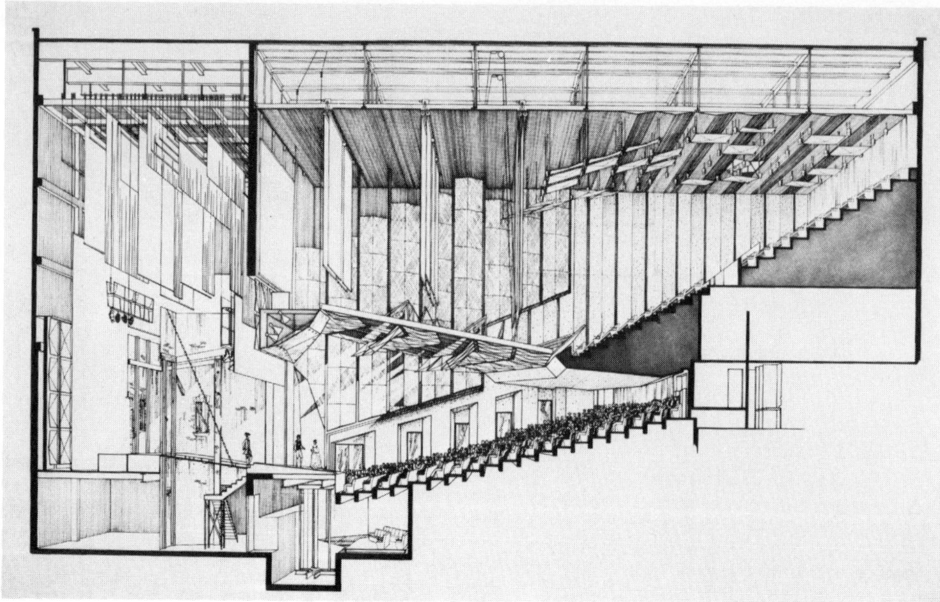

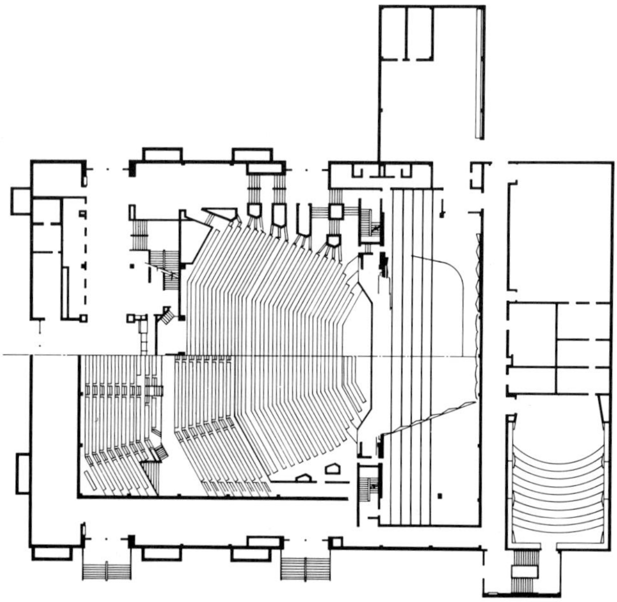

Plan

that can move about sixty orchestra seats and replace them with an open stage of extreme thrust. Other solutions, when a smaller theatre is needed, are a movable ceiling to cut off the balcony and movable platforms to convert the orchestra pit (and orchestra seats) to a forestage (Figure 11-10). Such equipment is very expensive, sometimes costing almost as much as building two theatres.

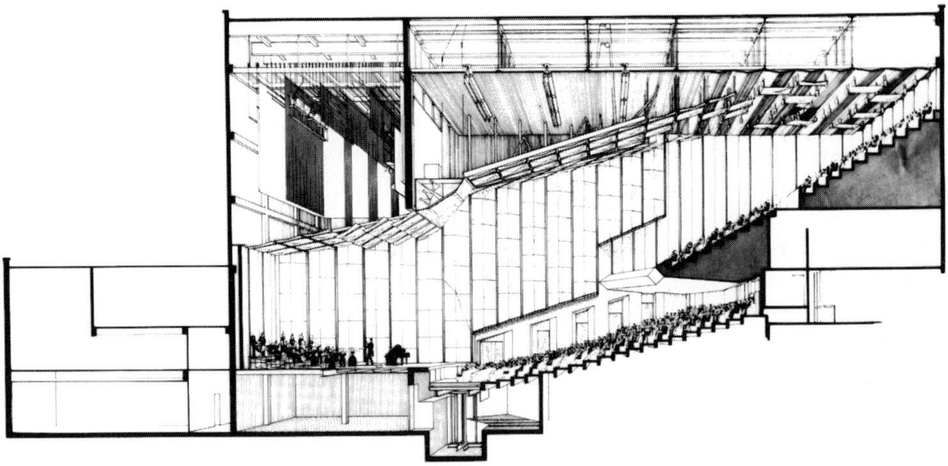

11-10 The convertible concert hall and theatre. With the ceiling up and the pit down (above), it is a concert hall seating 1800. With the ceiling down, the forestage raised, and the front rows stored in the basement (top left), it is a theatre seating 900. Kansas State University Concert Hall–Theatre. Wolfenbarger & McCully, architects. George C. Izenour, theatre consultant.

All theatre people agree that the multiform plan is excellent for the small studio theatre, especially as an experimental theatre for students. Several universities have small studio theatres with sections of the floor mechanized to change quickly, providing many different combinations of levels. For the small room that seats one hundred or less it is possible to make many changes by hand, to move platforms, steps, and ramps for the acting areas, and to put tiers of audience seats down one side, all at the end, or on two or three sides, or even to change between scenes to provide whatever audience-actor relationship the director wants to try. Grotowski, as we shall see, gives his small audiences a different position and a different role to play in each production. For such a functional room many directors would want to use plain, flexible screens and pylons to suggest environment. But there is nothing to prevent the designer from providing portable sculptural forms or even free-standing painted pictures as scenery. At first it may be a pleasure to see the crude, unadorned lighting equipment, but it is easy to cover the lights directly above the acting area in an egg-crate masking box, and some designers like to plan more pleasing sculptural forms to contain the sources of light.

The only complete solution, it seems, is to have more than one theatre and to use each one for the kind of play and production it best serves. Many schools and communities need an auditorium seating two thousand or more for large meetings, concerts, operas, and spectacles. But that size is virtually impossible for plays and even for the more intimate operas. The ideal lyric theatre for musicals, small operas, dance programs, and some plays should not seat more than 1,200 to 1,500. For amateur actors, dramatic theatres are being built to seat from 300 to 600, and the most popular arena theatres are even smaller. Lincoln Center is merely an extension of the interest, developed in many colleges and community centers, in having a number of theatres, each devised for a special purpose. Lincoln Center offers in one planned area Philharmonic Hall for concerts, the Metropolitan Opera House, the New York State Theatre for operetta and dance, several halls and theatres in the music school, and the Vivian Beaumont Theatre, containing not only the changeable form just described but also "The Forum," a small open-apron stage planned especially for readings and tryouts of new plays. The Kennedy Center for the Performing Arts in Washington contains four theatres in one building: a large concert hall, an opera house, a proscenium theatre seating 1,100, and a 500-seat convertible experimental theatre.

Poetic Drama

While the scene designers were quick to learn from Appia and Craig that a poetic symbol is better than a reproduction of reality, few of the plays they worked with had any poetic quality beyond the impressionist moods of nature. The modern poet has had a difficult time in writing for the stage. Realism drove traditional poetry out of the theatre; the half-suppressed tensions and stumbling impulses that realistic actors learned were not designed for speaking any kind of verse. Yet poetry has always been important in the theatre, and the poets have kept trying not only to find suitable verse forms but also to create theatre conventions that would make poetry possible. In church drama and radio drama the poet has had some success, and isolated experiments in the regular theatres have led the way to the freer theatrical productions of the sixties and seventies.

At first it seemed possible that realism might achieve poetry through a selection from the poetic idiom of the peasant. In Ireland, John Millington Synge transcended the limits of realistic prose by catching the "wild joy" of the speech of western Ireland. He believed that "in a good play every speech should be as fully flavored as a nut or an apple." His rhythmic prose in Irish dialect was very successful in the ironic comedy *Playboy of the*

11-11 A peasant tragedy with poetry, songs, and symbolism. Lorca's *Blood Wedding.* Indiana University production, directed and lighted by Gary Gaiser and designed by William E. Kinzer.

Western World (1907) and in the somber tragedy *Riders to the Sea* (1904). William Butler Yeats wrote such cottage plays as *The Land of Heart's Desire* (1894). But Yeats was a poet and was not satisfied with the limitations of the realistic form. He knew that poetry could be spoken more easily in a theatre of dance and song. When he discovered the Japanese Noh drama, he began to write similar plays about Irish legends for a simple room, with musicians to sing poetic statements and the unfolding and folding of a cloth to symbolize the beginning and ending of the play. His guests were interested, but few later actors or dancers have ventured to try to recreate a Western equivalent of the Noh.

More theatre people have been challenged to produce the poetic tragedies of the Spanish poet Federico García Lorca. Like Yeats, he moved from fairly realistic plays, using peasant speech and folklore, to a more poetic form. In *Blood Wedding* (1933), besides poetic dialogue he used choral rituals in the wedding and death scenes and the Requiem, and a number of symbolic and supernatural commentators (Figure 11-11). But Lorca was killed by Franco's forces and his plays remain isolated examples, too exotic for the general public.

One completely successful poetic play did come out of the lore and language of a peasant village. Dylan Thomas' radio play, *Under Milk Wood* (1954), has had a number of full stage productions, but it is essentially a play for voices and is most effective as a dramatic reading for six or eight readers (Figure 11-12). It is unsurpassed in its lightning-quick creation of character and evocation of situation in the shift from description to dialogue to dream to song. Some thirty-odd characters are developed fully while many others appear briefly as the listener ranges the high street and shops of the little Welsh town, overhearing the public conflicts and private hopes of the townspeople. Women gossip at the pump, and postman Willy

11-12 Readers' theatre for poetic drama. Actors in pools of light. Dylan Thomas' *Under Milk Wood.* Arkansas Arts Center, Little Rock. Directed and designed by Charlotte MacArthur, and lighted by Dwight Jackson. Photo Don Gucker.

Nilly carries news from house to house. A girl dreams of her lover "tall as the town clock tower, Samson-syrup-gold-maned, whacking thighed and piping hot, thunderbolt bass'd and barnacle-breasted, flailing up the cockles with his eyes like blowlamps and scooping down over her lonely loving hotwater-bottled body." Mrs. Pugh calls her husband a pig—"You should wait until you retire to your sty"—while he dreams of poisoning her—"Sly and silent he foxes into his chemist's den and there, in a hiss and prussic circle of cauldrons and phials brimful with pox and the Black Death, cooks up a fricassee of deadly nightshade, nicotine, hot frog, cyanide and bat-spit for his needling stalactite hag and bednag of a pokerbacked nutcracker wife." Polly Garter, who takes on all the lonely farm boys or drunk husbands, sings her wistful song:

> But I always think as we tumble into bed
> Of little Willy Wee who is dead, dead, dead.

Thomas, like Synge, Yeats, and Lorca, found it natural to combine the earthy language of the villagers with his own vivid poetry.

Expressionism, with its repetitive, staccato, telegraphic rhythms, seemed as unpoetic as the stammering prose of naturalism, and the repetitive inanities of some of Ionesco's plays were as unlyrical as the rows of soup cans on a pop-art canvas. Yet occasionally someone is able to gain a lyrical effect from the repetition of short phrases. In *Waiting for Godot,* there are moments of descending peace as the two tramps try not to hear all the dead voices of the past:

> They make a noise like wings
> Like leaves
> Like sand
> Like leaves,

which is echoed a moment later by:

> Like leaves
> Like ashes
> Like leaves.

In *Marat/Sade* free or rhymed verse is used effectively for every conceivable form of discourse, from oration, public proclamation, and debate to songs and angry chants. For speeches shouted with intense emotion verse is far more appropriate than prose. The irregularity of the verse, with rapid shifts from free verse to epigrammatic rhymed couplets, emphasizes the irony that pervades the play and gives the effect of hectic excitement and knowing madness that Weiss desires. An insane patient chants:

> I've helped commit a million murders
> The earth is spread
> The earth is spread thick
> With squashed human guts.

A herald ironically lectures the revolutionaries:

> Work for and trust the powerful few
> What's best for them is best for you.

The revolutionists in their turn cry:

> We want our rights and we don't care how
> We want our Revolution NOW.

Religious Drama

One kind of poetic drama that has found an effective new form is religious drama, played in the chancel of the church, borrowing from the liturgy of church worship as well as from the religious drama of medieval Christians and ancient Greeks. While the social hall of the parish building is a good place to put on realistic prose plays about modern ethical problems, a drama for the chancel of the church calls for choirs, choral processions, exalted subjects, and verse.

The most powerful means of achieving a spiritual level seems to be to return to one of the basic patterns of early Greek tragedy, to set a god or a saintly character in opposition to a chanting, dancing chorus of mortals whose spiritual problems are involved with him. That is the strategy used by T. S. Eliot. For the Canterbury Festival in 1935 he wrote *Murder in the Cathedral,* a poetic dramatization, half epic theatre, half medieval miracle play, of the martyrdom of Thomas à Becket, Archbishop of Canterbury, in 1170.

For the soliloquies and confrontations of Becket, Eliot used the sharp stanzaic and rhetorical forms of medieval and Shakespearean verse. To a chorus of Canterbury women drawn to witness the martyrdom, he gives his most vivid free-form verse. They feel the significance of the martyrdom as a ritual sacrifice of the seasons:

> Winter shall come bringing death from the sea,
>
> . . .
>
> And the world must be cleaned in the winter, or we shall have only
> A sour spring, a parched summer, an empty harvest.

What is expressed in abstract rhetoric by the main characters is physically sensed by these fearful women:

> I have smelt them, the death-bringers, senses are quickened
> By subtle forebodings . . .
>
> . . .
>
> What is woven on the loom of fate
> What is woven in the councils of princes
> Is woven also in our veins, our brains,
> Is woven like a pattern of living worms
> In the guts of the women of Canterbury.

The American poet Archibald MacLeish used a similar pattern for his religious drama *J. B.* (1958), which was discussed in Chapter 7. He presented another great sufferer, Job, as a modern American businessman and surrounded him with choral figures who prod him, argue with him, comment on him, and are deeply involved in his fate. *J. B.* was not written for a church but uses the image of a provincial circus, easily staged on either a proscenium or an open stage. Like Eliot, MacLeish achieved some of his most significant and vivid moments when a watcher, fearful of what the sufferer will do, feels drawn into the action. The character Nickles, the modern representative of Satan, refuses to believe that Job will accept his life again after all he has learned about suffering. He protests:

Job won't take it. Job won't touch it.
Job will . . . fling it in God's face
With half his guts to make it spatter.
He'd rather suffocate in dung,
Drown in ordure . . .

When Eliot wrote his choruses he had in mind the strong English tradition of choral reading and trained speakers. If he or MacLeish had had dancers in mind, they could have added another dimension, for dance is as powerful as poetry in dealing with religious and metaphysical subjects. The recent religious productions of Joseph Chaikin's Open Theatre and of Jerzy Grotowski's Polish Laboratory Theatre are even more theatres of dance than of poetry. Before we examine them, we must realize that, while theatre people have scarcely noticed it, America has developed a modern dance theatre of major importance.

Modern Dance Theatre

Total theatre needs dance as well as poetry. Early in this century both Craig and Appia called for a new approach to basic movement for the theatre, and Appia worked for a time with Émile Jaques Dalcroze, the inventor of eurhythmics, a method of teaching musical rhythms by body movement. In the 1930s Antonin Artaud insisted that movement was more fundamental for the stage than words and that the theatre should be based on the wild, cruel ecstasy of a barbaric ritual, with words chanted only for their exciting or mesmerizing sound. But realistic acting, which has dominated the theatre since the 1920s, has ruled out all contrived or lyric movement, even the art of pantomime, which dancers and actors had used for centuries. In the 1960s and 70s a number of small groups have resolutely set out to create a theatre of intense movement—a theatre of dance. They discover that they have much in common with the dedicated groups of modern dancers who, since the 1920s, have separated themselves from both the realistic stage and the romantic world of ballet and musical comedy.

The way to modern dance was opened by Isadora Duncan, an Irish-American girl from San Francisco who for the first three decades of the century had the artistic world of Europe at her feet—her bare feet. As a symbol of freedom and rebellion, she threw off the slippers, tight bodices, and fixed positions of the ballet and openly defied conventional morality in her personal life. She started schools in many places and tried to train large groups of children. On both continents there was a great interest in "aesthetic dancing," and "interpretive dancers" in loose robes and veils

11-13 Dance theatre using extreme intensities. *Top:* Paul Taylor and his company explore celestial space in *Orbs.* Photo Jack Mitchell. *Bottom:* Martha Graham and Merce Cunningham in *Letter to the World,* a dance interpretation of the life of Emily Dickinson. Photo Barbara Morgan.

floated about while a piano or small orchestra played light classical music. With her remarkable personality, Isadora had a great influence on the public, but no one was able to follow her with a professional group.

A company of some stability was created by Ruth St. Denis and Ted Shawn, and in the 1910s and 20s it trouped the country with carefully prepared numbers based on local color, many with Oriental or American Indian themes. But the "Denishawn" style of dance was still too pretty and soft for some younger members of the company. In the late 1920s three broke away and started in new directions of their own. They became the founders of modern dance. Martha Graham set up her own school and for four decades remained the top performer of modern dance. Together Doris Humphrey and Charles Weidman set up a school and a performing company. From the first, these studio companies were as dedicated as religious monks, ardently working out new techniques for achieving their new form of theatre. Although they used regular theatres for their few major performances, they broke away from the scenic patterns of the Broadway theatre as disdainfully as they broke away from the techniques of the classic ballet. Decades before the "poor theatre" of Jerzy Grotowski, they created a theatre stripped to its essentials. They refused to wear pretty costumes and flaunted their stark leotards. Instead of picture scenery, they used drapes, blocks, and abstract shapes; instead of soft string orchestras and waltz tunes, they called for percussion and harsh dissonance; instead of lightness, daintiness, and delicate poses, they offered weight, struggle, and tension. At first their performances seemed as abstract as cubist paintings, as violent and machinelike as expressionistic plays, as wild and ecstatic as primitive rituals, as heavy and straining as wrestling matches. They explored the natural relation of movement to breathing, to tension and relaxation, to work and play. They were especially interested in gravity—that natural force which ballet hides or denies—and hence in falls.

Martha Graham was the most distinctive figure. "Martha," as she was called, embodied the tight nervousness of modern life with her rigid lips, stiff hands, and stark costumes, her percussive movements, with sudden jerks, sharp accents, and short, broken gestures. She did falls, she stamped her feet and clapped her hands, she walked on her knees, she crouched, she sprang, she suddenly pulled her head between her knees. If Doris Humphrey was not so startling as Martha Graham, not so angular, not so taut and neurotic, she was just as fresh in her search for free, natural movements. Her movements—falls and leaps, off-balance tensions and recoveries—were very much like the rise and fall of waves, smooth but elemental. In 1931 the American movement was strengthened by the visit of the German dancer Mary Wigman, who in the bitter moods of pre-Hitler Germany had developed a more somber approach to dance. Her stark, demonic intensity demonstrated that a dance can evolve out of its own materials and does not have to depend on music, story, or surface charm.

As soon as audiences got used to the new approach to movement, they realized that the modern dancers had much to say—about modern life, but most of all about modern feelings, about revolt and independence, sympathy for the struggling masses, the vital sweep of America, religious idealism, the half-hidden fears in the depths of the soul.

Basic, primary movement is the central interest in modern dance—movement with little use of pantomime, story, or words. Yet sometimes poetry is used as an indirect comment on the movement. Lorca's poem about the death of a bullfighter is used in *Lament for Ignacio*, and phrases from *Othello* are used in *The Moor's Pavane*, both danced by José Limón. Alwin Nikolais has exploited other elements of the theatre—especially costumes and properties (see p. 1). His performers seem grotesque animated forms as they move about encased in geometrical shapes, flexible cords, wrappings, and balloons. But at other times Nikolais lets the human element emerge in exciting movements and groupings, with stunning costumes and settings and dynamic lighting. Most theatrical of all is the Nikolais sound track on electronic tape, made up of actual sounds combined with electronic sounds that have never been heard before.

Some avant-garde dancers have carried the reaction against romantic emotions and neat compositions much further. They show the natural impulse of all theatre people to wake up an audience that has become accustomed to a set of conventions and is therefore passive. Why not let the performers dance among the seats or suddenly look at the audience and imitate their reactions? Put many things on the stage, and let the audience choose what it wants to watch. Bring back spontaneity for both performers and audience. Set a dozen musicians playing anything they want to play, mix in a few radios, electronic sounds on very loud speakers, and a siren or two. Develop a "dance by chance," leaving some movements to the whim of the performers, or let dice or cards determine the next move. Or give the audience moments of rest, with nothing whatever to see.

The leader of this dance theatre of the absurd, this antidance, is Merce Cunningham, who danced for years with Martha Graham. With the avant-garde musician John Cage, and later with the experimental artist and sculptor Robert Rauschenberg, he presented programs designed to shock the conservative, amaze the young, and perhaps now and then point out a step beyond nihilism. He used emptiness not for Zen harmony and peace but for the shock of discontinuity, with the impudent effrontery, for instance, of having a dancer stand still for several minutes and then make one jump. The wonderful leaps Cunningham had done with Graham's company were now used for violent kinetic contrasts, as he began by suggesting what dancing he could do, then interrupted himself and threw away the expectation he had created.

Other dancers have learned to use some of the discontinuity of the antidance movement without giving up all traditional order. Paul Taylor, who has created some of the most impressive new dances of the late 1960s and early 70s, uses some startling absurdities as minor elements of comedy and surprise, but his major compositions have an impressive sense of order. *Orbs* delineates in its first movement a large idea of sun, moon, planets, and open space that gives us a bold perspective for the more mundane human and satiric later movements. In his new way Taylor even achieves an old-fashioned charm and dignity.

From the institutional point of view, modern dance had one great disadvantage in comparison with ballet. It is easy to get a large ballet company together and put on stunning theatrical spectacles, for ballet dancers are trained in standardized techniques. But modern dance has encouraged individuality by allowing each dancer to release his own feelings and special techniques. Hence the modern dancer has been inclined to work independently, creating new works for himself alone or for small groups rather than settling down as a performer of someone else's choreography.

Although modern dancers have not found the institutional stability of the symphony orchestras or the major ballet companies, they have created rich new forms of theatre, and, perhaps more important for the theatre as a whole, they have developed methods of training, derived from many traditions of both East and West, that allow for creativity within a strict discipline. Many dramas of the sixties and seventies call for physical intensities unimagined by the realistic actors of a decade ago. As a result, the training of an actor in today's theatre—for example, in Grotowski's Polish Laboratory Theatre—can be as rigorous as the training of a good modern dancer.

Total Theatre in Dedicated Groups

The great dream of the twentieth-century American actor is a permanent organization of dedicated theatre craftsmen, developing their abilities and discovering new spiritual depths in themselves as they create new plays or new versions of old plays for a devoted audience. This dream has been realized in some European theatres. For example, both before and after the Russian Revolution the Moscow Art Theatre received subsidies that made it possible to work for six to ten months in perfecting a play. The company kept a number of plays in repertory, and an actor was often allowed to play several roles in a play, thus giving him a chance to develop his abilities with a serious company for many years. In contrast, the commercial world of Broadway, with its frantic competition, rushed rehearsals, and frequent flops, seems designed to kill off all but the hardiest actors. A hit can be as deadening as a flop as an actor is frozen in one role for months or years or, after the New York run, spends a year or more on the road. With a small subsidy, the National Theatre Company and the Royal Shakespeare Company of England do remarkably well; but unfortunately, as such subsidized companies become established, they tend to settle into a routine of ancient and modern classics. A more exciting alternative, especially in America, where subsidies are rare and unpredictable, is to follow the example of the modern dancers, who form small groups that, with monastic devotion, defy the commercial world and vow to work together for years to perfect their techniques and create new forms of theatre. Many such groups have been revolutionary, reacting violently to the social and political world around them or withdrawing into themselves to create artistic forms for their own spiritual satisfaction. Since they are usually small avant-garde groups with little financial support, they make a virtue of poverty and strive to see what they can create as actors with little or no help from scenery or spectacular effects.

The chaos of Broadway does not seem inevitable, and there have been many attempts to organize the New York theatre so that there might be regular support and continuity of effort. The New York Theatre Guild, founded in 1919, maintained a high level of achievement for several decades. By organizing a subscription audience, it was able to abolish the star system and let its directors and designers prepare a production with greater care than commercial producers were accustomed to. The Guild started with recent European plays neglected by Broadway and, as new American playwrights appeared, gave their plays good productions. But it hired actors for each play, just as the regular producers did, and except for its very high standards, was merely a special Broadway showcase, not a real alternative to commercial theatre.

In the 1930s, as the depression focused attention on serious American problems, a group of actors and directors formed the Group Theatre to produce new plays about social problems and to work together to develop their acting abilities by Stanislavsky's method. For ten years they held together, working all summer in the country on acting problems, often living in New York in one cheap apartment house, borrowing or begging money when their plays failed and enjoying more affluence when they had a success. They discovered that one of their actors, Clifford Odets, was a very good playwright. He wrote *Waiting for Lefty*, the short labor-union drama in epic form that was described in Chapter 2. Even more characteristic of the depression decade were his Chekhovian studies of family frustration and hope, such as *Awake and Sing* (1935)—realistic comedies that made good use of actors trained in the Stanislavsky method. They could never make enough money to plan ahead but had to find commercial backing for each show. Eventually they gave up the struggle. But for a few years this small commune of dedicated souls survived in a chaotic world and created a distinctive style of ensemble acting. Their difficulties and ultimate breakup, vividly described in Harold Clurman's *The Fervent Years*, have been a warning that no dedicated group has a chance in the commercial chaos of Broadway.

Though the Group Theatre did not survive the war, its ideal of systematic training in method acting continued. In fact, this ideal completely dominated American acting in the forties and fifties, with Lee Strasberg running the Actors Studio as a center of theory and practice. But two developments in the 1950s shook the confidence of the method actors. First, the theatre of the absurd, originating in Paris, aroused great interest in America. Because its characters were cut off from any real environment, were exploding fragments of a meaningless universe, nobody knew what kind of acting to use or how to train for it.

The other unsettling development of the 1950s was the impact of Brecht and the Berliner Ensemble. For decades Brecht had called for a new approach to acting for his epic theatre, but except for the popular musical satire *The Three-Penny Opera*, his innovations drew the attention of only a few people. In 1949, however, the government of East Germany invited Brecht to return from America and head a new theatre company in East Berlin. In 1955 the Berliner Ensemble played in Paris and in 1956 in London, and the repercussions are still being felt. Here was acting that was as much oriented to the audience as to the other actors. Here were interruptions, by songs, projected slides, and parallel actions, with rapid shifts from narrative to action to commentary—all kinds of "alienation" that nevertheless presented the drama with strong emotional impact. Here was an amazing group, which in a few years had become the most exciting theatrical company in Europe. Now it was clear that there were other approaches to good acting besides Stanislavsky's. Because the Berliner Ensemble was from a communist country, it could not be brought to America during the fifties, but many Americans saw it in Europe, and many more began reading Brecht's plays and essays to find out what had impressed him about Chinese acting and what he had borrowed from the lecture hall, the demonstration platform, and the sports arena.

Far more startling than absurdist acting or Brechtian ensembles have been the recent frenzied productions of small dedicated groups in New York, which have displayed an infectious, youthful enthusiasm. Several grew out of the lively experiments at Ellen Stewart's Café La Mama. After starting at La Mama, Tom O'Horgan trouped a small company of young American actors over Europe, exploring group acting of the most acrobatic and ecstatic kind. Back in New York, he directed three plays in 1968 with an energy that appealed to a young audience. *Tom Paine* had little of the eighteenth-century revolution but much of the anger and rebellion of all youth; *Futz*, the story of a farmer who loved a pig, showed a joyous defiance of conventional neighbors; *Hair*, which O'Horgan restaged for Broadway, gave the public its first "American tribal love-rock musical." All these productions were characterized by a new freedom in acting, with little resemblance to the careful character creation of the Stanislavsky method.

Joseph Chaikin developed his Open Theatre more slowly and found several playwrights eager to work with his group, reshaping and rewriting as rehearsal and improvisation explored new possibilities. His *America Hurrah* (1966), three one-act plays written by Jean-Claude van Itallie, found a wide public. The first two plays were of the rather deeply felt expressionistic type familiar in the twenties and thirties. The third play was a novel work in which the action was presented by two larger-than-life manikins who tear apart a motel room and then strip limbs and pieces of cardboard off each other. What pertinence has Stanislavsky training for such inhuman creatures? Van Itallie's *The Serpent* (1968), called a ceremony, kept the whole company on stage like an expressionistic chorus or a religious dance group. The actors moved together like a long writhing serpent, separated for individual characters like Adam and Eve or Cain and Abel, or divided into pairs to explore the newly created world of sex.

Of all the dedicated groups the Living Theatre has been the most controversial and the most persistent in its attack on the established social order. From 1951 until 1963, Julian Beck and his wife, Judith Malina, kept the Living Theatre together in New York, paying their actors a little when they could, moving quickly from loft to warehouse if the tax collector got too close. They produced a wide range of plays, from poetic drama to classic tragedy, challenging their actors to work constantly on new techniques. Two plays made a strong impression as being well prepared and yet allowing improvisation and interplay with the audience. *The Brig* showed the cruel dehumanization of prisoners in a U.S. Marine stockade. *The Connection* seemed completely improvised as a movie photographer came from the audience to make a documentary study of the desperate dope addicts who chat and play jazz while waiting for their "connection." The Beck group's fresh approach and defiance of convention won it an ardent following.

Closed down in New York in 1963, the Living Theatre found a more responsive audience in Europe. They developed new plays or new versions

11-14 Total theatre in dedicated groups. The Becks conduct an outdoor rehearsal of *Paradise Now* for the 1968 Avignon Festival in France. Photo Fred W. McDarrah.

11-15 The audience participates. The climactic "mass love melee" from the Living Theatre's *Paradise Now.* New York, 1968. Photo *The New York Times.*

of old plays designed to shock the audience into new political or emotional attitudes. Invited to perform at the Avignon festival of 1968, they outraged the authorities by insisting on nude scenes and on extra performances as "free theatre in the streets." The engagement was canceled when demonstrations in the street defied the police. The company and all its followers —hundreds of young anarchists from all over Europe—were ordered to leave town. Back in America in the fall of 1968, the company produced an even more sensational effect. Some people were annoyed that the suffering, crying, cooing, caressing actors came into direct contact with the audience or invited the audience onto the stage. Others were outraged at the long scenes of the writhing, almost naked, scrawny bodies in a drama that seemed never to get anywhere. It was clearly a theatre of dedication, not of entertainment.

For the dedicated audience, such revelation was a release from an oppressive society, a promise of the brotherhood of man in a new mystic communion of joy. *Paradise Now*, the most characteristic production, began with thirty-seven long-haired, near-naked actors coming down the aisle, saying to each member of the audience, "We are not allowed to travel without a passport"; "I do not know how to stop war"; "I do not have the right to take off my clothes"; "One cannot live without money." Suddenly the audience was aware of policemen at the doors and joined in the chant, voicing their sympathy with all anarchists and rebels against authority. Here was pop mysticism with the hypnotic power of ancient rituals, with images of sex, savagery, and salvation.

It is no wonder that many young people joined the company, glad to work with no pay, in the hope of becoming fellow evangelists. Yet, in Europe again in 1970, Beck announced that the company was breaking up. Many radicals were not satisfied with the nonviolent revolt of the Becks. In order to feed a large company even the bare necessities, the Becks had to play in regular theatres and depend on the establishment. Some of the company planned to settle in small groups in the subculture of Europe. A few, tired of attacking "the malignant cancer of the West," set out for India. The Becks planned to join the guerrilla theatres in America, staging events in the streets, in factories, parks, and subways. Instead of reflecting reality, they wished to reshape it, to start the theatre all over again, in the midst of life itself.

Where the Living Theatre saw modern man in his outer relation to a corrupt society, the "poor theatre" of Jerzy Grotowski set out to study man in his religious relation to his inner self. The actors of Grotowski's Polish Laboratory Theatre, far more than followers of the Becks, dedicated themselves to concentrated work in a small group for a very small selected audience. Subsidized by the Polish government, Grotowski works in a small

Polish city and produces not in regular theatres but in small rooms, where he can bring forty to a hundred people into an intimate relationship to the play—for each play, a different relationship. They watch the torture and martyrdom in *The Constant Prince* as if looking down from the wall of a hospital operating room or a cockpit; they watch the hallucinations in *Kordian* as fellow inmates between the beds of an insane asylum; they watch the confessions and damnation of Dr. Faustus as friends seated at two long monastery tables for his last supper. In contrast to the Living Theatre, the

11-16
"Poor theatre." Jerzy Grotowski's Polish Laboratory Theatre enacts the great myths while building an extermination chamber of rusty pipes in Wyspianski's *Akropolis.* London, 1968. Photo Douglas H. Jeffery.

productions of the Polish Laboratory Theatre keep the actors in the play, with no direct contact with the audience, though they may be acting only a foot away.

The visit of the Polish Laboratory Theatre to America in the fall of 1969, though only a very few people saw the performances, produced more discussion than any other theatrical event in many years. Here was a group even more dedicated as "holy actors" than those of the Living Theatre. Here were new plays created by director and actors and classics completely reshaped as new creations. Here were subjects that seemed extremely pertinent to the spiritual crises of our day—actors performing a classic Polish play about the high points of civilization while they were constructing a gas chamber out of rusty pipe. Here was a perfection that could come only from years of work, with long technical training, one that was neither the improvised naturalism of Stanislavsky nor the traditional technical discipline of Oriental theatre but a training that released the creative potential of each actor. In that way it was similar to the training of the modern dancer, who borrows and invents new exercises for each new problem and expects to develop his individual role within the larger ideas of the choreographer. Unlike the modern dancer, Grotowski's actors do not eliminate language, though words are not always the central element. Following the disputed theory of Artaud that gesture and incantation are more basic than speech, Grotowski often uses words for mere sound and rhythm, with long passages unintelligible to his Polish audience. For *Apocalypsis cum Figuris,* the actors developed the play with sounds and improvised phrases. In the final rehearsals they substituted quotations from Job, St. John, *The Brothers Karamazov,* and poetic passages from T. S. Eliot and Simone Weil—at least recognizing that poetry has its place, even if theirs is not primarily a poetic theatre.

On the production side the "poor theatre" is equally startling. Having decided early on that it would be ridiculous for the theatre to compete with film and television in effects, Grotowski has eliminated everything that the actors cannot handle or create themselves—classic texts, costumes and sets, musical accompaniment, and lighting effects. The poor theatre is stripped to the two essentials—actors and spectators.

As director of a religious theatre dealing with the metaphysical problem of dedication of the self, Grotowski picks up where T. S. Eliot left off. Like *Murder in the Cathedral,* his plays often show a saintlike figure surrounded by a chorus of only slightly differentiated characters—a Christian prince who brings a blessing to the common people who torture and devour him but finally glorify him, or a Christlike village simpleton who provokes the villagers into crucifying him. The difference is that Grotowski cannot view the old myths without bitter awareness of the gas chambers of the modern world. That awareness gives a mocking tone and contorted tensions to acting that is already extremely acrobatic and tense. The "confrontation style" of costume and setting with rough, coarse, rusty texture, so popular with designers for more than a decade, seems completely appropriate to this mock-religious mood.

In acting, the Polish Laboratory Theatre is an even more radical development, breaking away from the tradition of individuality that has dominated Western theatre since the Renaissance. Grotowski's actors do not present individuals who suffer but the essence of suffering itself, and that brings acting very close to dance. While Stanislavsky had practically eliminated gesture, making unconscious, everyday movements expressive, Grotowski goes back to the repertory of traditional gestures last seen in the old melodrama, the broad farce, or the early movies. But he simplifies and intensifies those gestures so that they may become universal hieroglyphs, powerful but impersonal and generalized expressions of emotion. Such acting does not have to be convincing in the realistic sense—that is, closely related to the range and quality of the actor—but can transcend the realistic, profane world in indicating an abstract spirituality. Not only intensive training of voice and body and in control of signs and gestures is necessary, but also spiritual exercises to free the actor from his inhibitions. Grotowski often works many months on a play, and for the constant training of his company he has borrowed from Yoga, from the Kathakali dancers of India, from Peking Opera, and from Noh, as well as from the nineteenth-century elocutionist Delsarte and many other western traditions.

There may never be one total theatre that brings together all the strands, new and old. The theatres of objective reality and romantic dream persist along with the newer types that show a more creative, imaginative control of reality. The complex, open form of play alternates with the compact, classic structure. What for the spectator is a great wealth of choice—television, movie, Broadway and Off-Broadway, resident company, festival theatre, community amateur theatre, church drama, or small dedicated groups—may be for the young actor a painful dilemma. Even if he is not destined to be one of the few glamorous stars, he may try for Hollywood or Broadway. The best pay is in work for the screen—movie and television character roles—but very few are hired. Broadway is not dead, in spite of perennial reports, and continues to do some distinguished productions every year. But it is so chaotic and unpredictable that many actors are destroyed in the attempt to get started, and even those who have started lose many years in fruitless waiting and struggle.

The main hope is the subsidized resident companies, which are gradually becoming established in the major cities. America is finally recognizing that theatres, like churches, libraries, research laboratories, hospitals, and symphony orchestras, must be supported with public subsidies and regular gifts. In organization, programming of plays, and kinds of acting, the resident theatres correspond very closely to the American college theatres. Without knowing it, we have been preparing students for the resident ideal since the beginning of the century.

A number of universities are taking the lead in establishing resident companies, offering theatres, directors and designers, and modest pay for actors, usually by means of graduate assistantships. The actors are willing to work for a few years at apprentice wages, hoping that the university-sponsored company may provide the transition to a fully professional company.

Resident companies do not expect to hire the glamorous personalities who win nation-wide fame on the television screen, but by offering good seasonal employment and the chance to work on a variety of plays, they can attract and develop first-rate actors. That is the challenge—to educate a wide public to enjoy good drama without famous stars. One task of the resident theatre staff and public is to keep alive interest in local actors, since they, even more than screen personalities, will do the interesting acting.

Since resident companies must have wide support and must serve, like a museum, to show the young the classics of the past and the standard works of our own century, they will never be very far ahead in presenting new plays or new forms of theatre. Originality has usually come from individuals and small groups, and some actors will get their greatest satisfaction from working in a small, dedicated theatre. Since the witch doctor or shaman in the earliest primitive tribe first put on a mask to speak the words of the gods, the actor, of all artists, has been a dedicated person.

Bibliography

Bibliography

The first edition of *Invitation to the Theatre,* with annotated lists of plays, books, and articles arranged by subject at the end of each chapter, is available in most libraries. The following is a selected list, including books published since 1966. An asterisk is used to indicate that a book is available in paperback.

Guides to Books on Theatre

Blanch Merritt Baker, *Theatre and Allied Arts: A Guide to Books* (1952). Oscar G. Brockett, Samuel L. Becker, and Donald C. Bryant, *A Bibliographical Guide to Research in Speech and Dramatic Art** (1963). Paul Meyers, *A Guide to Theatre Reading* (1949). A. E. Santaniello, *Theatre Books in Print* (several editions).

Drama Review and *Educational Theatre Journal* regularly carry notices of new books on theatre. *Revue d'Histoire du Théâtre* in each issue lists books and articles on theatre in western Europe and America. *Theatre Research* frequently has special bibliographies.

There are published indexes to *The New York Times* and the London *Times* and to books in the Library of Congress and the British Museum.

Encyclopedias

Phyllis Hartnoll, ed., *The Oxford Companion to the Theatre* (3rd ed., 1967). *Enciclopedia della Spettacola* (1954–62). Walter Rigdon, ed., *The Biographical Encyclopaedia and Who's Who of the American Theatre* (1966). *Who's Who in the Theatre* (London).

Theatre History

George Altman et al., *Theatre Pictorial* (1953). Edwin Duerr, *The Length and Depth of Acting* (1962). George Freedley and John Reeves, *A History of the Theatre* (rev. ed., 1955). John Gassner, *Masters of the Drama* (3rd ed., 1954). Allardyce Nicoll, *The Development of the Theatre* (4th ed., 1958). Nicoll, *World Drama* (1949).

Shorter Histories

Oscar G. Brockett, *History of the Theatre* (1968). Sheldon Cheney, *The Theatre* (rev. ed., 1952). James Laver, *Drama: Its Costume and Decor* (1951). Kenneth Macgowan and William Melnitz, *The Living Stage* (1955). Richard Southern, *The Seven Ages of the Theatre** (1961).

Anthologies of Historical Material

Barrett H. Clark, *European Theories of the Drama* (1918; 2nd ed., with American theories, 1947; 3rd ed., with later European theories, 1965). Toby Cole and Helen K. Chinoy, *Actors on Acting: The Theories, Techniques, and Practices of the Great Actors of All Times as Told in Their Own Words* (1949). Cole and Chinoy, eds., *Directors on Directing** (1963). Cole, *Playwrights on Playwriting: The Meaning and Making of Modern Drama** (1961). John Gassner and Ralph S. Allen, *Theatre and Drama in the Making** (1964). Barnard Hewitt, *Theatre USA, 1668–1957* (1959). Alois M. Nagler, *Sources of Theatrical History* (1952).

Chapters 1 and 2

Realism

André Antoine, *Memories of the Théâtre Libre* (1964). John Mason Brown, *The Modern Theatre in Revolt* (1929), reprinted in his *Dramatis Personae** (1963). Robert Brustein, *The Theatre of Revolt* (1964). Harold Clurman, *The Fervent Years** (1945). John Gassner, *Form and Idea in the Modern Theatre* (1956). Gassner, *The Theatre in Our Times** (1954). Mordecai Gorelik, *New Theatres for Old** (1940). Robert Lewis, *Method—or Madness?* (1960). Erika Munk, ed., *Stanislavski and America** (1968). Duncan Ross, "Towards an Organic Approach to Actor Training: A Criticism of the Stanislavski Scheme," *Educational Theatre Journal*, XX (special issue, August, 1968). Constantin Stanislavsky, *An Actor Prepares* (1936). Stanislavsky, *My Life in Art** (1923).

Oriental Theatre

L. C. Arlington, *The Chinese Theatre* (1930; repr., 1965). Peter D. Arnott, *The Theatres of Japan* (1970). Faubion Bowers, *Japanese Theatre** (1959). Bowers, *Theatre in the East* (1951). James R. Brandon, *The Theatre of Southeast Asia* (1967). Jack Chen, *The Chinese Theatre* (1922). Earle Ernst, *The Kabuki Theatre* (1957). Ernst, "The Influence of Japanese Theatrical Style in Western Theatre," *Educational Theatre Journal*, XXI (May, 1969). Kalvodová-Sís-Vaniš, *The Chi-*

nese Theatre (1959). Leonard Pronko, *Theatre East and West* (1967). Pronko, "Oriental Theatre for the West," *Educational Theatre Journal, XX* (October, 1968). A. C. Scott, *The Classical Theatre of China* (1957). Scott, *The Kabuki Theatre of Japan** (1955).

Epic Theatre

Eric Bentley, *The Playwright as Thinker** (1946). Brecht issue, *Tulane Drama Review*, T13 (Autumn, 1961). Martin Esslin, *Brecht: His Life and Work* (1967). Hallie Flanagan, *Arena* (1940). Ronald Gray, *Brecht** (1961). Mordecai Gorelik, *New Theatres for Old** (1940). Gorelik, "An Epic Catechism," *Tulane Drama Review*, T5 (Autumn, 1959). Leo Kerz, "Brecht and Piscator," *Educational Theatre Journal*, XX (October, 1968). Jack Willett, ed., *Brecht on Theatre* (1964). Willett, *The Theatre of Bertolt Brecht: A Study from Eight Aspects** (1959).

Chapter 3

Romance and Melodrama

Harry Birdoff, *The World's Greatest Hit: "Uncle Tom's Cabin"* (1947). Michael R. Booth, *English Melodrama* (1965). Booth, *Hiss the Villain* (1964). Maurice Disher, *Blood and Thunder: Mid-Victorian Melodrama and Its Origins* (1949). Disher, *Melodrama: Plots That Thrilled* (1954). David Grimsted, *Melodrama Unveiled* (1968). Barnard Hewitt, ed., *The Renaissance Stage* (1958). Richard Moody, *America Takes the Stage: Romanticism in American Drama and Theatre 1750–1900* (1955). Nicolas A. Vardac, *Stage to Screen: Theatrical Method from Garrick to Griffith* (1949). Garff Wilson, *A History of American Acting* (1966). Marian Hannah Winter, *The Theatre of Marvels* (1964).

Opera and Ballet

Agnes de Mille, *The Book of the Dance* (1963). De Mille, *Dance to the Piper* (1952). Edward J. Dent, *Opera** (1949). Albert Goldman and Evert Sprinchorn, *Wagner on Music and Drama** (1964). Joseph Kerman, *Opera as Drama** (1956). Joan Lawson, *Classical Ballet: Its Style and Technique* (1960). Lawson, *History of Ballet and Its Makers* (1964). John Martin, *Book of the Dance* (1963). Bernard Taper, *Balanchine* (1963). Stephen Williams, *Come to the Opera* (1961).

Chapter 4

Tragedy

Sylvan Barnet, Morton Berman, and William Burto, eds., *Eight Great Tragedies** (1957). Robert W. Corrigan, *Tragedy, Vision and Form** (1965). Walter Kerr, *Tragedy and Comedy** (1967). Richard Levin, ed., *Tragedy: Plays, Theory and Criticism** (1965). Laurence Michel and Richard B. Sewall, eds., *Tragedy: Modern Essays in Criticism* (1963).

Greek Tragedy

Peter D. Arnott, *An Introduction to the Greek Theatre* (1959). Arnott, *Greek Scenic Conventions of the Fifth Century* (1962). Gerald F. Else, *The Origin and Early Form of Greek Tragedy* (1965). Edith Hamilton, *The Greek Way** (1937). George R. Kernodle, "The Fifth-Century Skene: A New Model," *Educational Theatre Journal*, XX (December, 1968). H. D. F. Kitto, *Greek Tragedy** (1950). Gilbert Murray, *Euripides and His Age* (1913).

Chapter 5

Medieval, Shakespearean, Neoclassic, and Modern Tragedy

Bernard Beckerman, *Shakespeare at the Globe, 1589–1609** (1962). O. B. Hardison, *Christian Rite and Christian Drama in the Middle Ages** (1965). C. Walter Hodges, *The Globe Restored* (2nd ed., 1968). Bertram Joseph, *Elizabethan Acting* (1951). Joseph, *Acting Shakespeare** (1960). George R. Kernodle, *From Art to Theatre* (1944). Kernodle, "The Open Stage: Elizabethan or Existentialist?" *Shakespeare Survey*, XII (1959). Kernodle, "Seven Medieval Theatres in One Social Structure," *Theatre Research*, II (1960). A. M. Nagler, *Shakespeare's Stage** (1958). A. P. Rossiter, *English Drama from Its Earliest Times to the Elizabethans** (1950). I. A. Shapiro, "Robert Fludd's Stage-Illustration," *Shakespeare Studies*, II (1966). Richard Southern, *The Medieval Theatre in the Round* (1957). Martin Turnell, *The Classical Moment: Studies in Corneille, Molière, and Racine* (1948). Glynne Wickham, *Early English Stages, 1300–1660* (1959–1962).

Chapter 6

Comedy

Robert W. Corrigan, *Comedy: Meaning and Form** (1965). J. C. Enck, Elizabeth T. Porter, and A. Whitley, *The Comic in Theory and Practice** (1960). Marvin Felheim, ed., *Comedy: Plays, Theory and Criticism** (1962). George R. Kernodle, "Excruciatingly Funny; or, the 47 Keys to Comedy," *Theatre Arts*, XXX (December, 1946). Walter Kerr, *Tragedy and Comedy** (1967). Arthur Koestler, *The Act of Creation* (1964). Louis Kronenberger, *The Thread of Laughter** (1952). Paul Lauter, *Theories of Comedy** (1964). Wylie Sypher, *Comedy** (1956).

Chapter 7

Disruption and Reconstruction

Antonin Artaud, *The Theatre and Its Double** (1938; tr. by Mary C. Richards, 1958). Eric Bentley, *In Search of Theatre** (1953). Bentley, *The Playwright as Thinker** (1946). Robert Brustein, *The Theatre of Revolt* (1964). Robert W. Corrigan, ed.,

*Theatre in the Twentieth Century** (1963). Martin Esslin, *The Theatre of the Absurd** (1961). Genêt and Ionesco issue of *Tulane Drama Review*, T19 (Spring, 1963). Eugène Ionesco, *Notes and Counternotes: Writings on the Theatre* (1964). Norman James, "The Fusion of Pirandello and Brecht in *Marat/Sade* and *The Plebeians Rehearse the Uprising*," *Educational Theatre Journal*, XXI (December, 1969). Lawrence Kitchin, *Drama in the Sixties: Form and Interpretation** (1966). Jan Kott, *Shakespeare Our Contemporary** (1964). Charles Marowitz, ed., *The Encore Reader* (1965). Walter W. Sokel, ed., *An Anthology of German Expressionist Drama** (1963). John Russell Taylor, *Anger and After** (1965).

Chapters 8 and 9

Planning and Directing the Play

H. D. Albright, W. P. Halstead, and Lee Mitchell, *Principles of Theatre Arts* (2nd ed., 1968). Bernard Beckerman, *Dynamics of Drama** (1970). Eric Bentley, *The Life of the Drama* (1965). James H. Clay and Daniel Krempel, *The Theatrical Image* (1967). Toby Cole and Helen K. Chinoy, eds., *Directing the Play: A Source Book of Stagecraft* (1953). Alexander Dean, *Fundamentals of Play Directing* (rev. ed., 1965). Northrop Frye, *Anatomy of Criticism: Four Essays** (1957). John Gassner, ed., *Producing the Play* (1953). George R. Kernodle, "Style, Stylization and Styles of Acting," *Educational Theatre Journal*, XII (December, 1960). Susanne Langer, *Feeling and Form** (1953). John Howard Lawson, *Theory and Technique of Playwriting** (1960). Frank McMullan, *The Directorial Image* (1962). Michel Saint-Denis, *Theatre: The Rediscovery of Style** (1960). Richard Schechner, *Public Domain* (1969). Lee Simonson, *The Stage Is Set** (1932). J. L. Styan, *The Elements of Drama** (1960).

Acting

Bertolt Brecht, "On Chinese Acting," *Tulane Drama Review*, T13 (Autumn, 1961). Michael Chekhov, *To the Actor: On the Technique of Acting* (1953). Toby Cole and Helen K. Chinoy, eds., *Actors on Acting: The Theories, Techniques, and Practices of the Great Actors of All Times as Told in Their Own Words* (1949). Edwin Duerr, *The Length and Depth of Acting* (1962). Lewis Funke and John E. Booth, *Actors Talk About Acting* (1961). Ted Shawn, *Every Little Movement Has a Meaning All Its Own** (1963). Constantin Stanislavsky, *An Actor Prepares* (1936). Stanislavsky, *Building a Character* (1949). Stanislavsky, *Creating a Role* (1961).

Chapter 10

Design

Irene Corey, *The Mask of Reality: An Approach to Design for Theatre* (1968). A. S. Gillette, *An Introduction to Scenic Design* (1967). Robert Edmond Jones, *The Dramatic Imagination* (1941). Orville K. Larson, *Scene Design for Stage and Screen* (1961). Jo Mielziner, *Designing for the Theatre* (1965). Oren Parker and Harvey K.

Smith, *Scene Design and Stage Lighting* (1968). Samuel Selden and H. D. Sellman, *Stage Scenery and Lighting* (3rd ed., 1959). Lee Simonson, *The Stage Is Set** (1932).

Lighting

Willard F. Bellman, *Lighting the Stage* (1967). Stanley R. McCandless, *A Method of Lighting the Stage* (4th ed., 1958). Edward F. Kook, *Images in Light for the Living Stage: A Survey of the Use of Scenic Projection* (1963). Joel E. Rubin and Leland Watson, *Theatrical Lighting Practice* (1954). Thomas Wilfred, *Projected Scenery: A Technical Manual* (2nd ed., 1965). Projection issue, *Theatre Crafts,* IV, No. 1 (January–February, 1970).

Costume and Makeup

Lucy Barton, *Historic Costume for the Stage* (1935). Richard Corson, *Stage Make-up* (1967). Motley, *Designing and Making Stage Costumes* (1965). Berneice Prisk, *Stage Costume Handbook** (1966). Douglas Russell, "The Problem of Style in Costume Design," *Educational Theatre Journal,* XX (December, 1968). Serge Strenkovsky, *The Art of Make-Up* (1937).

Chapter 11

New Forms

The Drama Review (formerly *Tulane Drama Review*) and *Yale Theatre* emphasize new forms.

Antonin Artaud, *The Theatre and Its Double** (1938; tr. by Mary C. Richards, 1958). Eric Bentley, ed., *The Theory of the Modern Stage** (1968). Peter Brook, *The Empty Space** (1968). Robert Brustein, *The Third Theatre* (1969). Jerzy Grotowski, *Towards a Poor Theatre** (1969). E. T. Kirby, ed., *Total Theatre: A Critical Anthology** (1969). Michael Kirby, *The Art of Time: Essays on the Avant-Garde** (1969). David M. Knauf, ed., *Papers in Dramatic Theory and Criticism* (1968). Richard Kostelanetz, ed., *The Theatre of Mixed Means* (1967). Maria Ley-Piscator, *The Piscator Experiment: The Political Theatre* (1969). Marshall McLuhan, *Understanding Media** (1965). Erika Munk and Richard Schechner, *Guerrilla Theatre* (1969). James Roose-Evans, *Experimental Theatre from Stanislavsky to Today* (1970). Michel Saint-Denis, *Theatre: The Rediscovery of Style** (1960). Richard Schechner, *Public Domain* (1969).

Auditorium Forms

American Theatre Planning Board, *Theatre Check List: A Guide to the Planning and Construction of Proscenium and Open Stage Theatres** (1969). Walden P. Boyle, *Central and Flexible Staging* (1956). Harold Burris-Meyer and Edward C. Cole, *Theatres and Auditoriums* (2nd ed., 1964). Margaret Cogswell, *The Ideal Theatre: Eight Concepts* (1962). Margo Jones, *Theatre in the Round* (1951). Maxwell Silverman and Ned Bowman, *Contemporary Theatre Architecture: An Illustrated Survey* (1965). Richard Southern, *The Open Stage* (1959).

Broadway versus the Noncommercial Theatre

William J. Baumol and William C. Bowman, *Performing Arts—the Economic Dilemma** (1966). Ralph Benner, *The Young Actor's Guide to Hollywood* (1964). Jean Dalrymple, *Careers and Opportunities in the Theatre* (1969). Frederick Dorian, *Commitment to Culture* (1964). William Gibson, *The See-Saw Log: A Chronicle of the Stage Production with the Text of "Two for the See-Saw"* (1959). William Goldman, *The Season: A Candid Look at Broadway* (1969). Moss Hart, *Act One** (1959). Henry Lee Munson, *Money for the Arts: The What, How and Why of Government Aid to the Arts in Seven Free Countries of Europe* (n. d.). Julius Novick, *Beyond Broadway: The Quest for Permanent Theatres** (1968). The Rockefeller Panel, *The Performing Arts: Problems and Prospects* (1965). Alvin Toffler, *The Culture Consumers: Art and Affluence in America** (1965).

Index

Index

1
2
D 3
E 4
F 5
G 6
H 7
I 8
J 9